WHO'S WHO IN

Enid Blyton™

WHO'S WHO IN

Enid Blyton™

EVA RICE

ORION

The right of Eva Rice to be identified as the
author of this work has been asserted by her in accordance
with the Copyright, Designs and Patents Act 1988.

First published in Great Britain in 1997 by
Richard Cohen Books

This revised edition published in 2003 by
Orion Media
An imprint of Orion Books Ltd
Orion House, 5 Upper St Martin's Lane,
London WC2H 9EA

A CIP catalogue record for this book is
available from the British Library.

ISBN: 0 75285 648 0 (trade paperback)
ISBN: 0 75286 061 5 (hardback)

Enid Blyton's signature is a trademark of Enid Blyton Ltd

Noddy © Enid Blyton Ltd

The Famous Five, The Secret Seven and
The Naughtiest Girl © Hodder & Stoughton Ltd

Typeset by Selwood Systems,
Midsomer Norton

Printed in Great Britain by Butler & Tanner Ltd,
Frome & London

To Joan Rice,
my grandmother

'An Adventure was one thing,
but an adventure without anything to eat
was quite another thing.
That wouldn't do at all.'

THE VALLEY OF ADVENTURE

CONTENTS

FOREWORD

I am as excited as Timmy the Dog with a new bone to be introducing this revised edition of *Who's Who in Enid Blyton*. First published in 1997 by Richard Cohen Books, it generated huge interest among Blyton fans, old and young, and I was surprised and delighted to receive letters and emails from a huge cross-section of devotees writing from far and wide. To every one of you, thank you.

When Orion showed interest in republishing, I suggested that I add two more of Blyton's most popular series to the work. The result is the inclusion of the 'Barney' Mystery books and her 'Farm' novels. I have loved working on these series, which I consider to be among Blyton's very best work.

I must extend huge thanks once again to my cousin and fellow Blyton know-all Alex Rice whose single-handed tackling of the Famous Five enabled me to get the book finished for its first publication in 1997, in time for Blyton's 100th anniversary celebrations. Alex has reread his notes with the enthusiasm of Mr Plod booking Noddy for speeding, occasionally making the odd comment in my direction – 'It's OK, I've done Dirty Dick' being perhaps the most memorable. Further thanks must go to James Preece whose knowledge of all things Enchanted remains unparalleled.

It is worth mentioning that I am not pretending to have included every single Blyton character in my work. I have written in detail about all the children, animals, fairy-folk and creatures from the following series: Noddy, The Secret Seven, The Famous Five, Malory Towers, St Clare's, The Naughtiest Girl, The Enchanted Wood, The Wishing Chair, The 'Barney' Mystery books, and the Mistletoe Farm and Willow Farm series. I have taken note of, and will mention characters from, a number of other series, including Amelia Jane, Brer Rabbit, the Misters Pinkwhistle, Meddle and Twiddle, The Three Golliwogs, The Five Find-Outers and The Put-Em-Rights. But everyone has a favourite Blyton character and I know that I will be upsetting someone by not including, for instance, Barker the black spaniel from Hollow Tree House, or Prickles the hedgehog who appeared in many of Blyton's short stories. Distressing though it was, I had to draw the line somewhere. Blyton wrote over seven hundred books and hundreds of short stories (many of which have been lost), plus pantomimes, plays and magazine articles.

Another issue that I must clear up is that this book is in no way a study of Blyton's personal life, although, where particularly relevant, I may add a detail about her character. When this book first came out, the press somehow got hold of the wrong end of the stick and imagined that I was going to be putting the characters into the 'psychiatrist's chair' and discussing issues including Big Ears' 'suspect' relationship with Noddy and whether George from The Famous Five had equally 'suspicious' traits. The book is nothing as sensational as all that. I am writing as a fan of Blyton's work, and would rather fly to the moon than dissect her work in such a laborious and pedantic manner. I can see how there is an inherent danger even in applying a quasi-academic technique to her work, so I have indulged in another agenda of laughing at the whole enterprise of putting Mr Plod and his pals under scrutiny. I write as an addict, but with an anarchic element, which I hope will give certain readers additional enjoyment.

I am aware that over the years Enid Blyton has been seen as highly politically incorrect because of her relentless portrayal of life in cosy, middle-class backgrounds where every household has a round-faced cook and everything is all right as long as there is a constant supply of biscuits and freshly squeezed lemonade with mysteries lurking round every corner. I am not interested in whether her stories are 'right' in this sense because they possess a timeless quality that transcends any amount of formal analysis.

So, if you fancy a trip to Kirren Island with the Five, a quick French lesson with Mam'zelle Dupont or a peek to see which land has stopped at the top of the Faraway Tree, you need only read on. I can certainly say that no other author has seized my imagination so strongly or thrown me headlong into other worlds with such force, then taken me home for icy ginger beer, sardine sandwiches and sticky buns. Today, more than one hundred years after her birth, Blyton's popularity remains undimmed, her books still sell worldwide and her extraordinary gift for storytelling is as potent as ever. After all, isn't Harry Potter just Malory Towers and the Enchanted Wood mixed together? In the words of the great Alicia Johns from Malory Towers: 'Long live our appetites! And may our shadows never grow less!'

Eva Rice

ACKNOWLEDGEMENTS

Bouquets to Laura Meehan, Trevor Dolby and Pam Ally.

Special thanks to James Preece for his enthusiasm and continued support in the Blyton arena, and to Alex Rice, cousin, co-author and Big-Ears to my Noddy.

ILLUSTRATION CREDITS

The author and publishers would like to thank the following for permission to reproduce illustrations:

Chris Beetles Ltd for *Five on a Treasure Island* (Hodder and Stoughton, 1942, illustrated by Eileen Soper) and *Five Go to Mystery Moor* (Brockhampton Press, 1967, illustrated by Eileen Soper)

Hodder and Stoughton Ltd for *The Secret Seven* (Hodder Children's Books, 1949, illustrated by George Brook) and *Secret Seven Mystery* (Hodder Children's Books, 1957, illustrated by Burgess Sharrocks)

Macmillan Children's Books for *The Island of Adventure* (Macmillan and Co Ltd, 1944, illustrated by Stuart Tresilian)

Award Publications Ltd for *The Put-Em Rights* (Award Publications Limited, 1999, illustrated by Chris Rothero)

Egmont Books for *The Mysteries Collection* (first published by Methuen, this edition published 2002), *Summer Term at St Clare's* (Methuen & Co Ltd, 1943, illustrated by W Lindsay Cable), *The O'Sullivan Twins* (Methuen & Co Ltd, 1942, W Lindsay Cable), *Third Year at Malory Towers* (Methuen Children's Books, 1948, Jenny Chapple), *Upper Fourth At Malory Towers* (Methuen Children's Books, 1949, Jenny Chapple), *The Magic Faraway Tree* (George Newnes, 1943, illustrated by Dorothy M Wheeler), *The Adventures of the Wishing Chair* (George Newnes, 1937, illustrated by Hilda McGavin), *Amelia Jane Again!* (George Newnes, 1946, Sylvia I Venus), *The Children of Willow Farm* (Country Life Limited, 1942, illustrated by Harry Rountree), *The Naughtiest Girl Again* (George Newnes Limited, 1942, illustrated by W Lindsay Cable), *Mr Pink-Whistle Interferes* (Dean & Son Limited, 1950, illustrated by Dorothy M Wheeler), *Hello, Mr Twiddle* (Dean & Son Limited, 1968), *Mr Meddle's Muddles* (Dean & Son Ltd, 1970, illustrated by Rene Cloke), *The Three Golliwogs* (Dean & Son Limited, 1978, illustrated by Rene Cloke), *Brer Rabbit's A Rascal* (Dean & Son Ltd, 1965, illustrated by Grace Lodge)

Collins Children's for *The Adventurous Four Again!* (George Newnes Limited, 1947, illustrated by Jessie Land), *The Rockingdown Mystery* (Collins, 1965, illustrated by Gilbert Dunlop), *The Ring O'Bells Mystery* (Wm Collins Sons & Co Ltd, 1966, illustrated by Gilbert Dunlop), *The Rilloby Fair Mystery* (Collins, 1965, illustrated by Gilbert Dunlop), *Six Cousins at Mistletoe Farm* (Evans Brothers Limited, 1948, illustrated by Peter Beigel), *Six Cousins Again* (Evans Brothers Limited, 1950, illustrated by Maurice Tulloch)

Enid Blyton Limited (a Chorion company) for *A Tale of Little Noddy* (Sampson Low, Marston & Co Ltd and CA Publications Ltd).

ADVENTURE STORIES

THE ADVENTURE BOOKS
THE FAMOUS FIVE
THE SECRET SEVEN
THE ADVENTUROUS FOUR
THE PUT-EM-RIGHTS
THE FIVE FIND-OUTERS

'Honey sandwiches, sardine sandwiches – and I hope you won't go for those too much, Peter, you're a pig over sardines,' said Janet. 'Buns, buttered and jammed all in halves. New doughnuts. A chocolate cake baked today. A smashing jam sponge sandwich, already cut into seven by Mummy. Doesn't it look lovely? Oh, and a plate of mixed biscuits.'

GO AHEAD, SECRET SEVEN

THE ADVENTURE BOOKS

The Island of Adventure (1944)
The Castle of Adventure (1946)
The Valley of Adventure (1947)
The Sea of Adventure (1948)
The Mountain of Adventure (1949)
The Ship of Adventure (1950)
The Circus of Adventure (1952)
The River of Adventure (1955)

Philip and Dinah Mannering, Jack and Lucy-Ann Trent and Kiki the parrot are the regular stars of the Adventure books who, like the Famous Five, find themselves embroiled in mysterious escapades during school holidays. Comparisons with the Famous Five do not end there, as the two groups are of similar age and personality. From Jack with his crime-cracking abilities and love of food to Dinah with her quick temper and dramatic mood swings and Lucy-Ann with her reluctance to get involved with anything too exciting, one could be forgiven for thinking that this particular gang are modelled closely on Blyton's Kirrin Island adventurers. The diverse plots of the eight books take the children all over the world with Kiki their feathered friend there to share in the fun, seemingly understanding everything that is going on around her. The children work in tandem with their detective friend Bill Smugs, who cannot help but marvel at their tremendous ability to solve mysteries that have been beyond even the highly trained police force. Indeed, what would Bill Smugs do without this band of intrepid explorers who, as he puts it, 'simply fell into adventures'?

Gus (Prince Aloysius Gramondie Racemolie Torquinel of Tauri-Hessia)

Prince of Tauri-Hessia, and heir to the Tauri-Hessian throne, who appears in *The Circus of Adventure*. To the probable relief of all concerned, he is known simply as Gus after being renamed Gustavus Barmilevo by police detective Bill Smugs, whose job it is to protect him from potential kidnappers.

Aloysius is also the name of Sebastian Flyte's famous teddy bear in Evelyn Waugh's *Brideshead Revisited*, published seven years before *The Circus of*

Adventure, but it is more likely that Blyton took the name from a book she read in her own childhood about the adventures of characters called Aloysius and Theodora.

Jake

Criminal in *The Island of Adventure* who is about as successful as his two namesakes in the Famous Five series. This Jake has a black patch over one eye, and his mouth is so tight-lipped it almost seems as if he has no lips at all.

Uncle Jocelyn

Uncle to Philip and Dinah Mannering, Jocelyn lives at Craggy Tops where the children often spend their school holidays. His similarity to Uncle Quentin from the Famous Five is remarkable, from his devotion to hard work which conveniently confines him to his study, to his having little time for the children. Whereas Quentin is a hard-working scientist, Jocelyn is a hard-working historian, and he has made it his life's work to study the history of the Cornish coast where they live.

Kiki

A parrot with attitude, Kiki is the feathered friend of the four children in the Adventure series. She is a beautiful white parrot with a yellow-crested head and is never far from the shoulder of her owner, the bird-loving Jack. Kiki possesses a wide-ranging vocabulary, including a great deal of rude language learned from Uncle Geoffrey, 'the crossest man in the world'.

Kiki has a 'most human manner' and, like Timmy in the Famous Five, seems to understand all that goes on around her. She has an uncanny ability to make pertinent comments at the right time, such as when Dinah sneezes in *The Island of Adventure*, and Kiki asks, 'Where's your handkerchief?'

Kiki enjoys being the centre of attention and loves playing to an audience in *The Circus of Adventure*. She becomes rather doleful when she is ignored. On more than one occasion she proves her worth by frightening off criminals with her convincing imitations and eerie screeching noises.

Mannering, Dinah

Twelve-year-old sister of Philip and one of the two girls in the Adventure series, Dinah is not the easiest of characters, displaying a fearful quick temper and sulky disposition. However, she bears no malice and her furies are soon

over, particularly when picnic meals appear. She detests all animals and insects, as much as her brother loves them, causing much contention between the pair. She and her brother each earn the nickname of Tufty at their respective schools, a reference to their hair which resolutely refuses to sit flat on their heads but sticks up in an amusing way.

> *'I suppose,' said Dinah at last, after a long silence in which the only noise was the sound of Kiki's beak scraping against the bottom of one of the pineapple tins, 'I suppose we had better set out as soon as it is dark – but I do feel quaky about it!'*
>
> THE SEA OF ADVENTURE

Dinah displays a confidence that makes her appear to be much older than Lucy-Ann, although there is only a year between them. It is mentioned that Dinah 'always likes to be doing something' and does not like to show when she is afraid, preferring to display the resourceful and independent side to her character. She is also far less emotional than Lucy-Ann, and it is stated in *The Castle of Adventure* that Dinah gives her mother a 'quick peck on the cheek' when she sees her at the beginning of the holidays, unlike Lucy-Ann who flings herself upon Mrs Mannering in joy.

Mannering, Philip

One of the four children who feature in the Adventure series, Philip is the thirteen-year-old brother of Dinah and son of Mrs Allie Mannering, although holidays tend to be spent with Uncle Jocelyn and Aunt Polly. Philip and Dinah are constantly quarrelling, in sharp contrast to their great friends, devoted brother and sister Lucy-Ann and Jack Trent. Fortunately, these arguments are always quickly resolved.

Philip is a great nature-lover, and animals in turn seem to like Philip. His pockets are constantly brimming with wildlife of all descriptions, including Lizzie the Lizard from *The Valley of Adventure*, and in *The Island of Adventure* Philip attempts to train earwigs.

Undoubtedly a valuable member of the Adventurous team, Philip remains calm and optimistic in a crisis. After being locked in a cave by Jake in *The Island of Adventure* he simply exclaims: 'What a bit of bad luck!' He also harbours a great interest in food, like all Blyton children, and insists on tucking into a whole loaf, a pound of butter and a jar of jam before setting off to rescue Jack from the Isle of Gloom where he is trapped on his own. Philip is

quite prepared to stand up for himself and the other children against grown-ups, as can be seen when he snaps irately at the burly and interfering handy man, Jo, who seems intent on spoiling their plans.

Smugs, Bill

Bill Smugs plays a prominent role in all eight books in the Adventure series. He is a clean-shaven man with a 'red, jolly face…twinkling eyes and a bald head'. As a general rule, Blyton crooks tend to be bearded and Smugs soon establishes himself as a close friend of the four children. A member of the police force, his real name is Bill Cunningham but he uses the pseudonym of Smugs to avoid suspicion from criminals. This is revealed in *The Island of Adventure*, but the children prefer the name Smugs and it remains with him throughout the series.

He finds the children's detective work a great help and their discoveries aid him in his work. He in turn is able to use his wealth of experience to help the children out of a number of sticky situations. Bill Smugs' character is allegedly based on a man whom Enid Blyton met on holiday and who asked to be put in one of her books, 'bald head and all'.

Tassie

A wild girl who features in *The Castle of Adventure*, Tassie is as sure-footed as a mountain goat, and spends her summer scampering over the hillside with the four children. She is forced by Mrs Mannering to have a bath, much to her disgust, and emerges a different girl. She strikes up a great friendship with Philip, sharing his love of animals, and also loves Kiki, who in turn befriends her pet fox cub, Button.

Trent, Jack

Eldest member of the Adventure gang at fourteen, Jack is red-haired and freckled, like his younger sister Lucy-Ann, earning him the nickname

Freckles. Jack is described as 'clever but inattentive' at school, as he can think of nothing but birds, and he longs for the holidays when he can explore the countryside for fascinating species. He goes 'brick red with excitement' at the prospect of seeing a great auk near Craggy Tops and is enthralled by the sighting of eagles in *The Castle of Adventure*. In keeping with his passion for birds, Jack is the proud owner of Kiki the parrot who accompanies the four children on all their escapades.

Jack's finest hour comes when he uncovers hidden machines used to print counterfeit notes in *The Island of Adventure*, thereby solving a mystery that had puzzled the government and the police for five years. Such mystery-solving is hungry work, and Jack certainly has an appetite. After one particular meal, Blyton comments that he has to undo his belt by two or three holes.

Trent, Lucy-Ann

Eleven years old and the youngest child in the Adventure series, Lucy-Ann is the devoted sister of Jack. Their closeness can be explained by the death of their parents in a plane crash when the two children were very young. Lucy-Ann is enraptured by the beauty of the world around her, and frankly is not cut out for the hectic pace of the adventures the children encounter. As she herself states, 'Adventures are too exciting when they are happening,' and she is much happier when they are over, a sentiment shared by Anne in the Famous Five. She even enquires as to whether they may 'have a little rest' when they are being chased down a dark passage by a potentially violent criminal called Jake.

Prone to sea-sickness and air-sickness, she is not the most hardened of travellers, and tends to turn on the tears in frightening moments. She nevertheless has plenty of pluck and nothing would ever persuade her to let the others go without her.

THE FAMOUS FIVE

Five on a Treasure Island (1942)
Five Go Adventuring Again (1943)
Five Run Away Together (1944)
Five Go to Smuggler's Top (1945)
Five Go off in a Caravan (1946)
Five on Kirrin Island Again (1947)
Five Go off to Camp (1948)
Five Get into Trouble (1949)
Five Fall into Adventure (1950)
Five on a Hike Together (1951)
Five Have a Wonderful Time (1952)
Five Go Down to the Sea (1953)
Five Go to Mystery Moor (1954)
Five Have Plenty of Fun (1955)
Five on a Secret Trail (1956)
Five Go to Billycock Hill (1957)
Five Get into a Fix (1958)
Five on Finniston Farm (1960)
Five Go to Demon's Rocks (1961)
Five Have a Mystery to Solve (1962)
Five Are Together Again (1963)

Julian, Dick and Anne Kirrin, together with their cousin George Kirrin and her dog Timmy, are the most famous of Enid Blyton's mystery-solving gangs. The Famous Five first appeared in 1942 in *Five on a Treasure Island*. They completed their twenty-first adventure, *Five Are Together Again*, in 1963.

Adventures always take place in the school holidays and appear to span twelve years, though if this were strictly the case, the oldest member, Julian, would have been twenty-four by the last adventure, and Timmy the Dog a rather grey thirteen. As with the adventures themselves, it is best to suspend belief on the chronology front, for there is always plenty to enjoy without worrying about detail.

Julian, Dick, George, Anne and Timmy have an amazing ability to attract adventure wherever they go, but then, as Blyton says at the end of *Five Go to*

Smuggler's Top, 'adventures always come to the adventurous'. Even when the Five deliberately try to avoid adventure they seem to find it. 'Adventures are off this time. Definitely off,' insists Julian in *Five Go Down to the Sea*, but they just can't resist uncovering a major drug-smuggling operation a few pages later. 'An adventure comes up all of a sudden, like a wind blowing up in the sky, and we're all in it, whether we like it or not,' explains Anne in *Five Have Plenty of Fun*.

The Famous Five deal with some tough criminals, and regularly have their lives put in danger. Police involvement is kept to a minimum, with Julian and Dick in particular keen to solve many of the mysteries themselves. In *Five Fall into Adventure* Anne begs Dick to go to the police rather than try to free their good friend Ragamuffin Jo by himself, but Dick is adamant they go it alone. The Famous Five have a terrific success rate, so he is probably justified in doing so. They are helped on many occasions by tremendous luck, and admit as much in *Five Have a Wonderful Time* when spotting the imprisoned Terry-Kane in Faynight's Castle while bird-watching.

Not everyone is captivated by the Famous Five's activities. In *Five on a Secret Trail* George gets upset with her mother for not seeming at all interested in their latest adventure. 'Oh, I am, dear,' Fanny replies. 'But you do have such a lot, you know.' That's for sure.

Aggie

A poor, miserable-looking woman who works at Owl's Dene in *Five Get into Trouble*. Badly treated by the criminal types who surround her, she shows compassion towards the children and proves to be a good ally. She is one of the few kitchen-workers in the Famous Five series who are not jolly.

Aily

Wild-looking little Welsh girl who befriends the Famous Five during their stay at Magga Glen in *Five Get into a Fix*. The daughter of a shepherd, she plays truant from school and spends her days in the hills with her dog, Dave, and lamb, Fany. She knows the countryside extremely well, and her knowledge of the land near Old Towers is a great help to the Five.

Alf/James

A fourteen-year-old fisherboy who appears from time to time in the series, not necessarily with the same name! In *Five on a Treasure Island* Timmy the dog is looked after by a fisherboy named Alf when banished from Kirrin Cottage by Uncle Quentin. Yet five adventures later, Alf would seem to have completely changed name. We now read how 'Timmy had never forgotten the time when James looked after him so well'. Clearly Timmy's memory is no better than Blyton's. Even for someone who did not care much for precise detail, this seems an extraordinary lapse for her.

Alfredo

Fire-eater at the circus, Alfredo features in *Five Have a Wonderful Time*. Enormous fellow who looks exactly as Dick imagines a fire-eater to look. Somewhat ironically, this master of fire manages to burn his breakfast regularly, much to the annoyance of his fierce little wife, Mrs Alfredo.

Alfredo is the uncle of Ragamuffin Jo who just happens to be staying with him during *Five Have a Wonderful Time*, and is therefore able to assist the Five in their adventure.

Mr Andrews

Mr Andrews owns and lives at Olly's Farm, as featured in *Five Go off to Camp*, together with his wife, Mrs Andrews, and her son (his stepson), Jock Robins. He doesn't take much interest in the work of the farm, primarily because he is too busily involved with illegal black market activities down at Olly's yard.

His criminal activities are exposed by the children, and he is last seen being led away in tears by the police. Jock is ashamed of him, not so much because of his criminal activity, but because he cries in public. For any of Enid Blyton's male characters, crying is about as low as you can go, for it shows a complete lack of strength and pluck. There is certainly no place for the modern man in the Famous Five's world.

Mrs Andrews

Mrs Andrews lives and works at Olly's Farm with her husband, Mr Andrews, and son from her first marriage, Jock Robins. Unlike her husband, she takes a strong interest in farm work, and loves working in the dairy.

Armstrong, Jennifer Mary

The daughter of millionaire Harry Armstrong, Jenny is kidnapped by the Sticks in *Five Run Away Together*, and held prisoner on Kirrin Island. Police comb the country for her, but it is the Famous Five who find and rescue her. Like Anne, she has a love of dolls and is extremely pleased to be reunited with Josephine, Angela, Rosebud and Marigold.

Mr Barling

Smuggler and gun-brandishing criminal in *Five Go to Smuggler's Top*, who objects to Uncle Quentin and Mr Lenoir's plans to drain the marshes, which would badly affect business. Too artful for the police, he is no match for Timmy who pins him to the ground and takes a painful nip at his shoulder.

The Barnies

Travelling players who put on a simple but extremely good-natured show in *Five Go Down to the Sea*. The Barnies' performance features nightingale-singer Edith Wells, old-time dancer Bonnie Carter, fiddler Janie Coster, comedian George Roth, and the 'finest tenor in the world', John Walters. The star of the show though is Clopper, the hilarious pantomime horse, worked by Sid and Mr Binks.

Beauty

Python owned by the appropriately named Mr Slither and star of many fairs, but Beauty's crowning moment comes when capturing Pottersham and his men in *Five Have a Wonderful Time*.

Ben

Given a brief name check in *Five Go Adventuring Again*, Ben is one of the Kirrin Farm dogs who plays happily with Timmy.

Ben

Ben is also the name of the Scottie dog at Tremannon Farm in *Five Go Down to the Sea*.

> *'We have to climb up this rocky wall now,' said Julian, 'go through that dark hole there, keep on climbing – and goodness knows where we'll come out!'* FIVE GO ADVENTURING AGAIN

Betsy-May

A doll given to Anne for Christmas in *Five Go Adventuring Again*, and named Betsy-May by Anne because 'she looks just like a Betsy-May'. Not to be confused with the little girl who likes to feel grown-up in *Tales of Betsy May*.

Biddy

The four-year-old dog owned by Jock Robins in *Five Go off to Camp*, Biddy appears with five little puppies in tow, having recently given birth. She was given to Jock by Farmer Burrows when he lived at Owl Farm.

Bill

Farmhand who gives the children a tour of the farm in a Land-Rover in *Five on Finniston Farm*.

Mr Binks

Mr Binks operates the front legs and head of Clopper the pantomime horse in *Five Go Down to the Sea*. He works extremely well with Sid, who operates Clopper's back half, but decides to give up the act after discovering that Clopper's head had been used by the Guv'nor to store drugs.

Binky

Collie dog owned by Toby Thomas in *Five Go to Billycock Hill*, who has a wonderful time with Timmy. The only criticism of Binky is that he's a bit of a dud ratter – he just can't seem to nip a rat.

Block

A mysterious figure involved in criminal activities in *Five Go to Smuggler's Top*, Block stays with the Lenoirs at Smuggler's Top, having 'just appeared one day'. The children find his face most curious, and there are many references to his cold, narrow eyes.

Supposedly deaf, it later transpires that he can hear perfectly well and has in fact been spying on Mr Lenoir and his work for the rich smuggler Barling.

Bob

One of Morgan Jones's seven dogs in *Five Get into a Fix*.

Boogle, Jeremiah

Wise old sailor in *Five Go to Demon's Rocks* who both entertains and frightens the children with the dramatic history of Demon's Rocks. He smokes a long pipe, has a fine beard and such enormous shaggy eyebrows that it is difficult to see his eyes beneath them.

Bouncer

Sheepdog at Tremannon Farm in *Five Go Down to the Sea*. A beautiful collie with a plumy tail.

Brent, Peter

Runs the butterfly farm with Mr Gringle in *Five Go to Billycock Hill*, but is often away on business.

Carl

Burly fellow who works for the villain, Red Towers, in *Five Fall into Adventure*.

Charlie the Chimp

Amiable chimpanzee who tours with the travelling circus in *Five Are Together Again*. He often helps the circus folk, but is used by the evil magician Mr Wooh to steal Professor Hayling's irreplaceable papers.

Clopper

Pantomime horse operated by Sid and Mr Binks in *Five Go Down to the Sea*. His antics have the children in stitches, and he regularly saves the Barnies' show. Unwittingly involved in criminal activity when his head is used to hide drugs. His two operators are so devastated by this discovery that they decide to move on. But Clopper could be back, as he's given to the Famous Five for Julian and Dick to use.

Coastguard

Coastguard in *Five on Kirrin Island Again*. He also makes toys.

Curly

Heroic pig who leads the Famous Five to captured RAF pilots Jeff Thomas and Ray Wells in *Five Go to Billycock Hill*. He is owned by little Benny Thomas.

The three children did their best to tug at the heavy stones.

Mr Curton

Threatens to blow up Kirrin Island in *Five on Kirrin Island Again*, and, as such, can be considered one of Blyton's more dangerous criminals. He is guardian to little Martin, but Curton's real interest lies in trying to get his hands on Uncle Quentin's secret new energy source. Curton is assisted in this operation by Peters and Johnson. All end up being led away by the police.

Dai

The oldest of Morgan Jones's seven dogs in *Five Get into a Fix*, Dai loves his master more than any of the others does.

Dave

Dog owned by the little Welsh girl, Aily, in *Five Get into a Fix*. She takes him everywhere with her.

Dearlove, Cecil

Rather wet and weedy, twelve-year-old Cecil arrives to play with Jock Robins in *Five Go off to Camp*. Jock has little time for him, but is asked to make an effort, as his stepfather is friendly with Cecil's father. Cecil arrives wearing a very clean and well-pressed grey flannel suit, but is later reduced to tears after a game of Red Indians.

Dirty Dick

A broad, short man, with hunched-up shoulders and a shock of hair, Dirty Dick needs only a beard to complete the look of the classic Blyton criminal. He appears in *Five on a Hike Together* in search of the Fallonia jewels, but problems begin when a message intended for him is intercepted by Dick from the Famous Five. He now finds himself directly in competition with the children to locate the jewels and, rather predictably, he comes second.

Doon

One of seven dogs owned by Welsh farmer Morgan Jones in *Five Get into a Fix*.

Dr Drew

Doctor who visits Julian, Dick, Anne and George when they are unwell in *Five Get into a Fix*. He advises a short break somewhere hilly to help them recover, and is therefore partly responsible for the adventure the Five experience at Magga Glen.

Durleston, Richard

A leading authority on antiques, he shows a great deal of interest in the site of old Finniston Castle with his friend Mr Henning in *Five on Finniston Farm*.

Aunt Fanny

George's mother is always more than happy to have the children with her at Kirrin Cottage during the school holidays, and is far more approachable than Uncle Quentin. Even she is kept in the dark about her husband's experiments.

Seriously ill in *Five Run Away Together*, she returns in later adventures displaying worryingly unsound judgement. Her decision to take a holiday with Quentin in *Five Have Plenty of Fun* and leave the children behind at Kirrin Cottage, despite threats towards them from dangerous criminals only a few days before, is one that only she can possibly explain.

Fany

Lamb belonging to Aily, the wild-looking little Welsh girl, in *Five Get into a Fix*.

Finniston, William

Descendant of the Finnistons of Finniston Castle, as featured in *Five on Finniston Farm*. Works in the little antique shop in the nearby town.

Mr Gaston

Awfully kind vet who patches up Timmy's injured leg in *Five on a Hike Together*. Lives at Spiggy House with his horses and his wife, Mrs Gaston, who lays on an excellent meal for the children.

Golf Pro

The Golf Pro appears in *Five Have a Mystery to Solve*. He rewards the children with a round of orangeade for finding lost golf balls, and gives the delighted Timmy a packet of biscuits.

Great Giddins Tea-Place Keeper

Serves up a super tea of home-made cakes and jams for the Famous Five when they drop in to her little tea-place in the village of Great Giddins in *Five Get into Trouble*. It should come as no surprise to learn that, like most Blyton cooks, she is a 'plump, cheerful soul'.

Great-Grandad

A burly old man with a shock of snowy white hair and a luxurious beard almost down to his waist. Lives with his family, the Philpots, at their farm in *Five on Finniston Farm*. He's very fond of Timmy, but he can't tolerate Finniston Farm's two American visitors.

Mr Gringle

Owner of the butterfly farm featured in *Five Go to Billycock Hill*, Mr Gringle is a peculiar figure with long untidy hair. He is far too engrossed in his butterflies to notice criminals plotting a large-scale operation in his very own farm. Short-tempered, he is not liked by the children.

Gringo

Owner of Gringo's Fair and an extremely inefficient criminal, Gringo is paid to kidnap Berta in *Five Have Plenty of Fun*, but kidnaps George by mistake.

Guv'nor

The boss of the Barnies in *Five Go Down to the Sea* shows none of the merriment and good nature associated with the Barnies' show. It is no surprise to find him being led away by police for his involvement in a drugs ring.

Hal

One of Morgan Jones's seven dogs, Hal is mentioned in *Five Get into a Fix*.

Harriet

Harriet is the little kitchen maid seen knitting in the kitchen corner in *Five Go to Smuggler's Top*. It is never revealed what Harriet is knitting, or whether she is any good at it.

Professor Hayling

A friend of Uncle Quentin, he and his son Tinker come to stay with the Kirrins in *Five Go to Demon's Rocks*. He returns the compliment in *Five Are Together Again* by having the Five to stay at his home, Big Hollow. Aunt Fanny finds him a difficult man. He regularly forgets to come in for meals, so engrossed is he in his work, and, like most scientists in the Famous Five books, he is rather short-tempered.

Hayling, Tinker

Nine-year-old son of Professor Hayling who stays with the Famous Five in *Five Go to Demon's Rocks*. He has an astonishingly loud voice and is mad on cars, regularly impersonating a Bentley or Jaguar. He is also the owner of the disused lighthouse at Demon's Rocks, which his father gave him and where the children spend their adventure.

His pet monkey, Mischief, provides much entertainment. The two return in *Five Are Together Again* when the Five spend their Easter holiday with them.

Henrietta (Henry)

Prominent in *Five Go to Mystery Moor*, where she meets the Five at Captain Johnson's riding school. Like George she tries to act like a boy, and insists on her name being shortened to Henry. Perhaps because of their similarities, there is an intense rivalry between George and Henry. George calls Henry by her full name to annoy her, and Henry is always quick to return the compliment. Henry's loud snoring at night does little to ease the tension, and so does the fact that she is by far the better rider, with lots of cups to her name. Relations between the two improve dramatically, however, when Henry helps rescue George and Anne from the clutches of the gypsies on the moor. George can't help but be very struck with Henry's courage.

Hunchy

A queer dwarf-like fellow with a hunched back and an evil face, Hunchy appears in *Five Get into Trouble*, living at Owl's Dene. He's short-tempered, particularly when Julian answers him back.

Mr India Rubber

One of the fair workers in *Five Have a Wonderful Time*, he is the grey of an ordinary school rubber and, with his flexible body, honestly looks as if he is made of rubber.

Jackson, George

Driver and extremely clever mechanic who takes the Famous Five to Demon's Rocks in the appropriately titled *Five Go to Demon's Rocks*. He is the great-grandson of the old sailor, Jeremiah Boogle.

Jake

Jake is the chief crook in *Five on a Treasure Island*, though for much of the book we know him just as the 'man who buys antique things', only learning of his name when his companion addresses him later on. His companion is never named, remaining simply as 'the other man'. When it comes to names, Blyton is not a stickler for detail.

Both are hardened criminals, holding George and Julian prisoner and even threatening to shoot Timmy with a revolver, all in a bid to capture the ingots from Kirrin Castle. But they make the mistake of underestimating the Famous Five ('You're only a child,' one of the men says to George. 'You surely don't think you can keep us from getting our way?') and become the first of many criminals to be thwarted by the children.

Jake

Another Famous Five criminal, this time appearing in *Five Fall into Adventure* as one of Red Towers's men, Jake is a gypsy fellow and friend of Ragamuffin Jo's father, Simmy.

Jake

This Jake is a worker at Green's Garage in Lowington, mentioned briefly in *Five Have Plenty of Fun*. As far as we know he has no criminal convictions, despite his name.

Jamie

Works at Finniston Farm, in *Five on Finniston Farm*, and helps free the children when they become trapped in a secret chamber on the site of old Finniston Castle.

Jan (or Yan)

A black-eyed boy burnt dark brown by the sun, Jan appears in *Five Go Down to the Sea*. He lives with his great-grandad, the shepherd at Tremannon Farm, and irritates the Famous Five by following them everywhere. They are extremely glad of his close attentions, though, when he arrives to free them from a locked cave. Not a classic adventurer, as he tends to be easily frightened, or 'frit' as he always put it, but Timmy likes him, which shows he must be a good sort.

Jan's Great-Grandad

The old shepherd at Tremannon Farm, he is known by everyone simply as Grandad. Even the big, red-faced villager at the Barnies' show calls him Grandad. It is extremely unlikely that he is genuinely the entire village's Grandad, although if he is, it might explain why he seems shrivelled up, 'like an apple stored too long'. He speaks in a slow Cornish voice, and the children like him at once.

Mrs Janes

The mother of villainous Will Janes works at the butterfly farm in *Five Go to Billycock Hill*, despite being unable to bear insects of any sort. She has the appearance of a witch, but as Dick comments, 'She is no witch, just a poor frightened old woman.' She warms to the children when they offer her sympathy.

Janes, Will

The tall and burly son of Mrs Janes in *Five Go to Billycock Hill*, Will used to work on the Thomases' farm at Billycock Hill, but now mixes with a bad crowd, making a dramatic change for the worse. He regularly beats his mother and is incriminated in the plot to steal RAF planes from the nearby airfield.

Janie

Small, talkative girl who briefly meets the Famous Five in her mother's village shop in *Five on Finniston Farm*.

Jenkins, Ifor

Welsh gardener at Julian, Dick and Anne's house. Originally from the Welsh mountains, he puts the children in touch with his aunt, Mrs Jones, and they spend most of *Five Get into a Fix* with her on her farm in Magga Glen, Wales.

Jess

Involved in the theft of Sir James Lawton-Harrison's important blue-prints in *Five on a Secret Trail*, Jess's unconvincing 'country woman' disguise fails miserably to throw the children off the scent.

Jet

Guy Lawdler's dog in *Five on a Secret Trail*. Thinks big Timmy is wonderful.

Jim

Makes a brief appearance in *Five on a Hike Together* when popping into the village shop to collect his sandwiches. He works at Blackbush Farm.

Jim

This Jim works at Kirrin Garage and helps Julian locate a suspicious-looking silver-grey American car in *Five Have Plenty of Fun*.

Joanna (Joan)

Probably the best-known Blyton cook, Joan works at Kirrin Cottage and therefore appears regularly in the Famous Five series. Although never really involved in the adventures herself, she does discover Quentin's ransacked study in *Five Fall into Adventure*, and is always on hand to listen to the children relay their incredible tales. As far as the quality of her cooking is concerned, Dick proposes in *Five on Kirrin Island Again* that she be given the OBCBE – Order of the Best Cooks of the British Empire.

Johnson

See Willis and Johnson.

Captain Johnson

Big, burly owner of the riding school, where the Famous Five stay in *Five Go to Mystery Moor*.

Joll

Another of Morgan Jones's seven dogs mentioned in *Five Get into a Fix*.

Jones, Glenys

Has the Famous Five to stay with her at Magga Glen Farm in *Five Get into a Fix*. A kind old woman, with eyes as sharp and bright as a blackbird's, she is the mother of Morgan Jones.

Jones, Morgan

An extremely strong, broad-shouldered Welsh farmer who investigates the strange goings-on at Old Towers in *Five Get into a Fix*. He lives with his mother at Magga Glen Farm. For some time Julian suspects him of being involved himself in the activities at Old Towers. He doesn't talk much, but he has a loud booming voice which he uses to great effect when trapped below the hill at Old Towers, calling his seven dogs who rush to his rescue.

Kennedy

A pupil at Dick and Julian's school, Kennedy is mentioned briefly in *Five Go Adventuring Again*. Kennedy's snails crawl up the walls of the classroom during geography.

Kent, Richard

The twelve-year-old son of one of the richest men in the country, Richard is central to the plot of *Five Get into Trouble*. For much of the adventure the Five think very little of him. George calls him 'a little coward with no spunk'; and when his lies and deceit put Dick in serious danger, Blyton comments, 'Nobody liked him – nobody believed him – nobody trusted him.'

> *'I say – another ice cream for me. You really are a sport, Julian. I'll have to share something with you quickly. What about going to my island tomorrow?'*
>
> FIVE ON A TREASURE ISLAND

He redeems himself in dramatic, daring fashion, however. With the children held against their wishes at Owl's Dene, he heroically escapes to raise the alarm by hiding in the boot of their captor Perton's car as it leaves the grounds. 'I think quite a bit of Richard now!' exclaims Julian, and once again the Famous Five seem to have brought out the best in one of their young acquaintances.

Kent, Thurlow

The father of Richard Kent, he is one of the richest men in the country. He spends most of *Five Get into Trouble* on business in America, appearing only briefly at the end to welcome Richard back from his ordeal. Like many fathers in Blyton's works, he has quite a temper on him, and Richard appears to be frightened of him.

Killin, Tom

Bully at Julian and Dick's school. Mentioned briefly in *Five Go off to Camp*. Hung up on a high peg at school by Mr Luffy, and deservedly so.

Kirrin, Anne

Anne is the youngest member of the Famous Five (excluding Timmy), and the most reluctant adventurer. As she herself says in *Five Have Plenty of Fun*, 'I'm not very keen on adventures. I prefer adventures when they're all over.' How unfortunate for Anne that she should get caught up in twenty-one of them.

Anne often feels 'rather small and scared' during the Five's adventures, but she is not a coward. As Julian observes in *Five Get into Trouble*, 'Anne is more worried about us than she is about herself – and that makes her brave. She couldn't be a coward if she tried.' Anne's concern for the well-being of others is seen throughout the series.

She attends the same boarding school as George and the two are good friends, but they couldn't be more different. George strives hard to appear like a boy, while Anne is in many ways a classic girl. She loves her dolls, likes wearing pretty dresses, and proves to be a marvellous little housekeeper in *Five Go off to Camp*, getting the food ready and making the others' beds, tasks which she enjoys.

Anne's most infuriating habit is her ability absent-mindedly to give away some of the Five's secrets to grown-ups. It earns her many kicks under the dinner table, and Julian tells her that 'the only way to stop you giving away secrets is to sew up your mouth, like Brer Rabbit wanted to do to Mister Dog!'

Kirrin, Dick

One of the Famous Five, Dick is the brother of Julian and Anne, and cousin of George. While older brother Julian is the natural leader of the group, Dick is the most athletic of the Five, being particularly good at gym at school. Many's the time that Dick's agility and general fitness are used to save not just himself, but the others too. His daring rescue of George and Julian from the castle dungeons in *Five on a Treasure Island* makes for particularly exciting reading.

There is more to Dick than athleticism, however. He has a sharp brain on him, geared to solving mysteries, and he excels in *Five on a Hike Together* when unravelling clues to locate the *Saucy Jane*. He absolutely loves the Five's many adventures, for, as he himself says, 'It makes life exciting.'

Dick can be short-tempered, but there is also a kind side to his nature. He takes pity on Ragamuffin Jo in *Five Fall into Adventure*, giving her a bar of chocolate and some biscuits, and this after being caught by a sharp right hook from her! Jo in turn warms to Dick, telling the Famous Five, 'I only like him – he's nice. Yah to the rest of you!'

'I'm sorry, I nearly made a mistake, George,' she said.

Kirrin, George

George is one of the Famous Five, and one of Enid Blyton's most interesting characters, not least because she is based on Blyton herself at that age. George's full name is Georgina, but she insists on the shortened version, so desperate is she to be considered a boy. Anyone calling her Georgina can expect the fearsome scowl that, according to Dick in *Five on Kirrin Island Again*, she puts on half a dozen times a day.

George is very convincing as a boy. She boasts to Anne that she can climb better than any boy, and swim faster, too, and she is not far wrong, being a stronger swimmer than both Julian and Dick. Her father, the normally reserved Uncle Quentin, is sufficiently impressed by her actions in *Five on Kirrin Island Again* to tell her, 'you do behave as bravely as any boy'; while, in *Five Fall into Adventure*, Dick admits that 'she has as much spunk as any boy'. This is the biggest compliment anyone can pay her.

Unlike her cousins, George is an only child and she likes time on her own occasionally, despite thoroughly enjoying the others' company. She always has time for her dog Timmy, though, and is absolutely devoted to him. On the rare occasions we see George cry, it is usually because someone has upset Timmy, and whenever the Famous Five are confronted with danger, George is far more concerned for Timmy's safety than her own. In *Five Go to Mystery Moor*, for example, George, having been kidnapped, is only interested in what her captors have done with Timmy, never once asking to be released herself.

George is also the proud owner of Kirrin Island, the scene of many a Famous Five adventure and a popular holiday haunt for the children. Such is her affection for her three cousins that she draws up a deed in *Five on a Treasure Island*, giving each a quarter share. As her mother says, 'She can be very rude and haughty – but she's kind at heart, very loyal and absolutely truthful.'

Kirrin, Julian

The oldest member of the Famous Five, Julian is the natural leader of the group, much respected by the other four, including Timmy. He is twelve when we first see him in *Five on a Treasure Island*, and considerably older by the end of the Five's twenty-first and last adventure, *Five Are Together Again*.

Julian has many leadership qualities. He is tall and strong for his age, and is always prepared to stand up for the children's rights, no matter whom he may be dealing with. He is extremely impressive in giving the evil Mrs Stick a piece of his mind in *Five Run Away Together* (Blyton describes 'a grim and determined Julian, a very grown-up Julian, a rather frightening Julian') and if there is ever any answering back to be done, Julian always obliges.

George saw, to her dismay, that the man had a shining revolver in his hand.

He can also be extremely diplomatic when he needs to be. He immediately gains the respect of the RAF guard in *Five Go to Billycock Hill* when apologising for trespassing, using his clear, pleasant voice. As Blyton says, 'There was something about the boy that reassured people.' Julian's real skill would appear to be his ability to size up a situation perfectly, and then deal with it in a fitting manner.

Julian is full of ideas, another sign of his qualities as a leader, and the rest of the children automatically turn to him when a decision needs to be made. He can be wrong, though, as in *Five Go Down to the Sea* when he jeopardises the Fives' friendship with the Penruthlans by incorrectly accusing Mr Penruthlan of being a smuggler. With so many important decisions to make in the course of twenty-one adventures, though, Julian is allowed the odd slip-up. Like most Blyton children, he has a tremendous appetite and is particularly fond of ginger beer.

Lawdler, Guy

Guy is the son of famous explorer Sir John Lawdler and twin brother of Harry Lawdler. About twelve or thirteen, he is sturdily built and has the cheekiest face Anne has ever seen. He shares his father's passion for archaeology, but this gets him into trouble in *Five on a Secret Trail* when he starts digging on a site close to hidden stolen blue-prints. Concerned that he might know too much, the blue-print thieves drag him away and lock him up, but he is soon freed by the Famous Five.

Lawdler, Harry

Twin brother of Guy in *Five on a Secret Trail*. The two have some fearsome quarrels, but Harry is devastated when Guy goes missing, soaking Anne's handkerchief three times with his tears. He helps the Five free Guy from his captors.

Lawton-Harrison, Sir James

Never seen in person, Sir James has a very important blue-print stolen in *Five on a Secret Trail*.

Mrs Layman

Invites the Famous Five to stay at her place in *Five Have a Mystery to Solve*. The house sits isolated high up a hill, with an excellent view of the mysterious

'There they are!' said Julian, in excitement.

Whispering Island. Not surprisingly, the Five jump at the chance to stay there.

Lenoir, Marybelle

Appears in *Five Go to Smuggler's Top*. In contrast to half-brother Sooty's dark features, Marybelle appears pale and delicate. Initially a shy girl, but by the end of the book she is described as a bit of a chatterbox.

Mr Lenoir

A scientist, Lenoir works with Uncle Quentin on a plan to drain the marshes in *Five Go to Smuggler's Top*. Like Quentin, he is a strict disciplinarian; and, like Quentin, he has a temper that frightens the children. George bears the brunt of one of his outbursts while staying at his house, Smuggler's Top, when sent to her room for the day with just bread and water. He can be kind and jolly too, however, and no doubt pleases George by believing throughout that she is a boy. Mr Lenoir is the stepfather of Sooty, and natural father of Marybelle.

Mrs Lenoir

Not as prominent in the plot of *Five Go to Smuggler's Top* as her husband and two children, perhaps the most interesting thing that can be said about Mrs Lenoir is that she had the smallest hands and feet Anne had ever seen on a grown-up.

Lenoir, Pierre (Sooty)

A school friend of Dick and Julian, he is known as Sooty because 'he's awfully dark', and because his surname is French for 'The Black One'. Mr Lenoir is Sooty's stepfather and also his natural father's cousin. As Anne comments when told about the relationships within the Lenoir family, 'It's rather muddled.'

As far as the plot is concerned, Sooty lives at Smuggler's Top and plays a big part in the Five's adventure there. An excellent climber, with an adventurous spirit, he's indebted to Timmy when held prisoner with Uncle Quentin in one of the secret passages under his own house.

Liz

Sniffer's dog in *Five Go to Mystery Moor*, Liz is described as 'a bit of a spaniel, a bit of a poodle, and odd bits of something else'.

Mr Lomax

Richard Kent's holiday tutor in *Five Get into Trouble*. Is pretty awful, according to Richard.

Lucas

Groundsman at the golf club in *Five Have a Mystery to Solve*. He has a well-tanned body, with a face as brown as a well-ripened nut, and is so friendly and completely natural that the children feel he is an old, old friend.

Mr Luffy

Master at Julian and Dick's school who accompanies the children on camp in the aptly titled *Five Go off to Camp*. He is an elderly fellow with a passion for studying insect life. 'Old Luffy seems to live in the world of insects, not in our world!' comments Julian. But the children find him good fun, and he in turn likes the children. Has the ability to waggle his right ear if he wants to.

Maggie

A shady criminal figure in *Five on a Hike Together*, Maggie accompanies Dirty Dick in the ultimately unsuccessful search for the Fallonia jewels. She wears sunglasses, which might suggest a cool, calm, collected persona, but, like many Blyton criminals, she is prone to going red with rage.

Maggy

Mother of Aily in *Five Get into a Fix*. She used to wait on Mrs Thomas at Old Towers.

Markhoff

One of Red Towers's men in *Five Fall into Adventure*, Markhoff is easily outwitted by the Famous Five.

Martin

Befriended by the Famous Five in *Five on Kirrin Island Again*, Martin is a sad figure. His mother died 'ages ago' and he lives with Mr Curton, a guardian. He often looks dull, miserable and sullen, and with Curton as his guardian, this is hardly surprising. An excellent artist, he is denied the chance to indulge his passion by Curton who sees painting as a weak and feeble thing for a man to do.

Once free of his guardian, he becomes quite a different boy. His face turns bright and cheerful, and the news that Uncle Quentin will try to get him into an art school cheers him further. In many ways, Martin's story is similar to that of Edgar Stick's (*Five Run Away Together*). Both have a bad start in life, but both are given a fresh start and a glimmer of hope by Blyton at the end.

Matthew

Man paid by Llewellyn Thomas to keep his mother, Bronwen Thomas, locked in her room in *Five Get into a Fix*.

Mischief

Monkey who accompanies the Famous Five and his owner, Tinker Hayling, to Demon's Rocks in *Five Go to Demon's Rocks*. As his name suggests, he regularly gets into trouble, whether raiding the larder at Kirrin Cottage, or blowing Constable Sharp's police whistle. Timmy mistakes Mischief for some sort of queer cat.

Nailer

Mentioned by name only in *Five on a Hike Together*, Nailer is the sender of the cryptic message concerning the whereabouts of the Fallonia jewels. The message in full reads: 'Two Trees. Gloomy Water. Saucy Jane. And Maggie knows too.'

Nellie

One of three collie sheepdogs at Tremannon Farm in *Five Go Down to the Sea*, Nellie gets on well with Timmy.

Old Ben

Eighty-year-old blacksmith in *Five Go to Mystery Moor*. A mighty figure of a man who tells the children all about the strange happenings at Mystery Moor.

Old Man Gupps

A solemn old man who walks into the village store to buy a packet of blanc-mange powder in *Five on a Hike Together*. He smokes a clay pipe and smells very unwashed. The blancmange powder purchase is as exciting as it gets for this particular character.

One-Ear Bill

Evil figure who featured heavily in Demon's Rocks' murky past. The Famous Five learn of him from Jeremiah Boogle. He used to lure ships to their doom on the rocks, and swiftly loot them. People used to say he himself was the Demon of Demon's Rocks. As for his name, he apparently had his left ear chewed off by a monkey.

Pat

A hall porter at a hotel in Graysfield, Pat finds himself involved in the plot of *Five Have Plenty of Fun* when he overhears two criminals discussing the whereabouts of kidnap victim George.

Paul

Steals Sir James Lawton-Harrison's extremely important blue-print in *Five on a Secret Trail* and nearly dies escaping with it.

Mr Penruthlan

The farmer and owner of Tremannon Farm, where the Five stay during *Five Go Down to the Sea*. Known as Mr Penruthlan throughout, even by his wife, Mrs Penruthlan. Conversation with him is very difficult when he forgets to put his false teeth in, but when he remembers he speaks well, except for lisping slightly over his s's.

Relations between him and the children are soured when Julian sees him acting suspiciously in Wreckers' Cove and wrongly accuses him of being a smuggler. In fact he is working with the police in an undercover operation. All is forgiven when Julian and the Five play a big part in the smugglers' capture.

Mrs Penruthlan

Gives the Famous Five a grand welcome at Tremannon Farm in *Five Go Down to the Sea*. The mother of seven grown-up children, she loves the children's company and provides wonderful meals for them.

Mr Perton

Lives at Owl's Dene, 'a house of secrets, of queer comings and goings' featured in *Five Get into Trouble*. An evil character, he instructs one of his men to put down poisoned food for Timmy. On a less serious note, he's also involved in the escape from prison of Solomon Weston.

Peters

Peters is one of the workers at Olly's Farm in *Five Go off to Camp*. Like most of the farm workers in Olly's Farm, he doesn't look like a farm worker, and is actually involved in criminal operations with the farm's owner, Mr Andrews.

Miss Peters

George and Anne's House Mistress at school appears briefly in *Five on a Hike Together*. Could this be the same Miss Peters who taught at Malory Towers a few years earlier?

Philpot, Harriet (Harry)

Has an almost telepathic understanding with her identical twin brother Henry, also called Harry, in *Five on Finniston Farm*, and shares in the Famous Five's adventure there.

Philpot, Henry (Harry)

The identical twin brother of Harriet. Both twins are known as Harry and live at Finniston Farm, where the Famous Five stay in *Five on Finniston Farm*. Initially not welcoming, he becomes a good friend and shares in the exciting adventure.

Mrs Philpot

Wife of Trevor Philpot who appears in *Five on Finniston Farm*. She has a kind, tired face and cries for joy when her family's financial worries are solved.

Philpot, Trevor

Farmer who runs Finniston Farm, scene of the Famous Five's adventure in *Five on Finniston Farm*. He is forced to take in guests, including the Famous Five, because of financial difficulties, but his problems are solved when the children discover valuable antiques on his land. He looks very like the two Harrys, his twin children.

Pottersham, Jeffrey

No-good traitor who holds fellow scientist Derek Terry-Kane captive in Faynight Castle in *Five Have a Wonderful Time*. The author of several books about old castles, his extensive knowledge of Faynight Castle's layout counts for nothing when Beauty the python chases him back to the tower room, where he is promptly bolted in by Ragamuffin Jo.

Uncle Quentin

Quentin Kirrin is the father of George, and a scientist of international renown. Spends most of the time locked in his study working on highly important experiments. In *Five on Kirrin Island Again*, for example, he works on a new energy source to replace coal, coke and oil. So important are his experiments that he is regularly kidnapped by men eager to get their hands on his work. Quentin is a true workaholic, and even takes a case of work with him when going on holiday to Spain with Aunt Fanny.

He is not very good with children, and regularly loses his temper with George and her cousins when they stay at Kirrin Cottage. The children consider him to be 'awfully fierce', but Quentin warms to them a great deal after hearing of their heroic efforts in *Five on a Treasure Island*.

Rafe

One of Welsh farmer Morgan Jones's seven dogs, Rafe lives at Magga Glen Farm where the Famous Five stay in *Five Get into a Fix*.

Ragamuffin Jo

With the exception of the Five themselves, Jo is one of the best-known characters in the Famous Five series. She excels on debut in *Five Fall into Adventure* by escaping from and then capturing Red Towers and his men, and returns two adventures later to capture more crooks, this time Pottersham and his

The door flew open and an angry, frowning face looked in.

men in *Five Have a Wonderful Time*. On both occasions her training as an acrobat in the circus serves her extremely well. Not surprisingly, the Five are tremendously impressed. Even George finds praise for her, describing her as 'the bravest girl I ever knew'.

Jo's first encounter with the Five, though, is not an amicable one. She is seen wearing torn dirty shorts and a filthy jersey, hence the name Ragamuffin, and immediately upsets George by sitting in her sandy hole on the beach. She follows this up by fighting with Dick, catching him with a good right fist on the jawbone. Yet there is some sympathy for Jo. She leads an awful life, stuck in a squalid caravan with her wicked father who beats her regularly, and denied the opportunities in life that the four children have had. Jo vows to show the children she's 'not as bad as they make out', and they in turn allow her the chance to do so. Julian best sums her up when he says, 'She's a pickle and a scamp and a scallywag – but her heart's in the right place.'

Ricky

One of the two Kirrin Farm dogs, mentioned briefly in *Five Go Adventuring Again*.

Robins, Jock

A farm boy, Jock becomes friendly with the Famous Five when they call at his farm for food supplies in *Five Go off to Camp*. By contrast, he objects strongly to having to spend time with Cecil Dearlove, the son of his stepfather's friend.

Jock used to live on Owl Farm but had to move when his father died. He now lives with his mother and Mr Andrews, his stepfather. There is no evidence to suggest that his old home Owl Farm is in any way connected with Owl's Dene, the house of queer comings and goings in *Five Get into Trouble*.

Mr Roland

The tutor hired by Uncle Quentin for the children during the holidays in *Five Go Adventuring Again* is described as 'rather a queer-looking man'. He is short and burly, with a beard, rather like a sailor.

Mr Roland is soon accepted by Julian, Dick and Anne, but significantly not at all by Timmy or George. When, for example, the children and Mr Roland throw sticks on a frozen pond for Timmy to fetch, Timmy returns them all apart from Mr Roland's. As events unfold, it becomes clear that Timmy is a sound judge of character, for it is Mr Roland who provides the criminal interest in this adventure.

In league with Mr Thomas and Mr Wilton, two artists from London Town staying at nearby Kirrin Farm, he steals top secret pages from Uncle Quentin's work, and when one considers that Quentin's work is work that could be used 'for the good of the country' (Aunt Fanny), this is a serious crime indeed. But thanks in particular to the stirling efforts of Timmy, Roland and his accomplices are thwarted by the Five and are last seen being led away by grateful police.

Rooky

The lead villain in *Five Get into Trouble,* Rooky's biggest mistake is to involve the Famous Five in his activities by accidentally kidnapping Dick. If only he had kidnapped young Richard Kent, as he had intended, he might have had more success.

His motives for wanting to capture Richard are simple. It was because of Richard's interference that he had lost his job as bodyguard to Richard's father, the wealthy business man Thurlow Kent. Now free after a short spell in prison, Rooky is looking to exact his revenge. He fails miserably, however, and a return to prison seems inevitable when he is also found to have been hiding escaped prisoner Solomon Weston.

Not one of Blyton's more sophisticated villains, Rooky has a fearsome appearance with big lips and a huge nose.

Sally

Expensive pedigree poodle owned by Berta Wright in *Five Have Plenty of Fun.* Timmy happily welcomes her to Kirrin Cottage.

Sanders, John

First appearing in *Five Go Adventuring Again,* John Sanders is an old farmer who lives at Kirrin Farm with 'the Missis'. He has known George since she was a baby, knew her mother when she was a baby, and knew her granny as well. So, as Anne rather untactfully points out, he must be 'very, very, old'. He is popular with George, especially as he addresses her as 'Master' and not 'Miss'.

Sarah

The cook at Smuggler's Top (*Five Go to Smuggler's Top*), like most Blyton cooks, is fat, round and jolly. Her delicious ginger buns are recommended.

Sid

Paperboy whose evening delivery round includes Kirrin Cottage. In *Five Fall into Adventure* he spends an evening at the cottage while Dick borrows his bike to follow George's kidnappers, and he thoroughly enjoys himself. A simple boy, he finds a game of draughts with the children too challenging, but excels at a game of snap.

Sid

This Sid works the back end of Clopper the pantomime horse, star of the Barnies' show in *Five Go Down to the Sea*. He does this extremely well and, while he would dearly love to operate Clopper's front, he does at least get to swish Clopper's tail.

Simmy

The father of Ragamuffin Jo, it is clear from Blyton's first description of him in *Five Fall into Adventure* that Simmy is an unfavourable sort: 'He slouched as he came, and dragged one foot. He had a straggly moustache and mean, clever little eyes.' His CV does not make good reading. He regularly beats Jo, is involved in the plot to steal Quentin's papers, and is finally led away by the police after being captured by Jo herself.

Skippy

Not, as one might expect, a kangaroo, but the little wife of Bufflo the fair worker in *Five Have a Wonderful Time*. All the fair folk join in when she strikes up a soft melody with a gay little chorus on her guitar.

Mr Slither

Snake-keeper with the travelling fair in *Five Have a Wonderful Time*. He gives the children a most entertaining talk on snakes, and is the owner of Beauty the python who plays an important role in the capture of Pottersham and his men.

Sniffer

A thin, skinny misery of a boy who appears in *Five Go to Mystery Moor*, he is called Sniffer because he sniffles all the time and is unable to remember his

real name. His sorry state can be attributed directly to his dark-faced gypsy father, 'a nasty bit of work' who regularly cuffs him. Reluctant to help the Five for fear of his father, he nevertheless manages to leave a trail of signs to lead the children safely off the moor.

The adventure ends with his father being arrested by the police, and it is hoped that this will give Sniffer the chance to make a fresh start in life.

Sniffer's Father

A surly-looking gypsy man in *Five Go to Mystery Moor*, with enormous gold rings hanging from his ears. His untidy hair is a sure sign of his wickedness. Caught up in the import of forged dollars from the north of France, he is arrested before the notes can be passed on to a waiting gang in London.

Snippet

Tiny black poodle, owned by the Philpots in *Five on Finniston Farm*. He is easily wound up by Nosey the Jackdaw.

Spiky

A short, plump boy, Spiky is a terrific help to the Famous Five in *Five Have Plenty of Fun* when he snoops around Gringo's Fair looking for the kidnapped George. He's known as Spiky because of his hair which resolutely refuses to be flattened, no matter how much hair-oil is applied.

Stick, Clara

Employed as home-help for the seriously ill Aunt Fanny in *Five Run Away Together*, Mrs Stick is short-tempered, harsh and hated by the children. She often sends them to bed without any supper and, when the children suspect her of trying to poison Timmy, matters come to a head. The Five decide to run away together to Kirrin Island.

As the plot unfolds, the full extent of Mrs Stick's evil nature is revealed. Not only does she attempt to poison Timmy (to many young readers this would probably be the most appalling act of all), she also helps herself to anything handy in Kirrin Cottage. Most seriously, she is involved in the kidnap of Jennifer Mary Armstrong, daughter of millionaire Harry Armstrong, and demands a £100,000 ransom.

She doesn't work alone; her husband, Mr Stick, is heavily involved too, as is her young son, Edgar, however reluctantly. As with all criminals in the

Famous Five series, though, Mrs Stick and her family are ultimately unsuccessful in their efforts. They are last seen being led away by the police, trying
to work out how they came to be denied by four children and a dog.

Stick, Edgar

Mrs Stick's boy is about thirteen or fourteen. He stays at Kirrin Cottage with
her in *Five Run Away Together* and is not liked by the other children. Julian
calls him Spotty-Face, a typically insensitive Blyton nickname, and George dislikes him because 'he does silly things, like putting out his tongue and calling
rude names'. Blyton describes him as a stupid, yet sly-looking youth, but he is
not totally without hope. Blaming his wretched character on his parents who
'had taught him nothing but bad things', Blyton suggests that there might be a
chance for him if he were set a good example instead of a bad one.

Mr Stick

The husband of Clara and father of Edgar is the orchestrator of the criminal
activity in *Five Run Away Together*. His appearance is unmistakably that of a
Blyton criminal: unshaven, bluish-black cheeks, black hands and fingernails,
and untidy hair. We never discover Mr Stick's first name, but we do know
that he is a sailor by profession.

Tang

One of Morgan Jones's seven dogs in *Five Get into a Fix*, Tang gives Timmy a
very hostile reception when he arrives at Magga Glen Farm.

Terry-Kane, Derek

Scientist who is kidnapped by his partner, Jeffrey Pottersham, in *Five Have a
Wonderful Time*. Being a scientist in the Famous Five series is certainly a high-
risk business, as regular kidnap victim Uncle Quentin will testify. Terry-Kane
is held in the hope that he will reveal details of his latest secret experiment to
interested parties on the Continent. But unlike Pottersham, he is no traitor
and is freed by the Famous Five with his secrets still intact.

Thomas, Benny

Younger brother of Toby Thomas in *Five Go to Billycock Hill*. He goes
everywhere with his pet pig, Curly. Anne in particular finds him adorable.

Thomas, Bronwen

Locked up in her own home, Old Towers, by her son Llewellyn Thomas in *Five Get into a Fix*, after refusing to agree to its sale. She is rightly concerned that the potential buyers are interested only in the rare, powerful metal below the house, which they would use to manufacture bombs.

Thomas, Jeff

Flight Lieutenant Jeff Thomas is the cousin of Toby Thomas, and is stationed at the RAF base near Billycock Farm. He is accused of stealing two valuable planes and passing them on to the enemy, but it is clear that he is innocent. After all, Timmy likes him and Timmy is an excellent judge of character.

Thomas, Llewellyn

The son of Bronwen Thomas, he is behind the criminal activity at Old Towers in *Five Get into a Fix*. For much of the time his mother is unaware of his involvement, believing him to have been killed for refusing to agree, like her, to the sale of the house. In fact Llewellyn is heavily involved in the illegal manufacture of bombs underneath Old Towers, and pays one of his men to keep his mother locked in her room so that she can't interfere.

Mr Thomas

The owner of Billycock Farm, visited by the Famous Five in *Five Go to Billycock Hill*, Mr Thomas is a farmer with a kindly brown face who helps in the search for his nephew, Jeff Thomas, and Ray Wells.

Thomas, Sarah

The mother of Toby and Benny, Mrs Thomas provides plenty of good meals for the Famous Five during their stay at the farm in *Five Go to Billycock Hill*. As one would expect of a good Blyton cook, she is a plump and jolly woman.

Thomas, Toby

A friend of Julian and Dick's, whom the Famous Five visit on his father's farm in *Five Go to Billycock Hill*. A bit of a joker who likes to play the fool, he soon upsets George with his spider. He hero-worships his cousin, Flight Lieutenant Jeff Thomas, and is devastated when he goes missing, presumed dead.

Thompson Minor

Briefly mentioned in *Five Go Adventuring Again*, Thompson Minor is the owner of white mice at Julian and Dick's school, despite no pets being allowed there. Matron squeals the place down when they escape.

Timmy

The canine member of the Famous Five, owned by George, who found him out on the moors when he was a puppy and absolutely adores him. When we first encounter Timmy in *Five on a Treasure Island* he is being looked after by Alf the fisherboy, having been banished from Kirrin Cottage by George's father, Quentin. Timmy, it seems, is far too mischievous for no-nonsense Uncle Quentin.

This is not the only time Timmy is banned from a household. When the Five stay at Smuggler's Top in *Five Go to Smuggler's Top*, Timmy is forced to stay in the secret passage behind George's room, as Mr Lenoir (like Quentin, a scientist, and similarly strict in character) simply won't tolerate dogs in the house.

On both occasions, though, Timmy wins favour with the strict landlords, and is allowed in. Quite right too, for Timmy really is a fine dog. Quite what type of dog he is, however, is difficult to tell. Blyton writes in *Five on a Treasure Island* that 'he was the wrong shape, his head was too big, his ears were too pricked, and his tail was too long'.

Timmy's value as a member of the Famous Five cannot be underestimated. If Timmy hadn't retrieved the map of Kirrin Castle after it fell overboard, the Five's first adventure might never have got underway. He can also be extremely fierce when he needs to be, and provides considerable security for the children.

Perhaps Timmy's most impressive attribute is being a remarkable judge of character. He is normally a very welcoming dog and the few characters he shuns invariably turn out to be dangerous criminals.

He leapt into the water and swam valiantly after the map.

Tinker

Mangy-looking dog owned by evil Clara Stick in *Five Run Away Together*. George calls him Stinker because 'he hardly ever has a bath, and he's jolly smelly'. His general appearance, with patchy, dirty white coat, and tail well between his legs, contrasts sharply with that of the strong, much-loved Timmy. When Timmy triumphs over Tinker in a memorable fight scene outside Kirrin Cottage kitchen, it is effectively good triumphing over bad.

Tom

Burly fellow who works for the rich villain Red Towers in *Five Fall into Adventure*.

Tom

Mentioned briefly by his mother, the shop lady, in *Five on a Hike Together*. He is a warder at the big prison on the moor.

Tom

Involved in the theft of the important blue-print in *Five on a Secret Trail*, this Tom has a struggle to prise up the heavy stone slab leading to the secret way, even with the use of a jemmy.

Mr Toms

Dick's form-master at school. In *Five Go to Smuggler's Top*, Dick recalls the time Mr Toms had his chair sabotaged by Sooty Lenoir, so that it collapsed as soon as he sat down.

Towers, Red

The man behind the plot to steal Uncle Quentin's papers in *Five Fall into Adventure*. Like many of Blyton's criminals he is bearded. And, like many of Blyton's criminals, his great plans are foiled by the children. He lives in a queer castle-like building, accessible only by boat, and gets fellows like Jo's father Simmy to do his dirty work for him.

Tremayne, Joe

Big red-faced villager who goes to watch the Barnies perform in *Five Go Down to the Sea*.

Wells, Ray

Flight Lieutenant Ray Wells appears in *Five Go to Billycock Hill*. He is accused, with Flight Lieutenant Jeff Thomas, of stealing two valuable planes from the RAF and passing them on to the enemy. In fact both are innocent, and are trapped in Billycock Caves by the real thieves until Curly the pig discovers them.

Weston, Solomon

Escaped prisoner discovered by Julian in a secret panel behind a bookcase at Owl's Dene, in *Five Get into Trouble*.

Wilfrid

In *Five Have a Mystery to Solve* Wilfrid is the young grandson of Mrs Layman, whom he (for reasons best known to himself and Blyton) refers to as his aunt. He is initially unhappy when the Famous Five come to stay with him at his grandmother's house while she is away, but soon warms to the wonderful Timmy. Exceptionally rude, he upsets Anne so much that the normally quiet little girl loses it completely and drenches him with water, much to everyone's amazement. His manners show a marked improvement afterwards. Wilfrid accompanies the Five to Whispering Island, and finds the adventure there tremendously exciting.

Wilkins

The policeman in *Five Go to Mystery Moor* who is one step behind the Famous Five. Julian explains the gypsies' secret operations to him.

Will

An old fellow with a shrivelled face, Will is one of the few good workers on Olly's Farm in *Five Go off to Camp*.

William

One of the children staying at Captain Johnson's Riding School with the Famous Five in *Five Go to Mystery Moor*, William shows maturity beyond his years when helping Henry to rescue George and Anne from the moor.

Willis and Johnson

Awful swotters at Julian and Dick's school who never have any time for fun, but are hailed by the boys in *Five on a Hike Together* when the school has a weekend off to celebrate their scholarships.

Willy

Sheepdog at Tremannon Farm in *Five Go Down to the Sea*. A beautiful collie who soon befriends Timmy.

Wooden-Leg Sam

Watchman who works by the deserted old railway line in *Five Go off to Camp*. Blyton's description of him is not particularly flattering. As well as having a wooden leg, he has two great arms 'that might quite well belong to a gorilla', a face as red as a tomato, and grey whiskers. He spends most of his time worrying about the mysterious spook-trains that go through the tunnel at night with nobody on board. 'I lock myself into my hut and get under the bed,' he tells the children, which might explain why he has so far failed to win any Watchman of the Year awards.

Mr Wooh

The magician with the travelling circus in *Five Are Together Again*, Mr Wooh is tall, commanding and handsome. He has a curiously deep voice, with a distinct foreign accent. But he is unable to magic his way out of prison when found guilty of using Charlie the Chimp to steal Professor Hayling's important charts and diagrams.

Wright, Berta

The daughter of important American scientist Elbur Wright, Berta stays at Kirrin Cottage in *Five Have Plenty of Fun* when threatened by kidnappers desperate to get their hands on her father's secret new scheme. A slim, pretty little girl with large blue eyes and wavy golden hair, she is twice forced to change identities in a bid to fool her potential kidnappers. The first change sees her dress as a boy and assume the name Lesley, something she absolutely hates. Her second change coincides with a visit to the Five's friend Ragamuffin Jo, in an attempt to throw the kidnappers off her trail once and for all.

The kidnappers are fooled to a certain extent; they capture George by mistake. This highly unsatisfactory state of affairs is resolved in the end, though, and Berta's father's secrets remain intact.

Berta has a strong American accent, and is prone to use American expressions like 'Great Snakes!' The children regularly take her to task over her pronunciation. Even Aunt Fanny tells the poor girl off, informing her, 'it's twenTY, not twenny'.

Wright, Elbur

One of the world's leading scientists, American Elbur Wright works on an important project with Uncle Quentin in *Five Have Plenty of Fun*. When men desperate to get their hands on details of his and Quentin's new scheme seriously threaten his daughter Berta, he is prepared to give the secrets away in return for his daughter's safety. He shows a great deal more sensitivity in this matter than Quentin who asks, 'How can he even think of giving away secrets for the sake of a silly girl?'

He and George agreed about every single thing except rabbits.

THE SECRET SEVEN

The Secret Seven (1949)
Secret Seven Adventure (1950)
Well Done, Secret Seven (1951)
Secret Seven on the Trail (1952)
Go Ahead, Secret Seven (1953)
Good Work, Secret Seven (1954)
Secret Seven Win Through (1955)
Three Cheers, Secret Seven (1956)
Secret Seven Mystery (1957)
Puzzle for the Secret Seven (1958)
Secret Seven Fireworks (1959)
Good Old Secret Seven (1960)
Shock for the Secret Seven (1961)
Look Out, Secret Seven (1962)
Fun for the Secret Seven (1963)

The Secret Seven is an exclusive club formed by Peter and his younger sister, Janet, concentrating on solving mysteries or puzzles in the neighbourhood in which they live. Peter and Janet are characters from two early Blyton works that were expanded to form the Seven series, which followed on from the popular Famous Five. The Seven are: Peter, Janet, Jack, Colin, George, Pam and Barbara. Unlike Timmy the dog in the Famous Five who is an official member of the gang, Scamper, Peter and Janet's golden spaniel, is not one of the Seven, but simply accompanies them on every adventure they encounter. The Seven meet every holiday in the shed at the bottom of Peter and Janet's garden, and no member is admitted into the gathering without whispering the secret password outside the door first. The meetings are always punctuated with endless and delicious supplies of food from the children's mother, and are frequently interrupted by Jack's mischievous little sister, Susie.

Alice

Woman who comes to do Secret Seven member Jack's family washing once a week and puts in her debut appearance in the eighth book, *Three Cheers,*

Secret Seven. She lives in a little cottage in Green Lane and delights the children by supplying them with gingerbread, 'sticky as can be', when they arrive to question her about her acquaintance Georgie Grim.

American Cousin of Jack and Susie

A generous relation from the other side of the big pond who kindly gives Jack a cowboy suit and Susie a wonderful toy aeroplane. This happens in the opening chapter of the eighth book, *Three Cheers, Secret Seven*, and his generosity sparks off the next adventure for the Secret Seven.

Antique Shopkeeper

The owner of an antique shop is disturbed when his shop is broken into in the middle of the night and a precious violin is stolen from the window in *Puzzle for the Secret Seven*, the tenth book in the series. Colin and Jack are there when the crime takes place, but in the darkness of the night it is impossible to see who the thief is.

Artistic-Looking Woman

A woman who looks as if she could be an artist appears in connection with the robbery of a number of valuable paintings in *Good Old Secret Seven*. The adventure begins when the children take a look through the telescope that Jack and Susie are given by their uncle Bob and spot curious goings-on in the castle on the other side of their village.

Baby

A plump and smiley baby features in *Puzzle for the Secret Seven* as the youngest offspring of Mr and Mrs Luke Bolan.

Barbara

Quiet Barbara is the most ineffectual member of the Secret Seven, rarely holding a key role in the unfolding of the numerous mysteries that the club is involved in, but still an integral part of the overall structure of the group. Her great friend is Pam; the two are rarely apart, and usually share the same views on what they are pleased about or afraid of. They even agree on the subject of Jack's troublesome little sister, Susie. As Barbara comments: 'Susie's very strong really.' This remarkable perception from one of the people whom Susie spends her time trying to outwit says a great deal for Barbara's sagacity and observation.

She is as giggly and silly as Pam, and the two are often quite crippled with hilarity at key moments in the Secret Seven's business because they seem to have quite a bad effect on each other's self-composition. She and Pam are often going to parties, much to their regret, as it sometimes prevents them from attending important Secret Seven meetings. They are also highly qualified gossipmongers who often have to be silenced by Peter for not concentrating on the important issues in hand. Barbara can be rather stupid and will ask questions such as 'How do we set about it?' when Peter allocates her a task. In return, he replies with great impatience: 'I can't explain such easy things to you.'

Binkie

The snuffly-nosed friend of Susie, Jack's younger sister, Binkie is a terrible chatterbox who 'only needed long furry ears' to look exactly like Peter and Janet's rabbit of the same name. She appears in two books in the series, *Puzzle for the Secret Seven*, the tenth book, and *Good Old Secret Seven*, the twelfth. It is said that: 'Susie was bad enough alone but when she and Binkie were together, the two were impossible.' Gushing and silly, Binkie is a potential threat to any sane plans that the Secret Seven make, as her inane banter is ceaseless and very irritating. She even composes a rude poem about the Seven which ends with the words: 'We think the Secret Seven / Are silly as can be.'

Uncle Bob

Secret Seven member Jack's uncle Bob appears in *Good Old Secret Seven* when he kindly gives Jack and Susie a telescope as a present. Jack and Susie appear to have generous relatives, as their American cousin too gives them presents (a model aeroplane and a cowboy suit) in *Three Cheers, Secret Seven*.

Bolan, Benny

A striking-looking, blind musical genius and son of Luke and Mrs Bolan, Benny appears in *Puzzle for the Secret Seven* where he is the subject of much debate and curiosity.

Bolan, Luke

Father of two and husband to a little fat woman who works at the local fair selling gingerbread. The Bolan family are the central characters in *Puzzle for the Secret Seven*, as their house is burnt down by a fire and the Seven step in to help. Luke Bolan is a 'good enough fellow' who finds himself on the wrong side of the law when he steals a valuable violin for his blind son to play.

Mrs Bolan

The wife of Luke Bolan, and mother of a dear little baby and of Benny, the blind child, Mrs Bolan appears in *Puzzle for the Secret Seven*. Generous and friendly, she gives the Seven free gingerbread at the fair because they had run out of money, and she is overwhelmed by the kind gesture of the Seven and Peter and Janet's parents to let them stay in Matt's old caravan when their shack is burnt down.

Bony

Aptly named French boy who is as thin as a rake and appears in the thirteenth adventure, *Shock for the Secret Seven*. Bony is staying with Jack and Susie and is quite confused when Susie tries to drag him along to interrupt a Secret Seven meeting. He has an amazing way with dogs, and any hound that comes near him seems to be bewitched by the boy. Perhaps it is he who is stealing local pedigree canines?

General Branksome

Adorable old General Branksome has his collection of medals stolen from him and is quite distraught until Colin visits him and promises that he will find them and bring them back to the old man. The General appears in *Look Out, Secret Seven*, the fourteenth and penultimate book in the series. He actually weeps in front of Colin when he speaks of the stolen medals and is quite overcome by the whole situation.

Briggs, Henry

The Secret Seven track down Henry Briggs when Peter and Janet's father's car is stolen and a glasses case with Briggs' name on is found in the front seat. However, when they find him and question him on the matter, it transpires that he is actually a friend of Peter and Janet's father, and had left the case in the car long before the crime was committed.

Brownie

Horse looked after by Old Man Tolly but owned by cruel farmer Dinneford who features in the fifteenth book in the series, *Fun for the Secret Seven*. Brownie is a handsome steed who has won many prizes in his time and, therefore, is a prime victim of the horse thieves who have appeared in the neighbourhood. However, with the Secret Seven on the case, the thieves are caught and Brownie celebrates his thirteenth birthday at the end of the book, looking forward to wearing the new saddle the Seven had raised funds for and being ridden by Peter and Janet.

Mr Burton

Works for Peter and Janet's father in *Secret Seven Fireworks* as a hedger and ditcher. He states that he likes 'sun, wind and rain' and is happy in his job as it 'takes him outdoors'. The Seven request some of the twigs that he has chopped down for their bonfire.

Caretaker

A cross-patch of a caretaker appears in *The Secret Seven*, book one in the series. He is furious to discover that 'meddling kids' are hunting around the house he is looking after, and cries out that he is going to 'teach you to make fun at me, you and your dog!' after they fire questions at him about the mystery they are trying to solve.

Mr Cartwright

Only referred to in *Shock for the Secret Seven*, when his dachshund is stolen by a mysterious dog thief.

Cheeky Charlie

Jack's aunt's dog whose name is used as a password by the Seven. Little do they realise that this canine has a namesake who is the leader of a gang, in *Secret Seven on the Trail*, planning to divert a train carrying valuable lead onto another line.

Circus Small Girl

Peter calls this lass over for a chat in *Secret Seven Adventure*, to enquire whether there are any one-legged men in the circus. She replies: 'All of us here have got our two legs – and need 'em!' Good point.

Codger

'A nice but ugly little mongrel dog who thought that his master was the finest man he had ever seen!', Codger appears in the fifteenth and last book in the series, *Fun for the Secret Seven*, and proves to be as faithful and loving to Old Man Tolly as Scamper is to Peter and Janet.

Colin

Colin is one of the four boys in the Secret Seven and appears in all fifteen books in the series. Like all members of the club, his mission is to rid the neighbourhood of crooks, thieves and criminals, and see them safely led away by the police, muttering that they cannot believe they have been outdone by cheeky kids. Colin is the least adventurous of the four boys, preferring to keep out of trouble and, as a result, always finding himself in extremely dodgy scenarios. He follows a man with a poodle down the street, thinking he could be a potential dog thief, only to be accused of trying to steal the dog himself. 'Gosh!' says Colin, scuttling home, 'I've done my bit today. I wonder how the others got on?'

Colin's moment of triumph comes in *Look Out, Secret Seven* when he makes a promise to General Branksome who lives next door to him that he will return the old man's stolen medals. The General replies: 'I believe you, boy! I believe you'll find them! Ah, you're a boy after my own heart! You'll be winning medals too, some day!' Although Colin makes his promise in an over-whelming surge of pity towards the General, he does return his medals to him, earning the respect and admiration of a man who has fought in many a battle.

Colin's Cousin

Colin's cousin is discussed briefly in *Secret Seven Win Through*, as the club are trying to think of a punishment for Jack's young sister, Susie, who they fear has been snooping around their new meeting place. Colin recalls a trick that his cousin played on a friend. The jester got a reel of cotton and wound it across the entrance of a summer house after covering the cotton with honey. When the unfortunate victim walked in, he thought he had walked into a giant spider's web.

Colin's Grandpa

Mentioned in *Go Ahead, Secret Seven* as having a quick, dry cough, similar to that of a suspicious character Colin has been shadowing.

Colin's Mother

Like all the Secret Seven mothers, Colin's is a smashing cook and provides some delicious ginger buns for the group in *Secret Seven Win Through*, the seventh book in the series.

Colin's Mother's Friend

Secret Seven member Colin comments that his mother's friend breeds bull terriers. This fascinating piece of information is revealed in *Go Ahead, Secret Seven*.

Mrs Cook

Mentioned in *Shock for the Secret Seven*. Works on the farm owned by Peter and Janet's parents and reports to Janet that Mr Kaye has had his prize Alsatian puppy stolen. News of this latest canine abduction travels fast through the village.

Mr Dinneford

Vindictive, mean and heartless local farmer who owns Brownie, the horse looked after by Old Man Tolly in *Fun for the Secret Seven*. Mr Dinneford

blames Tolly for Brownie's lameness, even though it is not his fault, and eventually sells Brownie to Peter and Janet's father who, in turn, sells the horse on to Tolly himself.

Dog-Breeder

A dog-breeder is mentioned in *Shock for the Secret Seven*. The Seven decide that he is a suspicious character and may be carrying out the dog robberies that have been occurring, but then realise that he breeds dogs and would not dream of stealing them. He does not take kindly to Pam and Barbara snooping around his kennels.

Dog-Handler

A dog-handler makes a sudden appearance in *Look Out, Secret Seven*. He is in charge of Sasha and Vanya, the two Alsatian dogs that come to the rescue of the Seven when they are trapped in Bramley Woods by a ferocious dog called Nabber. His smooth handling of the collective canines prompts George to comment: 'I'll jolly well train to be a dog-handler as soon as I'm old enough!'

Doris

Friend of Susie's, Jack's annoying little sister, and a member of Susie's rival gang in *Secret Seven Fireworks*. Susie, Doris and Hilda become the Tiresome Three and succeed in their mission of driving the Secret Seven around the bend. Doris is also mentioned in *Good Work Secret Seven*, the sixth book in the series, once again in connection with Susie and her annoying ways.

Miss Downey

Poor Miss Downey loses her priceless little scottie to the dog thief in *Shock for the Secret Seven*.

Miss Ely

Nanny to Susie, Jack's naughty little sister, Miss Ely is mentioned in the first book in the Secret Seven series, and is rather a tiresome woman. She favours Susie over Jack, considering Jack to be dirty, noisy and bad-mannered, and is furious when Jack kicks her under the table at supper. She sends him straight to bed as a punishment.

Emma

Nurse to General Branksome who is mentioned in *Look Out, Secret Seven*, Emma duly supplies the inevitable biscuits and lemonade when Colin goes to visit the General and discusses the theft of his medals.

Mrs Fellows

Seen cleaning her windows through Jack and Susie's telescope in *Good Old Secret Seven*.

Fingers

A dodgy man with half a finger missing on one hand and hair so short that he looks like an escaped prisoner, Fingers appears in *Good Work, Secret Seven*. He is found by the Seven when they dress up as a guy in a wheelbarrow, and listen in on various plans and schemes being made by this undesirable scumbag.

Fireman

Peter calls the fire brigade in the tenth book, *Puzzle for the Secret Seven*, when he spots a burning house after a visit to the funfair at Hilly Down. The firemen are quick to arrive on the scene and one of them questions Peter as to whether there could be a well in the vicinity from which to obtain water. Even in the face of such an awesome sight, Janet draws analogies with food, commenting that it is 'like a million bacon rashers frying at once'.

Mr Frampton

A smart name for a smart gentleman – Mr Frampton is a key figure in *Three Cheers, Secret Seven*. He makes the acquaintance of Peter and Jack when he and Mr Grim catch the two boys snooping around Bartlett Manor looking for clues as to why they have seen a gas fire burning in the supposedly deserted house. Frampton carries an umbrella, wears a bowler hat and works in the bank.

Fred

Delivery boy for the vet who features in *Fun for the Secret Seven*. When Fred goes away to stay with his grandfather for two weeks, he is replaced by Bob Smith who is hoping to earn enough money to help out Old Man Tolly and Brownie the horse.

Gardener

Peter and Janet's parents' gardener appears in the eleventh book in the series, *Secret Seven Fireworks*. He is not amused when the Seven wish to take his store of onions out of the shed that they use for their meetings.

George

George of the Secret Seven is one of the four boys that make up the club of children who spend their days solving local mysteries and puzzles. As he is a valuable member of the society, there is great distress when George is forced to resign after a man he was 'shadowing' as part of his Secret Seven work grabs him and takes him back home. George's father decides that his behaviour is disgraceful and that he should not be allowed to belong to a club where the members spend their time stalking members of the public. George's departure from the Seven means that they elect another member although, strangely enough, they do not elect anyone new when Jack temporarily leaves. In George's absence, the dependable Scamper takes his place so that the club does not need to change its name to the Secret Six. George is not forgotten, however, and by the end of the book, his father concedes that he should go along to the next meeting and get himself reinstated, much to the joy of the rest of the club.

George's Father

George is a valuable member of the Secret Seven, so the others are shocked when his father bans him from the club after he is caught 'shadowing' a sup- posedly innocent man down the street. George certainly would not dream of disobeying his parents in principle, but does go on to do some investigating of his own. It is mentioned that his father 'did not look kindly on any display of temper'.

George's Granny

George's granny is a provider of humbugs for a Secret Seven meeting in *Good Work, Secret Seven*.

George's Mother

Only mentioned properly in *Go Ahead, Secret Seven* when she is described as being 'shocked' by her son's behaviour when she hears that he has been 'shadowing' a man as part of his work for the Secret Seven. She agrees with George's father that he should not belong to the club any more if that is the sort of behaviour he is indulging in.

Greta

Colin's granny's Austrian helper who features briefly in *Secret Seven Fireworks*.

Grocer

Peter stumbles across a very rude grocer in *Good Work, Secret Seven* who tells him to 'Clear off!' after accusing Peter of stealing fruit from his stall.

Grim, Georgie

Mr and Mrs Grim emerge in the eighth book, *Three Cheers, Secret Seven*, as mysterious residents of the supposedly deserted Bartlett Lodge. Mr Grim is specified as being 'thick set and broad-shouldered with a ruddy, surly face and screwed-up eyes'.

Mrs Grim

Wife of the disturbingly erratic Georgie Grim, whom the Secret Seven find hard to figure out, Mrs Grim is revealed in the last few chapters of *Three Cheers, Secret Seven* as a weak and ailing old lady who is being looked after by her dependable husband.

Harris

Policeman who comes to the rescue of the Seven in *Look Out, Secret Seven*, when they are trapped in Bramley Woods on a dark night with a growling Alsatian looming over them.

Harris, Lucy Ann

See Lane, Emma.

Harris, Mary Margaret

See Lane, Emma.

Harry

Member of Susie's, Jack's sister's, rival gang to the Secret Seven, the Famous Five. They seem incapable of thinking up an original name, and christen themselves after the club that they have read so much about. Blyton obviously enjoyed referencing her own work.

Harry

Friendly and capable stable lad who appears in *Secret Seven Mystery*. Works alongside the rather less approachable Tom.

Headmaster

The Headmaster of Jack's school (which is also the school of the other three boys in the Secret Seven) is mentioned in *Good Work, Secret Seven*. Barbara suggests that he might be a member of a gang the Seven are tracking down, until Jack points out that he is his headmaster. 'Still,' Jack concedes, 'he does look a bit grim.'

Healey, Colonel James

Mentioned in the first book in the Secret Seven series as the owner of the stolen racehorse Kerry Blue. His reward to the Seven for recovering his nag is tickets to the circus, much to their collective delight.

Hilda

Crops up in *Secret Seven Mystery* in Warner's Riding Stables, where Janet and George are snooping around trying to gather information about the missing girl, Elizabeth Sonning. Two years below Janet at school. (There is also a Hilda mentioned in *Secret Seven Fireworks*, book eleven in the series, which could be the same girl, as she is a friend of Susie's who is younger than the other seven members.)

Mr Holikoff

Resident at 64 Heycom Street, Covelty, Mr Holikoff is a mysterious figure who never actually materialises in the first book in the series, but is important as he is the owner of the house where Kerry Blue, the stolen racehorse, is kept.

Inspector

The authority figure and voice of adulthood who features mainly in the closing chapters of the Secret Seven books, and makes comments such as: 'Dear me, what bright ideas you children have ... You seem to have done most of the work for me!' The Inspector is a good friend of the Seven despite the fact that they succeed in outwitting him and all his colleagues in solving every local mystery or crime throughout the fifteen books of the series.

Jack

Jack is second-in-command to Peter in the Secret Seven and appears as a focal character throughout all fifteen books in the series, not least because he is the unfortunate brother of Susie, who sets out to destroy the Secret Seven whenever she can. Poor Jack is constantly finding himself in difficult circumstances as a result, and at one point even resigns as a member of the Society because Peter gives him such a hard time when Susie invades one of their meetings with her skinny friend, the French boy, Bony. Jack's departure from the Seven leaves everyone extremely despondent, as he is a key figure in their mystery-solving lives, but naturally everything comes together again by the end of the book, and Jack is reinstated as a member.

Jack is brave and intrepid when it comes to the matter of cracking down on

local crime, sneaking out of his bedroom at night and disobeying his parents and Susie's nanny, Miss Ely, when he feels that he needs to gather more clues or information. Like all Secret Seven members, he has great respect for his parents and, although Susie is infuriating most of the time, he will not have anyone else being rude to or about her, simply because she is his sister, claiming that: 'Susie *can* be really sensible when she wants.'

Old James

Ancient blind man who works on Peter and Janet's parents' farm and is mentioned in *Secret Seven Win Through* in connection with the scarecrow that he has placed in the oat-field. According to James, the scarecrow has a robin's nest in each pocket.

Jack raced at top speed, his mind in a whirl. He couldn't forget what he had seen in that shed. He must tell someone, he must. If what he had seen meant what he thought it did, the great Dog Mystery was solved! SHOCK FOR THE SECRET SEVEN

Janet

Sister of Peter, the Secret Seven's creative director and chief, Janet is the most admirable of the three girls in the club as she is the only one who does not spend the majority of her time either giggling or crying. Janet is described as 'a fine kind of sister to have – a really good member of the Secret Seven', especially when compared with Jack's meddlesome sister Susie who succeeds in ruining as much of the Secret Seven's work as she can. Janet's contributions to meetings and investigations are always lively and constructive, and how proud she is when Peter tells her how well she has done! It is stated in *Go Ahead, Secret Seven* that 'Janet loved Peter to praise her.'

Janet, like her brother, is always looking forward to meetings of the Seven when she gathers together as much food and drink as she can for the members to feast on. There is nothing that Janet enjoys more than squeezing lemons into a big jug to make fresh lemonade, or carrying a tray of currant buns into the old shed for a meeting. Definitely a believer in food being a catalyst to constructive thought, she revels in providing the Seven with sustenance for their adventures.

Janet has been known to have sudden brainwaves that send the Secret Seven on the road to catching their bandits, as can be seen when she suddenly deciphers a mysterious message and realises what its true significance is: 'In the middle of all this, Janet suddenly sat up and said in a loud voice, "WELL I NEVER!"'

Jeff

Thin, pale, long-haired youth who appears in the third book in the series, *Well Done, Secret Seven*. Jeff lives in the same tree that the Seven decide to build a tree-house in during the hot summer holidays. He tells Peter and Colin that he has no father and, when his mother goes to hospital, he is sent to live with his bad uncle and aunt who he claims are criminals. Peter, Colin and the rest of the Seven set about making things right and foiling the master plan of these wicked people.

Jeff

Jeff appears in *Secret Seven on the Trail* as a friend of Jack's sister Susie and a member of her rival gang the Famous Five, named after their literary heroes. Jeff is probably quite a cowardly boy as, when he suggests that he might knock 'Stumpy Dick' (a make-believe criminal) to the ground, the rest of the gang dissolve into laughter. He appears again in the seventh book in the series, *Secret Seven Win Through*, as Susie's comrade.

Jim

A dodgy man mentioned in *Secret Seven Win Through* as one of the three criminals who commit a mail-bag robbery and hide the results beside the scarecrow in Peter and Janet's parents' farmland.

Jim

Jim is heard producing some 'enormous guffaws' when he and two others, under the guidance of Susie, succeed in fooling the Secret Seven into a false adventure. 'Oh what a joke! To think they had brought the stuck-up Secret Seven all the way to the shed just to see *them*!'

Johns

Johns is the amicable gardener and friend of Peter and Janet's father's cow-man who works in the grounds of Milton Manor, the house of Lady Lucy Thomas who has her necklace stolen in *Secret Seven Adventure*.

Jones, Harry

Spotted through Jack and Susie's telescope in *Good Old Secret Seven*, stealing an orange from the greengrocer's cart. He is not referred to again.

Jumbo

Unsurprisingly, Jumbo is an elephant who appears in the circus the Seven visit in the second book, *Secret Seven Adventure*.

Kate

Friend of Susie's, Jack's irritating little sister, mentioned in *Secret Seven on the Trail*. She and Susie form a rival club to the Secret Seven and christen it the Famous Five in memory of their favourite books.

Mr Kaye

Mr Kaye has his beautiful prize Alsatian puppy stolen by the mysterious dog thief in *Shock for the Secret Seven*.

Kerry Blue

Valuable and magnificent racehorse stolen in the first ever Secret Seven adventure. Kerry Blue is shut away as a prisoner in a deserted house, her coat sticky with dye. Fortunately, the Seven come to her rescue. When Peter and Jack are locked in the cellar of the house with the steed, Peter's calming voice and gentle touch manage to soothe her.

Mrs King

Spied through the telescope given to Jack and his little sister Susie in *Good Old Secret Seven*. Janet states that she can see she has twelve onions in the basket on her bicycle.

Kip

Enormous Alsatian who appears in the fifth book, *Go Ahead, Secret Seven*. Kip is told to guard Peter, Colin and Jack, who have come close to solving the mystery of the missing dogs in the neighbourhood.

Lane, Emma

Peter and Janet pay a visit to a Mrs Emma Lane in the third book, *Well Done, Secret Seven*, following up a clue given to them by Jeff, the boy who has run away from his unkind aunt and uncle. They are attempting to get to the bottom of some strange words Jeff has overheard involving Emma Lane, and are confused by the fact that no one of this name lives in the house. Instead, it is occupied by Mrs Lane's daughter, Mary Margaret Harris, and her grand-daughter, Lucy Ann Harris.

Larkworthy, Albert

Crippled husband of the grumpy Mrs Larkworthy of the Scarecrow Inn. The Secret Seven realise that they are on the wrong track when they see that he and his wife could not possibly be in the throes of carrying out a devious crime.

Mrs Larkworthy

Landlady of the Scarecrow Inn, in *Secret Seven Win Through*, with a very dis-agreeable face. She shouts at the children when they ask her questions about a man called Albert, who turns out to be her husband. 'Now don't you be saucy!' she cries.

Larry

Larry and his partner in crime, Zeb, form elaborate plans to steal hundreds of pounds' worth of lead from a train by switching the train onto another line and confusing the system in the fourth book, *Secret Seven on the Trail*. The Seven step into the adventure quite unwittingly after following up some false clues, given to them by Jack's irritating little sister, Susie, that lead them to the meeting place of the two men. Little do Larry and Zeb know that the Seven are lying in wait for them on the night of their plotting.

Larry

Boy who helps at Lane's Garage and features in *Good Work, Secret Seven*. He is described as having 'a shock of fair hair and a very dirty face and twinkling eyes'. He is visited by the Seven who are on a trail of a mystery that they do not realise has been set up by the fun-loving Susie.

Mrs Lawson

An elaborate description of Mrs Lawson is given by Janet in *Go Ahead, Secret Seven*, the fifth book in the series. Janet is asked to try out her powers of observation on the other members of the group and does extremely well, describing a woman with 'a round face, a big nose with a wart on one side, and grey curly hair. She wore a green coat with a belt, a hat with lots of red cherries round it…' She gets no further as the others all yell out, 'Mrs Lawson!'

Lennie and Richard

We know nothing about Lennie and Richard other than that they are suggested as possible new members of the Secret Seven to replace George when he is forced to resign from the club. Fortunately, neither of these two are agreed upon by Peter, and Scamper takes George's place in the meantime.

Little Woman

Looks after Old Man Tolly in the fifteenth and final book in the series, *Fun for the Secret Seven*. She jokingly warns him of horse thieves, and it turns out that she has hit upon the theme of the next Secret Seven adventure.

Liz

Postman's sister who makes her Secret Seven debut in *Shock for the Secret Seven* as an accomplice in the postman's dastardly deeds involving the theft of several dogs in the neighbourhood.

Lord Lofty

Beautiful, proud-looking horse belonging to the local vet in *Fun for the Secret Seven*. Pam suggests that she should bring him sugar lumps on a silver plate because he is so magnificent.

Lorry Driver

A big, hefty and cheerful lorry driver features in *Good Work, Secret Seven* and is extremely helpful in that he informs the Seven of a venue called Sid's Place where they believe lies the clue to their latest mystery.

Auntie Lou

Chocolate-providing godmother to Peter and Janet, Auntie Lou appears at the beginning of *Look Out, Secret Seven* with a box of goodies for the children. Her generosity prompts Peter and Janet to hold a Secret Seven meeting so that the whole club can share the food.

Louis

Sullen tightrope-walker and thief who steals Lady Lucy Thomas's precious pearl necklace from her bedroom by scaling the walls of her estate on stilts. Louis realises that he has been outwitted by the Secret Seven when they suggest that he has hidden the pearls in the lion's den and the water trough reveals a false bottom. He is led away by two policemen.

Lord Lunwood

Unfortunate victim of five uncouth robbers who steal his collection of paintings in *Good Old Secret Seven*. Luckily, the Seven spy the sinister happenings through Jack and Susie's telescope and decide to investigate.

Mr Luton

Violin-playing church warden in Peter and Janet's village; mentioned in *Puzzle for the Secret Seven*. He and his wife are swiftly dismissed as possible criminals because it is difficult for Peter to imagine them breaking a window to steal a valuable violin.

Mac

Partner in crime with Nibs, Mac appears as one of the pair who steal the famous racehorse, Kerry Blue, dye her to avert suspicion, and hide her in a deserted house where they think she will remain concealed from the public. Mac and Nibs are the first two criminals the Secret Seven have to deal with as they feature in the first book in the series. Their lack of respect for the children's integrity and their assumption that kids are 'little pests' give the Seven a taste of things to come. Most criminals in Blyton's books work on the premise that children will never be able to unravel their complicated plots. How wrong they are!

Man Trailed by Colin

Colin sets about trailing a man, in *Shock for the Secret Seven*, in connection with the disappearance of several pedigree dogs in the area. The man is in possession of a poodle Colin fears could be stolen, but the man leads him and the poodle to the house of an old lady who clutches the poodle to her heart and accuses Colin of being the thief!

Matt

A shepherd on the farm belonging to Peter and Janet's parents, Matt is mentioned with regularity throughout the series. He is particularly prominent in *Puzzle for the Secret Seven*, when he helps the Bolan family by suggesting they live in his old caravan as their shack has been burnt down. Matt also features in one of the most touching Blyton moments ever, when his stolen sheepdog, Shadow, returns to his master: 'I missed you, old friend, I missed you. Like a brother I grieved for you, and my heart was full of sorrow. Where have you come from, this cold night of stars? Did you guess I was waiting for you every hour of the day and night?'

Nabber

Alsatian belonging to Wily, the murky character who is involved in stealing General Branksome's medals in *Look Out, Secret Seven*. Nabber is a ferocious beast, by all accounts, and is made to guard members of the Seven as they attempt to outwit the criminals in Bramley Wood in the dead of night.

Nibs

Appears in the first book as one of the two master criminals who steal the famous racehorse Kerry Blue and attempt to dye her to conceal her identity. He works with another character bearing the equally dubious name of Mac.

Pace, John Wilfred

'Poor old John Pace', aged seventy-one, crops up in the fifth book, *Go Ahead, Secret Seven*. He is a little bald fellow who fits a description given by the police in connection with the theft of several valuable dogs: 'Small and bent. Bald with shaggy eyebrows and beard. Very hoarse voice. Shuffles badly when walking. Scar across the right cheek.' How John Pace came to look like this must surely be another story.

Pam

One of the three girls in the Secret Seven club, and the most typically 'girlie', Pam is prone to tears and giggling fits which leave Peter, as head of the club,

exasperated. Pam's close friend is Barbara, and the two always work together on mystery-solving exercises when they can. Like every other member of the group, she is always delighted and proud to receive praise from Peter whom she looks up to very much, as can be seen in *Three Cheers, Secret Seven* when Pam does her own bit of problem-solving by asking her granny questions about the elusive Mr Grim. She is clearly a capable girl when she puts her mind to things, but possesses the dangerous vices of jealousy and silliness, as is stressed in *Go Ahead, Secret Seven* when she and Barbara do not produce sensible notes and Peter states that their work is 'very poor, both of you'. Pam is not amused when Janet shows that she has worked very well and thoroughly on the task of 'shadowing' people in the neighbourhood: '"Janet would be able to tell them [the police] everything," said Pam, rather jealously.'

Pam has the intelligence to realise that Jack's sister Susie, who is in her class at school, may be a terrible nuisance to the Secret Seven but is not altogether *bad* and would never lie. The fact that Susie and Pam are in the same class at school suggests that she, Barbara and Janet are actually younger than Peter and the other boys, as they are mentioned as being older than Susie. Pam is quite undone when disaster strikes in *Shock for the Secret Seven* and Scamper is stolen from Peter and Janet; she is almost constantly crying. Has hazelnuts growing in her garden.

Pam's Father

We know nothing about Pam's father except that he is a big man, as is revealed in *Secret Seven Fireworks* when he donates an old pair of trousers to the guy that the Seven are constructing.

Pam's Granny

Archetypal little old lady who supplies the Secret Seven with a tin of peppermints in *Secret Seven Win Through* and is very helpful concerning her old gardener, George Grim, whom the Seven have their suspicions about in *Three Cheers, Secret Seven*, the eighth book in the series. 'You and your mysteries!' says Pam's granny. 'You really amuse me!'

Mrs Penton

Elderly woman who used to look after Peter and Janet's mother when she was a girl. Peter and Janet visit her for tea in *Good Work, Secret Seven* and she provides a delicious spread, including the inevitable cream buns and chocolate eclairs. She regales them with stories of how naughty Janet and Peter's mother was when she was little, telling of how she ate too many eclairs and made herself ill, much to their amazement.

Peter

The undisputed leader of the Secret Seven, Peter is renowned for his quick thinking and crisp words to his fellow club members when they lose their badge or forget the secret password. Woe betide any member who finds themselves on the wrong side of their commander, who has little patience with silliness or giggles from the girls. Peter appears as the principal character in all fifteen books in the series, with Jack as his second-in-command. He displays great concern and respect for his sister, Janet, although his opinion of girls in general is fairly low and he shows particular exasperation with the constant sniggering of Barbara and Pam.

Peter's pride in the Secret Seven is apparent all the way through the series, with comments such as 'The best society in the world! Hurrah for the Secret Seven!' being stock phrases in his day-to-day existence. It is also remarked upon that Peter 'liked getting his own way', although he shows great distress when anything threatens to destroy the harmony of the group. Unfortunately, his hot temper gets the better of him on a number of occasions, and at one point in *Shock for the Secret Seven* he drives Jack to leave the Secret Seven altogether through his harsh words: 'How *dare* you let anyone know we'd a meeting here today? And *why* aren't you wearing your badge? You don't *deserve* to be a Secret Seven member!'

It is also made clear in *Fun for the Secret Seven*, the fifteenth and last book in the series, that Peter is excessively untidy, treading a bar of nougat into the carpet and leaving it there for days, much to the amusement of his sister. He has great admiration for his father and will most probably follow in his footsteps and work on his own farm when he finally outgrows the Secret Seven. He is good with animals, as can be seen by the adoration of the faithful Scamper, and he shows remarkable prowess when calming the great stolen racehorse, Kerry Blue, when the boys find themselves prisoners with this formidable steed. Peter is the ideal head of the Secret Society, and his leadership sees the Seven through fifteen independent mysteries, several of which have left the police vexed for weeks. Indeed, the only character in any danger of showing more quick-wittedness and dexterity than Peter is Jack's naughty sister, Susie.

Peter and Janet's Father

Peter and Janet's father is the Secret Seven parent who is involved in the majority of their plans, but not until the very end when the Seven have already figured everything out for themselves: 'You're a set of meddling youngsters, you know, but somehow your heads and hearts are sound and you do the right thing in the end.' He is a farmer by profession, and a good one at that, having great relationships with all those who work on his estate. Nothing pleases Peter and Janet more than to be praised by their father whom they hold in very high regard.

Peter and Janet's Mother

It is stated that 'Everyone liked Peter and Janet's kind, generous mother.' Like all good Blyton mothers she is kept very much on the periphery of the stories, popping up at the beginning of every book with suggestions of food for the children to have in their meetings, and helping them organise huge, cool jugs of home-made lemonade. She is soft-hearted and expansive, wanting to help the Bolan family in *Puzzle for the Secret Seven* as much as she can when their house is burnt down in a fire at Hilly Down. She comments that she is glad to have 'a decent son who runs a decent club helped by his decent sister,' in response to Peter's over-use of the word 'decent'. Peter and Janet's mother is the only outsider who is regularly admitted to Secret Seven meetings, as she is always bearing trays of goodies such as jam tarts or ginger cakes.

Policemen

In *Puzzle for the Secret Seven*, 'A policeman appeared as if by magic' when an antique shop is broken into in the middle of the night. Policemen are figures of jurisdiction and prestige, respected highly by the children as pillars of the community, but they are never quicker than the Secret Seven at picking up on clues, and are constantly amazed at how well the mystery-solving children tackle crime. In the same book, the policeman at the scene of this incident tells Colin and George to 'Get off home. You can't help us, only hinder us.' How wrong can you be?

Postie

The postman (real name Tommy) is the most unlikely candidate for crime, and yet in *Shock for the Secret Seven* he proves himself to be a master criminal of his time. It is he who is stealing all the pedigree dogs in the neighbourhood and with remarkable ease, as all of the dogs love and respect him, and follow him into his van without hesitation. Jack is the one who realises that Postie is not as innocent as he seems and that his van contains a good deal more than a few brown envelopes and parcels.

Mr Quentin

Suspicious character who features in *Good Work, Secret Seven*, Mr Q is the accomplice of Fingers who is in charge of hiding stolen goods. When Quentin is found by the police, he crumples up and tells them everything they want to know. The police would not have found him without the help of the Seven, of course.

Rachel

Peter and Janet's parents' cook, Rachel, is mentioned in *Look Out, Secret Seven*, rolling out pastry.

Riccardo

Lion-tamer at the circus who makes a brief appearance in *Secret Seven Adventure*, when he is asked to open up the lion's cage and search for the stolen pearl necklace lost by Lady Lucy Thomas. Much to his astonishment, it is revealed in the lion's water trough.

Richard

See Lennie.

Robber

Stout, tall man with red hair and a moustache. One of a gang of robbers whom the Secret Seven chance upon in *Secret Seven Fireworks*. There are three criminals in this gang, and one of them is caught in the clothes from the guy that the Seven have made for bonfire night. The villains break into the home of Mrs Strangeway, Colin's granny, and steal all her most precious family jewellery and possessions. Fortunately, the Seven are on the trail.

Mr Roneo

Mentioned in *Good Old Secret Seven*, when he is seen through Jack and Susie's telescope painting his greenhouse on a wobbly ladder.

Ronnie

The infuriating friend of Susie's, Jack's sister, Ronnie is featured briefly in *Good Work, Secret Seven*, as he, Doris, Jim and Susie roar with laughter at how they succeed in tricking the Seven into thinking they are solving a mystery.

Rover

Pam's dog Rover is mentioned in the fourth book, *Secret Seven on the Trail*, when Pam suggests that Rover's name should be used as the new password for the club. Nobody else seems to agree that it is a good idea.

Sam

A school friend of Susie's, Jack's younger sister, Sam appears in *Secret Seven on the Trail* as part of Susie's rival gang, the Famous Five. Sam is given to emitting explosive snorts when he feels the urge to laugh. (For other characters with this major flaw *see* Irene and Nora from Malory Towers.)

Sasha and Vanya

Russian-named Sasha and Vanya are two Alsatians belonging to Harris, the policeman who comes to the rescue of the Secret Seven in *Look Out, Secret Seven*. Sasha and Vanya outwit fellow Alsatian hound Nabber, who has been set to guard the group of children by dodgy Wily and Tom Smith, his partners in crime.

Scamper

Although Golden Spaniel Scamper is not officially a member of the Secret Seven, his presence is constant throughout the fifteen books in the series, being faithful and loving to Janet and Peter, guarding the shed where they hold their meetings as if it were his own kennel. He has a remarkable understanding of the children and their secret society, woofing at appropriate moments to voice his agreement in certain pivotal situations. He is always included in the feasts supplied by the club members, and is not averse to a chocolate biscuit, ginger bun or cup cake. It is stated in *Good Work, Secret Seven* that 'Scamper, who had also been asked to tea, had his own plate of dog biscuits with shrimp paste on each. He was simply delighted and crunched them non-stop.' Scamper also has his fair share of excitement, particularly in *Shock for the Secret Seven* when he is the centre of attention as one of the many victims of a local dog thief who is abducting pedigree hounds and keeping them in hiding. The distress felt by the Seven, and in particular Janet and Peter, is palpable in this most potent of episodes, but inevitably the gang succeed in returning Scamper and the other missing canines.

Scamper is the only creature whom the Seven see as fit to replace George when he is forced to resign from the club for the duration of one book. Scamper wears his badge with pride, but is happy to see George reinstated when his father admits he deserves to be a member once again. With Scamper by their sides, the Seven feel brave and able to conquer any mysteries that come their way, as he appears to have a real feeling for good and bad, and is instantly aware of any underlying dangers. He knows that Susie, Jack's naughty sister, is to be chased away whenever she appears outside the Secret Seven shed, and proves himself very useful in warning the club members of her whereabouts. Without Scamper, nothing is really *right* somehow.

Much of Scamper was based on Blyton's own spaniel, Laddie, although Loony in the Barney series is the real Laddie, according to Blyton herself.

Mr Scraper

Violin teacher at the school attended by the Secret Seven boys. Considered very briefly as a possible thief of the valuable violin that vanishes from an antique shop.

Smith, Bob

A school friend of Jack, Peter, George and Colin, Bob Smith seeks help from the Secret Seven when he hears that Old Man Tolly is having trouble paying the vet's bill for his horse. Bob Smith is made a temporary member of the Secret Seven for the duration of the last book in the series, *Fun for the Secret Seven*, as he sets about helping Tolly and his trusty steed Brownie. Bob is a great admirer of the Seven, and it is mentioned that his knees shake as he addresses the little group in the shed at the bottom of Peter and Janet's garden. He comments that he wished he had the brains of the Seven, but Pam counteracts this by telling him that he has something much more worthwhile: 'A very kind heart!'

Smith, Tom

Turns from friendly to furious in the twinkling of an eye in *Look Out, Secret Seven*. Members of the gang settle down to enjoy their picnic lunch with Tom whom they meet in the woods and take an interest in because he expresses his enjoyment of bird-watching. But he turns from sweet to sour when the boys mention the stolen medals belonging to General Branksome, and before too long the Seven are caught up in another adventure, feeling sure that all the clues lie in the large hands of Mr Smith.

Mrs Sonning

Grandmother of Elizabeth Sonning who appears in *Secret Seven Mystery* and lives in Bramble Cottage, Blackberry Lane, Belling Village. Mrs Sonning is visited by Jack and Peter when they hear that it is her granddaughter who has vanished, and find her in a state of great distress.

Sonning, Charles

Brother of the enigmatic Elizabeth Sonning whose disappearance is the theme of *Secret Seven Mystery*. Charles Sonning lives in France, but comes over to England when he hears that his beloved sister is missing.

Sonning, Elizabeth Mary Wilhelmina

Materialises in *Secret Seven Mystery*, the ninth book in the series, under the dubious guise of Tom the stable boy. She has been missing from home after she was accused of stealing at school and runs away to be with the horses that she loves. She is a 'merry laughing girl' with a mass of fluffy hair. (For other fluffy-looking girls, *see* Maureen Little and Nora of Malory Towers.)

Spade-Carrying Man

Seen in an allotment by Colin and Jack in *Secret Seven Win Through*. He shouts out that the boys should 'clear off' and then asks perhaps the most cryptic question in the whole of Blyton's writing: 'Are you the two kids who have been taking broccoli from here?'

Stoopy Man

When Janet describes a 'stoopy man who walked a bit lame with a large over-coat on and an old soft hat pulled well over his face', it is evident that he is going to be the cause of later debate. He appears in *Go Ahead, Secret Seven* and, although Janet initially has no idea that he is a suspicious character, her description comes in very useful when he resurfaces in a deserted coal mine where stolen dogs are being hidden.

Mrs Strangeway

Colin's granny is mentioned in *Secret Seven Fireworks* as she has her house broken into by thieves. Naturally, the Seven are on the case immediately.

Stumpy Dick and Twisty Tom

Characters with names like these can have been invented only by Jack's younger sister, Susie, in *Secret Seven on the Trail*. Stumpy Dick and Twisty Tom are merely figments of Susie's imagination and she is unaware that her silly idea of pretending that her gang, the Famous Five, is on their track will lead the Secret Seven to a real adventure.

Susie

The original Spice Girl and troublemaker, Susie is the younger sister of Secret Seven member Jack, and appears regularly in the series; she is both exasperating and amusing. Although not a member of the Seven herself, she is the most complex of all the characters, as she is a perfect pest much of the time, and yet is very proud and would never tell a lie or be a coward. Barbara makes an astute observation that leaves the rest of the gang thinking hard when she comments: 'Susie's very strong really. She's brave and bold and don't-carish, and she doesn't cry if she hurts herself and she sticks by her friends through thick and thin. In some ways I admire her, but at times, she's just a nuisance.'

Susie is extremely intelligent and succeeds in out-smarting the Seven, including Peter and her own brother Jack, on more than one occasion. It is mentioned of the boys that 'secretly they felt that she might be a bit too clever for them!' Susie is often accompanied by various bizarre friends, including the rabbit-faced and highly irritating chatterbox, Binkie, and in *Shock for the Secret Seven* she is constantly found with the French boy, Bony, on whom she delights in practising her rather dubious French: '"*Le petit chien s'en va!*" said Susie, very pleased with herself, "*il est...* er ... *stolen.*"' Susie revels in annoying and confounding the Secret Seven with her elaborate fake mysteries. Coincidentally, she inadvertently leads the Seven on the trail of *real* criminals on one occasion, after leaving a series of fake clues in their path that lead the Seven to Tigger's Barn and a genuine adventure.

Jack is ambivalent about his sister. Although he is always longing to pull her hair and tell her just how awful she is being, and is frequently heard groaning that 'She's the worst sister possible!', he does not take kindly to others being rude about her behind her back. She is still his sister and a brother should, of course, look after his sister at all times. Susie is not a girl who needs a great deal of looking after, however, as she is manipulative (sucking up to the au pair and getting Jack into trouble), cunning (starting her own club called the Famous Five, named after the books of the same title, to rival the Secret Seven), and infuriating (inventing a rude song with Binkie about the Seven and singing it loudly at every turn). However, she is ingenious, too, and honest deep down, and even reveals her good side on a couple of occasions, coming to the rescue of the Secret Seven when they find themselves in trouble.

Tanner, Albert

Appears in the seventh book, *Secret Seven Win Through*. Classic Blyton criminal with all the trimmings who takes part in a mail-bag robbery with his side-kick, Ted Yorks, but chooses the wrong hiding place in a cave near Peter and Janet's house, for the Seven have chosen the very same cave to be their summer meeting place. Peter and Janet's father exclaims in amazement when he sees Albert, for the man used to work on his farm but had to be dismissed because of his dishonesty. As Albert Tanner is led away by the police he looks 'sullen and silent', no doubt cursing those pesky kids who have wrecked his evil plans.

Mr Taylor

Appears in *Go Ahead, Secret Seven*, the fifth book in the series, where he is described as being 'a young fellow, strong and determined-looking', and is later mentioned as having a thin mouth and cold eyes. He is responsible for George's brief resignation from the society as he spots George 'shadowing' him in the street and grabs hold of him in fury. Although George was only practising his Secret work, Mr Taylor is very annoyed and makes George show him where he lives so that he may speak to his father. George's father is, in turn, extremely cross with his son and bans him from the Secret Seven. They elect Scamper as a temporary member of the gang, but are determined to get George reinstated. The members of the Seven attempt to talk to the young man and tell him that George had not meant any harm, but to no avail. Naturally, it later transpires that Mr Taylor is as suspect as can be and is involved in the theft of a number of valuable dogs in the area. No wonder he was upset by George's behaviour.

Mrs Thom

Has her 'lovely dog' stolen in *Shock for the Secret Seven*.

Thomas, Lady Lucy

Lady Lucy's pearl necklace is stolen from her bedroom in Milton Manor in the second book in the Secret Seven series, *Secret Seven Adventure*, but with the help of the children it is recovered soon after from the water trough in the lion's cage at the local circus.

Mr Tiptree

Owner of a local riding school, Mr Tiptree is visited by Janet and George in *Secret Seven Mystery* as the Seven suspect that the missing Elizabeth Sonning may have got work at his stables.

Mr Tizer

Crook and embezzler who features in the third book, *Well Done, Secret Seven*, Tizer is talked about by Jeff, the boy whom the Secret Seven find hiding in their tree-house, and is described as a bad man who is planning a crime in the near future. It is up to the Seven to stop his plans.

Tolly

Central to the fifteenth book, *Fun for the Secret Seven*. Old Man Tolly is the proud owner of Brownie the horse and Codger the mongrel. When he finds himself in financial difficulties, these are swiftly sorted out by the ever-ready Secret Seven. Tolly is a kindly man who is liked by everyone, and is quite overwhelmed by the help he receives from the children. In return he assists them by helping to catch the horse thieves who have been operating in the area, 'going for the thieves with a pitchfork and making them dance in pain!'

Tom

Sullen-looking boy with a bad attitude in *Secret Seven Mystery*. He works at Warner's Riding Stables and is questioned by the Secret Seven about his knowledge of the missing Elizabeth Sonning.

Trinculo

Bald-headed acrobat from the local circus who features in *Secret Seven Adventure*, the second book in the series. At first the children suspect Trinculo as the thief who stole Lady Lucy Thomas's pearl necklace, as when he is performing he is wearing a dark wig which fits the children's description of the thief. However, when they chat to him at the end of the evening and discover that he is amusing, friendly and bald, they think again.

Twisty Tom

See Stumpy Dick.

Ungracious, Impatient Woman

A woman with the vices of impatience and rudeness appears in Starlings Hotel in *Go Ahead, Secret Seven*. She answers Colin and Peter very tersely when they ask after the whereabouts of a man whom the woman reveals to be a Mr Taylor.

Vanya

See Sasha.

Wardle, Emma

Mrs Sonning's companion, Emma Wardle, answers the door to Peter and Jack in *Secret Seven Mystery*. The boys hope that Mrs Sonning may help to throw some light on the curious disappearance of her granddaughter. Emma Wardle is an organiser of jumble.

Mr Warner

Owner of Warner's Stables, which leads the Secret Seven to Elizabeth Sonning in *Secret Seven Mystery*.

Mr Whistler

Vet who appears in the fifteenth book in the series, *Fun for the Secret Seven*. Mr Whistler has been forced to charge Old Man Tolly a hundred and seventy-five pounds for the hours he has spent looking after Brownie, Old

Man Tolly's horse, but the Seven resolve the situation so well that the vet says he will not accept any further payment for Brownie as he is so fond of the horse and so impressed by the children's kindness. Tolly responds by calling the vet 'a gentleman he is! A right-down, slap-up gentleman!'

Will

On guard at Mrs Sonning's house during the Secret Seven's night-time search for the missing Elizabeth Sonning, her granddaughter. Dismissed when the policeman decides that nothing constructive has been seen or found.

One-Leg William

Resident of Chimney Cottage, he is an unlikely suspect for the theft of Lady Lucy Thomas's pearl necklace which has disappeared from her home, Milton Manor. One-Leg William is so called because he lost a leg to a shark and had it replaced with a wooden alternative. The disabled man is a possible criminal in the eyes of the Seven because his wooden leg makes little round marks very similar to those that surround the scene of the crime. It is later discovered that these marks were made by stilts and that William, therefore, is innocent.

Wily

The small-handed accomplice of the highly dubious Tom Smith, Wily appears in *Look Out, Secret Seven* as the character who is able to fit his hand inside the hole in a tree to retrieve the medals that he and Tom have stolen from Colin's neighbour, General Branksome. Wily is the owner of Nabber the Alsatian whom he sets on guard when he realises that the Seven are on his trail. But help arrives for the gang, Wily and Tom Smith are led away, and the medals are returned to the overjoyed General.

Yorks, Ted

Culpable fiend who participates in a mail-bag robbery with his side-kick, Albert Tanner. Both characters used to work on Peter's parents' farm, and were dismissed for dishonesty, although Peter's father concedes that Ted was 'a fine hedger and ditcher'. Ted is put into prison after the mail-bag incident and tries to signal the whereabouts of the mail-bag to Albert and another man named Jim.

Zeb

Linesman at the railway station near the village where the Secret Seven reside. Zeb is in on a plan, with his mate Larry, to switch a train carrying valuable lead onto another track.

THE ADVENTUROUS FOUR

The Adventurous Four (1941)
The Adventurous Four Again (1947)

Tom, Mary, Jill and Andy are a group of mystery-solving children who appear in two stories set in a small fishing village on the north-east coast of Scotland. Their first adventure is particularly memorable for its strong wartime references. When Tom stumbles upon some enemy submarines, Blyton writes, 'Tom felt frightened – but he wasn't going to show it! No – he was British, and these men shouldn't think they could scare him!' And later the children are informed: 'We have to be strong and courageous when we fight such a powerful and evil enemy as ours. You are on the right side and that is something to be proud of!' This was clearly Blyton's effort to boost the morale of the country.

By the time of the Adventurous Four's second adventure, the evil enemy had been defeated, but Blyton still serves up another dangerous and dramatic plot, this time involving a hidden firearms storehouse on the Cliff of Birds.

Andy

Mature for his fourteen years, this Scottish fisherboy is the oldest and wisest of the Adventurous Four, and takes charge in moments of crisis. In *The Adventurous Four* he exposes the hidden enemy submarines and is rewarded with a magnificent fishing boat from the Government.

Jill

One of the Adventurous Four, Jill is twin sister of fellow member Mary and younger sister of Tom. She has many good ideas, such as covering Andy's boat in seaweed to disguise it from the enemy. As Andy says, 'I didn't know girls could have such good ideas.'

Colonel Knox

Appearing in *The Adventurous Four Again*, he introduces himself to the children as 'someone in charge of very high-up affairs'. Blyton was never one to get bogged down in detail.

Tom held on firmly while
Andy looked down.

Mrs Macpherson

Works at the village shop in *The Adventurous Four*
and recommends tinned sausages to Tom.

Mary

Member of the Adventurous Four, with her twin
sister Jill and older brother Tom. At times she is
overwhelmed by some of the dramatic events
encountered in *The Adventurous Four*, but she
responds well to Andy's pep talks.

Tom

A small, wiry boy of twelve with red hair and a
passion for sausages. His younger twin sisters,
Mary and Jill, also in the Adventurous Four, insist
that he should have been called Carrots, Ginger or
Marmalade because of his red hair.

In *The Adventurous Four* he is captured by the
enemy when returning to an island to fetch his
camera. Describing himself as a 'perfect silly' for
running into such danger, he manages to escape
with the aid of a gramophone and a copy of the
record 'Hush! Hush! Hush! You Mustn't Say a Word!'

THE PUT-EM-RIGHTS

The Put-Em-Rights (1946)

Sally Wilson, Micky Gray, Amanda Gray, Claude 'Podge' Paget, Yolande Paget and Bobby Jones are six children who band together to try and make the world – or at least Under-Ridge village, where they live – a better place. The group's existence owes much to the Tramping Preacher, who conveniently stirs the children with a compelling talk at the beginning of the school holidays. Inspired by his teachings, the Put-Em-Rights spend the rest of the holidays endeavouring to help the people of Under-Ridge, adopting the motto 'Watch, Pray and Work'. Despite their good intentions, the children's efforts are often seen as interfering rather than helpful.

In truth, Under-Ridge is not a desperately exciting place to live and the Put-Em-Rights were never developed beyond the original book.

Gray, Amanda

Eleven-year-old member of the Put-Em-Rights. Daughter of the village rector, and exceptionally lazy.

Gray, Micky

Twelve-year-old elder brother of Amanda, and fellow member of the Put-Em-Rights, Micky tackles the Put-Em-Rights' first case, with eventual success, and as such can be considered the first Put-Em-Righter.

Jones, Bobby

Twelve-year-old member of the Put-Em-Rights who offers his resignation from the group after discovering that his father is not dead, as he had been led to believe, but actually in prison for fraud. He lives in Under-Ridge village with his mother.

Midge

Midge is the subject of the Put-Em-Rights' first case. Regularly beaten by his cruel owner Fellin, Midge the dog is saved when the gang succeed in making 'the man kind, and the dog happy'.

Paget, Claude (Podge)

This member of the Put-Em-Rights is known affectionately as Podge because, frankly, he's a bit fat. Podge is a careless, rather arrogant boy with rich parents and an easy life, but his genuine yearning to do something worthwhile makes him a valued Put-Em-Righter.

Paget, Yolande

The youngest member of the Put-Em-Rights, and cousin of fellow Put-Em-Righter Claude, Yolande has little confidence in her own ability and, although slightly more self-assured by the end, she is still the weakest of the Put-Em-Rights.

Wilson, Sally

Efficient but bossy member of the Put-Em-Rights, Sally is Head of Class at school and undoubtedly intelligent, but lacks the tact and sensitivity needed for some of the Put-Em-Rights' more delicate cases. Her mother is Head Teacher at the village school.

THE FIVE FIND-OUTERS

The Mystery of the Burnt Cottage (1943)
The Mystery of the Disappearing Cat (1944)
The Mystery of the Secret Room (1945)
The Mystery of the Spiteful Letters (1946)
The Mystery of the Missing Necklace (1947)
The Mystery of the Hidden House (1948)
The Mystery of the Pantomime Cat (1949)
The Mystery of the Invisible Thief (1950)
The Mystery of the Vanished Prince (1951)
The Mystery of the Strange Bundle (1952)
The Mystery of Holly Lane (1953)
The Mystery of Tally-Ho Cottage (1954)
The Mystery of the Missing Man (1956)
The Mystery of the Strange Messages (1957)
The Mystery of Banshee Towers (1961)

Larry Daykin, Margaret 'Daisy' Daykin, Pip Hilton, Bets Hilton and Frederick 'Fatty' Trotteville are the Five Find-Outers. Formed originally to solve a case in *The Mystery of the Burnt Cottage,* they go on to star in fifteen mystery adventures. They live in the village of Peterswood but, with the exception of youngest member, Bets, are away at boarding school during term time, so mystery-solving has to wait until the holidays. As with all Blyton's adventurous groups, there is never a shortage of mysteries to solve, and some are particularly dramatic. In their ninth adventure, for example, *The Mystery of the Vanished Prince,* we see an attempted kidnap by helicopter but, fortunately, Fatty is on hand to foil the international criminals involved.

The Find-Outers have many strange encounters, but Blyton never brings anything supernatural to the mysteries, always offering a practical explanation instead. In *The Mystery of Banshee Towers,* for instance, the strange wailing noise is found to come simply from a bit of machinery with a specially filled-up balloon and amplifier, all fitted neatly into an underground hole in a rock. 'I should find it very difficult to believe in a real banshee,' comments Fatty.

To Mr Goon, the Peterswood village policeman, the Five Find-Outers are nothing more than little nuisances, interfering with the law. If Peterswood was to rely on Mr Goon to solve its mysteries, however, the villagers would probably still be stuck on the very first mystery of them all. Peterswood and the world outside owe the Five Find-Outers a great deal indeed, and in particular the highly intelligent and amusing Fatty.

'Well! How could you think that boy was me, even in disguise, I don't know! He's an oaf! A clod! A lump! Not a brain in his head! Good gracious, surely I don't look in the least like him?
FATTY IN *THE MYSTERY OF THE HIDDEN HOUSE*

Buster

Dog who accompanies the Five Find-Outers on their mystery-solving. Buster is used by the group as a sort of bloodhound, but spends more time chasing rabbits. He is owned by Fatty and loved by all the children.

Daykin, Laurence (Larry)

The thirteen-year-old leader of the Five Find-Outers successfully sees off an early leadership challenge from Fatty by four votes to one. Larry is a natural leader, but needs to work on his man-management skills – he's quite capable of reducing Fatty to sulks and Bets to tears with his unsympathetic comments. Not a high-flyer at school, he prefers instead to concentrate his brain power on solving mysteries in the school holidays.

Daykin, Margaret (Daisy)

One of the Five Find-Outers and twelve-year-old younger sister of Larry Daykin, Daisy voted for her brother in the group's leadership contest, but nevertheless admires Fatty's intelligence. She offers logical comments and has a cool head in a crisis.

Goon, Theo

Mr Goon is the hapless village policeman who investigates the same cases as the Five Find-Outers, but usually with considerably less success. Known to the Find-Outers as 'Clear Orf', simply because this is what he is likely to shout when coming into contact with them. His nickname has wisely not been updated in recent editions to accommodate more modern-day phraseology.

Fatty brought out a live white rat.

Hilton, Elizabeth (Bets)

At just eight years of age, Bets is the youngest of the Five Find-Outers and frankly a bit of a liability. She asks questions like, 'What's a detective?' and 'What are clues?', which hardly inspires confidence in her mystery-solving ability. And like most of Blyton's youngest group members, she tends to respond to moments of crisis by bursting into tears. However, she does have the uncanny knack of stumbling upon important discoveries, and on more than one occasion has set the Find-Outers on the right track. She is also responsible for the Five Find-Outers' name.

'Well!' said Fatty and roared with laughter. 'You are a lot of mutts! Where is this poor fellow? We'd better put him right.'
THE MYSTERY OF HOLLY LANE

Hilton, Philip (Pip)

Aged twelve, Pip is not a natural academic but has a real appetite for solving mysteries. He is also a keen cricket fan who spends a lot of time studying bowling analyses in the newspaper. He is the elder brother of fellow Find-Outer Bets, but has little respect for her comments. To him, she's just a little girl who likes dolls and cries a lot when she falls down.

Inspector Jenks

This police inspector is based on a real-life friend of Enid Blyton, Police Inspector Stephen Jennings. When Inspector Jennings was promoted to Chief Inspector, Jenks was similarly elevated, appearing in *The Mystery of the Strange Bundle* as Chief Inspector Jenks for the first time.

Trotteville, Frederick (Fatty)

Frederick Algernon Trotteville is affectionately known to the other four as Fatty, because, as fellow Find-Outer Pip remarks, his initials F-A-T describe him rather well. Not one of Blyton's subtler nicknames, and nor are the names poor Frederick is known by at school – Tubby and Sausage. He does attempt to slim at one point, when selected for the school tennis team, but is simply unable to resist buns, lemonade and ice-cream for elevenses.

Early impressions of Fatty are not favourable. The other four see him as 'plump, conceited and stupid' and his regular boasting (despite his nicknames,

Fatty dipped his hand in again.

he excels at school) does not help matters. Over the fifteen adventures, however, Fatty develops into the undoubted star of the group, with more charisma than the other four put together. He grows in popularity as well, his practical jokes and master disguises providing much entertainment, particularly when they are at the expense of bumbling policeman Clear Orf, whom Fatty delights in upstaging. Larry may be the leader of the Find-Outers, but Fatty is the main reason for the group's impressive mystery-solving success rate. As Bets admiringly observes, 'Things always happen when Fatty's around.'

THE 'BARNEY' MYSTERY SERIES

The Rockingdown Mystery (1949)
The Rilloby Fair Mystery (1950)
The Ring O Bells Mystery (1951)
The Rubadub Mystery (1952)
The Rat A Tat Mystery (1956)
The Ragamuffin Mystery (1959)

Written for an older audience than the Secret Seven and Famous Five, the 'Barney' Mystery series was hugely popular for Blyton. The chief protagonists are Roger and Diana Lynton, their irrepressible cousin Snubby, their friend Barney, his monkey Miranda and Snubby's spaniel, Loony. Their mystery-solving takes place in a variety of unusual locations, and nearly always under the not particularly watchful eye of elderly governess Miss Hannah Pepper. Needless to say, food features heavily. Blyton serves up a typical dollop of tongue in cheek self-consciousness when Roger observes 'how weird' it is that every mystery they have solved 'begins with R'.

> *Snubby went over to the fire that was still gleaming in the grate, and faced the men. His red hair stood on end, and he felt very scared. But he put on a bold face, and even tried to whistle.*
>
> *THE RAT A TAT MYSTERY*

Ballinore, Sir Richard

See George Higgins.

Barlow, Naomi

Elderly resident of Ring O Bells who lives in a woodland cottage. Takes Barney in when he has nowhere to stay. Provider of great cinnamon biscuits and owner of the well that provides the key to the Ring O Bells Mystery.

Boatman

Takes the children and Miss Pepper out to the blow-hole in *The Rubadub Mystery*. Full of 'queer old tales' and has seen 'many a whirlpool' in his time. Could be called Binns as he is the boatman the Funny Man recommends at lunch in the Three Men in a Tub Inn.

Bruce

Very good school friend of Snubby's who is mentioned in *The Ragamuffin Mystery*, Bruce is nearly as much of a troublemaker as Snubby and sends him a letter in their secret code, which sparks off a series of events that lead to the eventual capture of several unsavoury criminals.

Colville, Thomas

'Hairy Man' who employs Tonnerre and Vosta to steal valuable papers in *The Rilloby Fair Mystery*. Not much is known of him except that he has a 'cultured' voice. (For other cultured criminals, *see* Benedict (real name Raymond Jones) in the Six Cousin Stories.)

Dai

The real Ragamuffin who is confused with Snubby in *The Ragamuffin Mystery*. Owns a black poodle called Woolly who is confused with Loony. Snubby decides that Dai is 'a bit simple' after they exchange words on the beach. Wears a big woolly jumper. (For a more famous ragamuffin, *see* Ragamuffin Jo in the Famous Five series.)

Dourley, Hugh

Lives with his granddaughter Mother Hubbard in Ring O Bells. More commonly known as 'Old Grandad' but refers to himself as 'Button'. Pink and bald with a 'mere button' nose, he has white, shaggy eyebrows and smokes a pipe. Gets mighty confused when the children bombard him with questions about his family and Ring O Bells, forgetting his own name in the process and transporting himself into the past so thoroughly that he finds it 'impossible to place the children in the present'. Diana marvels at how peculiar it must be to be so old. Claims to be a hundred years old, though the ever-tactful Snubby remarks that he 'looks two hundred!'

Dummy

'A good chap but never properly growed-up', Dummy appears in *The Rubadub Mystery* as a helper at the Three Men in a Tub Inn. Dummy lives up to his politically incorrect name by struggling over the simplest of sentences. Remarkably, his memory is improved by Snubby impersonating the banjo as it stirs memories of when Dummy himself used to play. It is suggested that Dummy was 'different' ever since he had fallen from the rope during a wire-walking act and hurt his head. Plays a significant part in reuniting Barney with his long-lost family as he used to know Barney's kind mother, Tessie. Miss Pepper considers him 'more like a gnome or brownie than a human being,' which is probably a compliment as Blyton wrote extensively about these supernatural beings (*see* Toys and Enchantment).

Fred (The Funny Man)

Clown who forms part of the Pierot show taking place on the pier in *The Rubadub Mystery*. The Funny Man quickly notices Snubby's comic potential and persuades him to enter the children's competition at the show which, naturally, he wins. Perhaps a career as a talent scout would be better suited to this man who rightly points out to the children that 'It isn't always funny to be funny. I get bored.'

Glump, Gloria (née Tregonnan)

Majestic-looking woman who is 'a mixture of "glum" and "plump"', Mrs Glump runs the Three Men in a Tub Inn in *Rubadub*. Snubby is said to be 'lost in admiration' at her large number of chins and gloomy face. Soon inspires the adjective 'glumpish'. Friend of Miss Pepper's when they were little girls. Owns a bull-mastiff called Mr Tubby. Good cook.

Professor Hallinan

Criminal who goes by the name of Professor Hallinan, a famous ornithologist, but is rumbled by Snubby and Barney when they question him about Dotty Shade Warblers and Short-Necked Curlikews. He fails to spot that these are made-up names, so the seeds of suspicion are sown.

Higgins, George

Goes by the name of Sir Richard Ballinore while he is staying in Wales with the Jones family. This bogus Knight of the Realm's thieving and treachery are uncovered by Barney and Roger in *The Ragamuffin Mystery* along with fellow fake 'Professor Hallinan'. Implicates Mr Jones in his criminal activities, much to his wife's dismay.

Hubbard, Mother

Resident of Ring O Bells who welcomes the children into her cottage at the start of their third Mystery. Wears a red shawl and printed skirt and speaks in a 'pleasant brogue'. Makes very good 'gingers' and lives with her grandfather, Old Grandad.

Mr Icy Cold

Snowman built by Roger, Diana and Snubby in *The Rat A Tat Mystery*. Mrs Tickle is given a terrible shock when she sees Mr Icy Cold at her window as she is making tea. A logical explanation for this surreal vision is provided at the end of the story when it becomes clear that it was not Mr Icy Cold but Jim and Stan dressed up in a white sheet. An easy mistake to make, Mrs Tickle.

Professor James

Initially introduced as rather deaf with a hot temper, the canine-hating Professor James features in *The Rubadub Mystery*. When Miss Twitt mentions that she 'loves children so', the Professor states that he 'would like to drown them all'. However, by the end of *The Rubadub Mystery* his wig and beard are shed to reveal a much younger man with brown hair, who is working for the police.

Jim

See Stan.

Jim

Sender of coded letters in *The Ragamuffin Mystery*. Unfortunately for Jim, his letter is intercepted by Snubby, who in return gives his school friend Bruce's coded letter to Dai, the messenger boy and ragamuffin of the book's title. Roger chortles to himself at the idea of Professor Hallinan and Sir Richard Ballinore attempting to decipher Bruce's letter. Perhaps jokes about the cricket team and propositions of tricks to play on the French master are not what the pair had in mind.

Jones, Dafydd

Young scamp of a son of Mr and Mrs Jones with a pet goose called Waddle. Appears in *The Ragamuffin Mystery* and, although he is considered a pest by the children, he eventually proves himself to be something of a mystery solver when he helps Barney and co. to uncover the evil doings of Professor Hallinan and Sir Richard Ballinore.

Jones, Llywellen

Superb cook who runs the Penrhyndendraith Inn with his talkative wife in *The Ragamuffin Mystery*. Tall and surly-looking with thick, untidy hair and glasses. Miss Pepper decides that 'however well Mr Jones cooked, she wasn't going to like him'. Gets himself thoroughly worked up when Miss Pepper refuses to move out of the room that makes noises in the middle of the night. Roger and Diana decide that he must have some 'secret sorrow'. Met his wife when he was the second chef at a smart hotel in London and she was a chambermaid. Was lent the money to buy the Inn from two very suspect men.

Jones, Lorna

Receives a very lukewarm round of applause when she wins the Girls' Prize at the Pierot show in *The Rubadub Mystery*. 'Certainly she had been very good,' concedes Blyton, 'but nobody had liked the little show-off.'

Mrs Jones

Runs the Penrhyndendraith Inn with her husband. Features in the last book in the series, *The Ragamuffin Mystery*. Likes to talk on a very regular basis about her husband's supreme cooking skills, much to the amusement of the children. As Diana claims, 'she goes on and on like a babbling stream, but she's quite interesting'. Has the last word in the whole series when she mentions at the end of the tale that 'somebody ought to write a book about those children and their doings!' Well Mrs Jones, writes Blyton, obviously enjoying herself, they have!

Jones, Myfanwy

Welsh shopkeeper with a wrinkled face and startling eyes who features in *The Ragamuffin Mystery*. Provides the children and Mr Martin with ice-creams which food critic Diana decides have 'not much taste' but are 'deliciously cold'. Mrs Jones speaks in a curious dialect ('Cooking good sit, very very good') which implies that Blyton considered the Welsh to be entirely foreign to the English heroes. Suggests that the gang stay in her son's guest house, which leads, inevitably, to great adventure.

Mr King

Tutor to the children in *The Rockingdown Mystery*, Mr King is a 'stocky, well-built man of about thirty-five or forty with hair going a little grey and a mouth that looked distinctly firm'. Turns out to be a secret agent, which explains his lack of interest in the classroom, and the fact that he is 'pretty innocent' to the sort of schoolboy stunts that Snubby pulls on him during lessons, like swapping Mr King's ruler for one that was 'mysteriously wrong in its measurements'. Roger feels that Mr King is someone 'very thrilling' when his true identity is revealed. All's well that ends well as aptly named criminals Jo, Frisky and Scarface are caught and handed over to the police.

Loopy

Golden cocker spaniel belonging to Miss Hannah Pepper. Quickly befriends Loony and the two form a mischievous alliance, taking on each other's bad habits and causing canine mayhem wherever they go.

Lorimer, Barnabus Hugo (Barney)

Circus boy of about 'fourteen or fifteen' when he is first introduced in *The Rockingdown Mystery* who becomes the firm friend of Roger and Diana Lynton and their cousin Snubby. He and his monkey, Miranda, seem exotic, romantic and fascinating to the three children who lead very ordinary lives in comparison, yet lonely Barney yearns for a family of his own. Usually described as being as 'brown as a berry' and the picture of health, Barney is a

nomadic young lad, sleeping under the stars or in the odd barn, earning his keep at local fairs. His acrobatic abilities come in handy on more than one occasion, as does his fearlessness and inside knowledge of the way circus folk operate. *The Rubadub Mystery* sees Barney reunited with his long-lost father, and his personality in the remaining two books seems much more grown up as a result. No other Blyton character generates such enthusiasm before appearing at the start of each book – it's 'good old Barney!' from the moment his name is mentioned. Great fan of Shakespeare, as the only clue he has to his father's identity is that he 'acted in Shakespeare's plays'. Not highly intuitive, he comes to the end of his third consecutive mystery holiday with the telling remark that 'I never thought that anything like this would happen when I popped down here to see you for a few days.' When will they learn?

Lorimer, Tessie

Circus girl and mother of Barney who ran away from her husband without telling him that she was pregnant, afraid that he would try to steal the baby back if he knew. In *The Rubadub Mystery*, Dummy reveals Tessie's reasons for running away, but fear of the mother-in-law still seems a rather weak excuse. It is more likely that Tessie missed circus life too much to settle down. Died when Barney was very young, but not without letting him know that his father was still alive. (For another character with half-circus blood, *see* Carlotta Brown in St Clare's.)

Lunatic (Loony)

Black cocker spaniel belonging to Snubby – the aptly named Loony Dog is a key player in the children's adventures. He and Snubby form a chaotic double act and hate being apart from each other although it is never revealed where Loony spends his time during the term when parentless Snubby is away at boarding school. Devoted though he is to Snubby, it is mentioned in *The Rubadub Mystery* that Loony 'had smelt an enticing fishy smell at the end of the pier and was going to examine it if it was the very last thing he did'. Like his owner, Loony is a great food fan. As the Lynton family cook says, 'I never in my life knew an animal that could slink into the larder when the door's shut like that dog of yours can. He's a living miracle!'

Given to barking madly whenever excited and hurling himself on top of people when they return to him, Loony also likes stealing brushes, towels and napkins from Miss Pepper and is frequently bemused by Miranda the monkey who enjoys jumping onto his back much to the mirth of the children.

Blyton based the character of Loony on her real-life cocker spaniel, Laddie, whom she felt 'deserved to be put into a book as a real character'. (For another black cocker spaniel *see* Crackers in the Six Cousins Stories. For another adventurous spaniel, *see* Scamper in the Secret Seven. For another insane spaniel, *see* Loopy in the Mystery series. Yes, Blyton liked the breed.)

Lynton, Diana

Sister of Roger, Diana or 'Di' Lynton is a well-rounded Blyton girl who laughs at her cousin Snubby's absurd jokes, cries when she's upset and adores ice-cream. Bearing in mind the fact that Diana is the only girl in the gang, she copes admirably, although it is mentioned in the first book in the series, *The Rockingdown Mystery*, that she 'moons over her peaches and cream', jealous of Snubby for taking away her brother's attention. However, her urges for 'parties and tennis' are never mentioned after chapter one. Who needs such things when there are mysteries to solve? There cannot be a reader out there who does not secretly hope that, years after their adventures end, she and Barney may marry.

Keen amateur ornithologist, good swimmer and presumably a good actress as it is mentioned that she played the part of Titania in *A Midsummer Night's Dream* at school. Believes that 'brothers are good things to have when things go wrong!'

Lynton, Richard

Impatient, irritable father to Diana and Roger Lynton. Finds his nephew Snubby a terrible strain, and Loony the dog even more so. Fan of good manners, newspapers and punctuality. It is mentioned in *The Ragamuffin Mystery* that 'Daddy's such fun on a holiday!', though we never find out if this is the case as he never features in any of the children's adventures. Finds his uncle Robert a 'terrible bore'. Becomes 'Good old Dad!' after stating when he meets Barney that 'any friend of Roger's is a friend of mine'. Quite capable of giving Snubby a 'good whacking' when he steps out of line.

Lynton, Robert (Great-Uncle)

Silver-haired, blundering fool and great-uncle to Diana and Roger on their father's side. Fooled by Snubby at the start of *The Rilloby Fair Mystery* into believing in a fictional gang (The Green Hands Gang) who are planning a crime involving an atom bomb. Claims to be writing his memoirs, which Roger cheekily gives the working title of 'Nodding over a Pipe'.

Lynton, Roger

All-round good sort. In keeping with many of Blyton's adventure characters, he is a fine, sensible boy with a knack of uncovering criminal activity before the police get a sniff at it. He and his sister Diana are much more conventional children than their great friend Barney, the circus boy and their madcap cousin Snubby. Roger is noted as being fifteen years old in *The Rubadub Mystery* which makes him three years older than his cousin Snubby who is consistently 'about twelve'. Apparently Roger is 'not quite as excitable' as his sister or Snubby, which can only be a good thing.

Lynton, Susan

Mother to Diana and Roger Lynton. Crops up at the start of every Mystery book but never develops into a significant character. We know that she has a soft heart (she cannot bear to throw away Diana's first pair of shoes), and a difficult husband. Any chance of her taking part in any mysterious goings-on in *The Ragamuffin Mystery* are thwarted by the sudden dangerous illness of her sister Pat.

Martin, Barnabus Frederick

Father of Barney. Discovered on the last pages of the fourth book in the series, *The Rubadub Mystery*. In the first three books, when Barney is living as a nomadic circus boy, he talks of his father and how he would love to meet him one day. All that Barney knows about him is that he is an actor who specialises in Shakespeare. Further information on Barney's father is revealed by the childlike Dummy, who used to know his wife, former circus girl Tessie. It emerges that Barney's father's mother deeply disapproved of the match between her son and Tessie so that Tessie eventually ran away. There cannot be a Blyton fan left unmoved by the touching reunion between Barney and his father. Barnabus Senior is unaware that he even has a son until he is contacted by Miss Pepper, which leaves a few question marks over the behaviour of Tessie Lorimer. It is mentioned that he has an unmarried sister plus a married brother with four children, providing the once-lonely Barney with an instant large, friendly family.

Mrs Martin

Barney's grandmother on his father's side who first appears in the penultimate book in the series, *The Rat A Tat Mystery*. With brown eyes, white hair and a lively smile, she is an instant favourite with Snubby, Diana and Roger. However, Dummy states in *The Rubadub Mystery* that Tessie, Barney's mother, ran away from her husband because his mother was unkind to Tessie whom she considered to be an unsuitable match for her son. It seems that Barney's father and Barney himself have forgiven Mrs Martin for this behaviour. Has a monkey, Jinny, who befriends Miranda in *The Rat a Tat Mystery*. Again, it seems odd that Blyton introduced a monkey as Mrs Martin's pet since the sort of eccentricity required to own such a creature does not fit in with Dummy's claim that Tessie's mother-in-law was rather stuffy. It could be that Blyton simply forgot between books that she had made Mrs Martin the reason for Barney's lonely childhood.

Miranda

Monkey belonging to Barney. Miranda wears a red skirt and bonnet and delights in jumping on Loony the spaniel's back when he is least expecting it. Miranda is easily frightened by strange noises but will do anything to protect Barney from danger. Works on the Hoopla stall in *The Rilloby Fair Mystery*, and makes firm friends with Barney's grandmother's monkey, Jinny, in *The Rat a Tat Mystery*. Diana is especially fond of 'dear little Miranda'. Likes

raisins, apples and sitting on Barney's shoulder. Provides great comfort to Barney when he has to sleep rough or in dark, spooky mansions (Rockingdown Hall, Ring O Bells House).

Morgan the Cripple

Bearded criminal in *The Ragamuffin Mystery* who confuses Snubby with the scruffy boy who is supposed to be delivering him a coded letter. Gets his name from the fact that he has a bad leg, so is unable to fish and lets out boats instead. Uncle of Dai the ragamuffin.

Naval Man

Clean-shaven traitor with a misshapen little finger who is involved with the grisly Mr Marvel in *The Rubadub Mystery*. Snubby is able to give a full description of him to Professor James as he first spots him on the train on the way to Rub a Dub.

Nightingale, Iris

Pretty girl of about twenty on whom Snubby develops a huge crush during *The Rubadub Mystery*. Snubby asks her to sing his favourite songs at the show, to which Roger replies, 'I hope she knows "Where did you come from, Baby dear?" Snubby is not amused and suggests that Roger wants 'a bang on the head'.

Old Ma

Frightening circus woman closely resembling a witch, who has a strange hold over Tonnerre in *The Rilloby Fair Mystery*. Old Ma has white hair, 'monkey eyes and a chin and nose that almost met'. Despite or maybe because of her hideous looks, Old Ma has a sharp tongue, but amuses everyone greatly by muddling Snubby and Loony's names. Like most old women, she becomes 'very twinkly' around Snubby. Cooks up a storm in her big iron pot. Cackles frequently.

Paulus (Mr Matthew Marvel)

Tall, thin with staring eyes. Pulls potatoes out from behind Snubby's ears and two small watches from out of his mouth, much to the boy's astonishment. Chief attraction at the Pierot show where he 'reads minds' dressed as an old-time enchanter with flowing cloak. Barney takes a job as Marvel's assistant and is fooled into believing that Marvel can find his father for him. This leads to one of Blyton's most gripping plots, as chapter twenty-seven ('Marooned by the Whirlpool') sees Barney and unlikely hero Dummy fighting for their lives. Mr Marvel is eventually revealed as a 'plausible, wily, traitorous rogue', much to the horror of his fellow guests at the Three Men in a Tub Inn.

Pepper, Hannah (Miss)

Cousin to Miss Rebecca Pepper and owner of the boarding house in Ring O Bells village, scene of the children's second adventure. Fatter and shorter than her cousin, Hannah is a jolly sort of lady who dislikes monkeys (Miranda) and owns a golden cocker spaniel called Loopy. She is elevated to 'Good Old Miss Hannah!' status at the end of *The Ring O Bells Mystery* when she suggests that homeless Barney stay on at her guest house with the other children for a further week of fun and merriment. No doubt by the end of these seven days she is presuming that Barney will have found himself alternative accommodation.

Pepper, Rebecca (Miss)

Old governess of Mrs Lynton who steps in to help out with Roger, Diana and Snubby during the holidays. Tall, thin, trim, and grey-haired with twinkling eyes and 'a nice smile that quite altered her rather prim face with the straight grey hair brushed away from it', Miss Pepper is a fairly typical Blyton adult – relaxed enough to allow her charges to fall into potentially life-threatening adventure every holiday, but strict enough to make sure that they are sent to bed early for misbehaving or being rude at mealtimes. She finds Snubby a particular trial, and is constantly amazed by how much he eats, though it is mentioned in *The Rockingdown Mystery* that Miss Pepper was 'once able to eat a whole tin of Nestlé's milk by herself'. When she lays down the law, Snubby refers to her as 'Peppery' and sneezes a great deal in her presence. Miss Pepper has a vital role in the discovery of Barney's father, when she 'quietly and efficiently' sets about tracking him down through friends in the village of Cherrydale. She is very fond of Barney, whom she considers a most unusual and interesting young man, though after unpacking a suitcase full of Diana's dirty, torn clothes she decides that 'Really, children nowadays are quite impossible!' A 'dangerously ill' sister emerges at a convenient point during *The Rockingdown Mystery*, which gets Miss Pepper out of the picture for just the right amount of time. (For another 'dangerously ill' relative who paves the way to a great mystery, *see* Susan Lynton.)

Piggott

Criminal who features in *The Ring O Bells Mystery*. Piggott drives an electrician's van and is forced to offer Barney a lift to Lillinghame when his van breaks down and Barney fixes the tyre. Makes suspicious trips round Europe; is usually at the centre of any 'little kidnapping'; hides papers and has a false bottom (in his van). The police claim to have 'had their eye on Piggott for some time' but it takes the know-how of four children, a monkey in a red skirt and a black cocker spaniel to put him behind bars, where he belongs. As Barney puts it, he is 'a nasty fellow'.

Detective Inspector Rawlings

Kidnapped detective who is held captive in a secret passage in *The Ring O Bells Mystery*. His life is saved by Barney and Roger who discover him and alert the rest of the police force as to his whereabouts. Contracts a terrible cough while he is held captive.

Mrs Round (Roundy)

Cook with a face 'as round as the harvest moon', Mrs Round has the mammoth task of feeding the children during their stay in Rockingdown village. Comes up with the inspired moniker of 'Master Sauce Box' for the ever-irreverent Snubby. Maker of sensational tomato soup.

Sardine

Black cat belonging to the Lyntons. Gets her name from her great fondness for sardines.

Snubby

Freckle-faced, snub-nosed cousin of Roger and Diana Lynton, Snubby has no parents so spends his school holidays with a variety of uncles and aunts, most of whom are frequently exasperated by his incessant gags and huge appetite. A natural leader who is 'adored by all the boys in his form but the despair of all the masters', Snubby is never far away from ice-cream, chaos and his black cocker spaniel, Loony. An inspired performer, Snubby impersonates the banjo, zither and harmonica to great acclaim and, despite being endlessly described as a 'caution' by Mrs Tickle in *The Rubadub Mystery*, remains a great favourite of every elderly lady for miles around. Barney's headmaster feels that he has a great deal of good in him but is, in the meantime, 'a pest' – a sentiment echoed by many a foiled criminal. Despite Roger stating that 'A little of you goes a long way Snubby. Too far!', Snubby remains one of Blyton's most endearing characters – troublesome and silly at times but full of surprises, unexpected courage and a great lust for life. Perhaps Snubby would be better behaved if he had a mother or father to keep him in order, but then would he be the Snubby that we know and love? He adores his cousins and secretly longs for parents of his own, but it is obvious that Snubby will, as even his headmaster concedes, 'turn out fine in the end'.

Only once is Snubby referred to by his real name of Peter, that is by Mr King in *The Rockingdown Mystery*. Possibly the most greedy Blyton character

ever, and that's saying something. Like Blyton herself, who had a strong con-
stitution and little sympathy for those who were ailing, Snubby claims that
'appendicitis was nothing' and that he enjoyed having it. However, Snubby
suffers from terribly 'wobbly legs' after his bout of illness at the start of *The
Ring O Bells Mystery*. Talented ice-skater and cricket fan.

Stan

Appears in *The Rat A Tat Mystery* with fellow lawbreaker Jim. 'Evidently men
with brains', they make the mistake of choosing Rat A Tat Cottage as the base
for their murky doings and get more than they had bargained for when
Barney, Snubby and the gang emerge. Stan and Jim attempt to scare them
away, but dressing up as snowmen and knocking on doors and running away
is not enough to frighten the gang, although Mrs Tickle is suitably alarmed. It
transpires that the two criminals have been hiding stolen weapons in boxes
under the ice.

Tell, Billy

Father of Young 'Un and son of Old Ma, Billy Tell appears in *The Rilloby Fair
Mystery* with a party trick that involves shooting apples off his son's head with
a gun rather than with the traditional bow and arrow as used by his namesake.
Dresses in a redskin suit and looks 'rather grand' but 'very dirty'.

Three Men in a Tub (Mr Tubby)

Bull-mastiff belonging to Mrs Glump in *The Rubadub Mystery*. Portly and wrinkled, he frightens Loony the spaniel into behaving himself. Omits 'rather human-sounding' groans when he lies by the fire.

Mrs Tickle

Resident of Rat A Tat Cottage who looks after the children when they come to stay. Astonishing cook who provides Snubby's favourite home-made macaroons for tea. Considers Snubby 'a caution' but becomes very fond of his impish ways. Says her prayers and applies hand cream at night.

Tonnerre

Owner of the fair that stops at Rilloby long enough for a mystery to unravel. Also owns a 'thunderous voice' and a 'fearful temper'. Underpays everyone who works for him. The only person he fears is the witch-like Old Ma. Goes from being 'not a pleasant fellow to work with', to a master criminal in 140 pages. Uses his chimps, Hurly and Burly, as unwitting accomplices to his thieving plans. Used to be a great acrobat and a superb dancer.

Miss Twitt

Aptly named woman who 'gushes' over children, birds, pretty butterflies, cats and dogs and smells strongly of Sweet Pea perfume. Covered in bracelets and necklaces, she dines with the children and Miss Pepper at the Three Men in a Tub Inn in *The Rubadub Mystery*. Blyton often dressed her 'silly' women characters in fussy beads with 'bits of chiffon' and floaty scarves (*see also* Mrs Lacey, mother of Gwendoline Mary in Malory Towers; and Rose Longfield in the Six Cousins series). Diana is disgusted at the way Miss Twitt talks to her as if she were about six, and Snubby seizes the chance to play her up, using his trademark sharp wit to rename her 'Miss Twitter'. Miss Twitt finally gives as good as she gets and remarks that Snubby has a very bad memory for names, but 'not all of us can have brains, can we?' One in the eye for Snubby, as Roger observes.

Vosta, Illia Juan

Fun-loving circus type who finds it 'impossible to say no to anyone', Vosta features in *The Rilloby Fair Mystery*. Trains and looks after the chimps, Hurly

and Burly, and is firmly under the thumb of the vicious Tonnerre who implicates him in his shady dealings. Fan of Snubby and Loony. Someone has to be.

Waddle

Goose belonging to Dafydd Jones. Stars in *The Ragamuffin Mystery*. Was nursed back to health by Dafydd as a gosling when he broke his leg and the two of them form a troublesome pair. (For other animals who have been nursed back to health by diligent children, *see* Skippetty the lamb in the Farm Stories.)

Young 'Un

Circus boy who features in *The Rilloby Fair Mystery* as the 'kid in charge of the shooting range'. Grandson of Old Ma and son of Billy Tell, he claims to have 'shot the weathercock off a steeple once'.

SCHOOL STORIES

ST CLARE'S
MALORY TOWERS
THE NAUGHTIEST GIRL IN THE SCHOOL

'And I promise, Darrell,' said Felicity, equally solemnly, 'I'll never let Malory Towers down. I'll carry the standard high, too.'

LAST TERM AT MALORY TOWERS

ST CLARE'S

The Twins at St Clare's (1941)
The O'Sullivan Twins (1942)
Summer Term at St Clare's (1943)
Second Form at St Clare's (1944)
Claudine at St Clare's (1944)
Fifth Formers at St Clare's (1945)

St Clare's is the seat of learning for a number of Blyton's most dynamic characters, including 'Don't Care' Bobby Ellis, 'Firm but Fair' Hilary Wentworth and 'Wild' Carlotta Brown. The exact setting of the school is not made clear, although the school coaches are mentioned 'rolling up the hill' at the beginning of the new term, and it is likely that the nearest town is within walking distance of the school grounds. Langley Hill is a popular spot for picnics and bathing in the cove, though, unlike Malory Towers, St Clare's is not situated on the coast. There is no clear House system, and the girls sleep in dormitories until the Fifth Form when they share studies, two to a room. The school is run by grey-haired Miss Theobald, who is able to see the potential in every girl and draws out the best in them.

St Clare's is unusual in that half of the books in the series take place when the girls are in the first form. We follow Pat, Isobel and co. up the school as far as the Fifth Form, but Blyton never writes about their life as Head Girls in the Sixth, much to the frustration of many readers. However, *Fifth Formers at St Clare's* is one of Blyton's most gripping works, featuring sleepwalking, anchovy toast, midnight feasts and Antoinette, the little sister of Claudine.

St Clare herself was a nun and disciple of St Francis who made her a member of his movement in 1212 when she was a young girl, too shy even to come up to the altar and receive communion. She founded the Poor Clares and went around barefoot, refusing all income. She died after a long spell of illness in 1253. The St Clare's of Blyton's writing is not a convent school and there are no references to nuns, past or present, but it is likely that St Clare herself would have been the kind of strong, brave woman Blyton admired.

Antoinette

Antoinette appears in only one book in the St Clare's series, and that is the last. In *Fifth Formers at St Clare's* Antoinette plays the kind of prominent role that her sister, Claudine, played in the previous book. She is as French and chic as Claudine, and as daring and naughty, causing delightful pandemonium when she spreads expensive face cream instead of shoe cream on snobby Angela Favorleigh's shoes, and then plasters the shoe cream all over the toast Angela asked her to prepare, pretending that she thought it was anchovy paste. Antoinette is only in the Second Form, but she tricks Angela quite superbly, and to the great amusement of the rest of the school. She is up to tricks again when she rings the fire bell in the middle of an important sports meeting called by Mirabel Unwin, resulting in the meeting being cancelled, once again, to the great entertainment of the rest of the girls.

Antoinette is also at the centre of the First Form's plans for a midnight feast, and she asks for Claudine's advice on storing the supplies of food. Claudine points out a cupboard near her room, but the girls are shocked to discover that someone else knows where the key is hidden and is pilfering the food (see Alma Pudden). We are left wondering whether Antoinette will ever acquire the 'sense of honour' that the English girls take such pride in possessing, but like Claudine, her intentions are always good, despite the bizarre nature of her actions.

Arnold, Prudence

'Sour milk' Prudence is the most unlikeable character in the entire St Clare's series. Introduced in *Summer Term at St Clare's* she masquerades as a very righteous and pious girl which she certainly is not. All of Blyton's most detestable characters are endowed with a sly cunning that enables them to get so far without being caught. Prudence is the most cunning of all, forcing Pam Boardman to become friends with her so that she can use Pam's brains to help her with her work and exams, knowing that the younger girl will be powerless once she is in Prudence's grasp. She is a terrible snob, constantly referring to Carlotta (whom she loathes) as a 'low-down circus girl', and sticking her nose in the air in disgust at the thought that she has to attend classes with a girl who used to ride horses in the ring. Indeed, Prudence's hatred of Carlotta, unquestionably stemming from jealousy, inspires her to begin stalking Carlotta when she disappears from the school and goes to the local circus ground in Jalebury, the neighbouring town, to ride the horses there. Unfortunately for Prudence, she does not quite get the reaction that she had planned when she reveals the secrets of Carlotta's past to the other girls. The girls are delighted by Carlotta, and dislike Prudence even more than before.

The final straw comes when Prudence is caught cheating, looking through the answers to a French exam in the middle of the night. Even after this incident, she refuses to mend her ways, and sets off one night to follow someone

Prudence shrank back, afraid.

she thinks is Carlotta on her way to meet up with her circus folk friends. Prudence actually steps unwittingly into the centre of a kidnapping incident involving Sadie Greene. Sadie is rescued by Carlotta's quick thinking, but Prudence is asked to leave St Clare's and is described as 'her own worst enemy, and always will be'.

Bertha

Goalkeeper during a lacrosse match in *The O'Sullivan Twins*.

Binks

Dog found by Kathleen Gregory in *The Twins at St Clare's*. He is injured when he first appears, having been shot by a local farmer who feared for his sheep. Kathleen takes the dog back to school, and nurses him back to health, keeping him hidden in the little box room. He is eventually discovered chasing the school cat by Miss Theobald, who decides that Kathleen may keep the dog until the end of term, when she can take him home as her pet. Kathleen is a great animal-lover and the little dog adores his mistress who names him Binks for no reason at all.

Brown, Carlotta

A central character of the St Clare's books after her arrival in the First Form for the summer term, Carlotta is a hot-tempered, dark-eyed, wild-haired, half-Spanish ex-circus girl who is as 'don't carish' as can be, and has gypsy blood running through her veins. She says exactly what she thinks, and stands no silliness from anyone, but because of her overriding goodness and sense of fun she is very much liked by all except Mam'zelle, who despairs of Carlotta's appalling grasp of French and her erratic behaviour. Carlotta and Mam'zelle come to blows one day when a frog is set loose in the classroom, and Carlotta receives the blame, although Roberta (Bobby) Ellis is really the guilty party. Carlotta lets off a torrent of excited Spanish in Mam'zelle's direction, most of which (unfortunately for her) is understood. Miss Roberts, the First Formers' tutor, appears on the scene, alarmed by the high-voltage drama electrifying what should have been a perfectly normal French class. Carlotta is forced to calm down.

At first Carlotta's circus days are kept a secret from the girls, but one day she astounds them all in the gym lesson by performing incredible cartwheels, shinning up the ropes like a monkey, and walking on her hands. Once the truth is out, the girls admire Carlotta even more, and beg her to tell stories of her romantic past in the circus. Her father and grandmother are mentioned frequently throughout Carlotta's school days as the 'sensible' influence in her life. Her father was a gentleman who ran off and married a gypsy, Carlotta's mother (*see* Barnabus Lorimer, in the 'Barney' Mystery series, for a similar background).

The only girl not impressed by Carlotta's past is the unpleasant Prudence Arnold who does her best to get the girl into all kinds of trouble. Inevitably, Carlotta learns to control her hot temper as her time at St Clare's progresses. She strikes up a friendship with Claudine when she arrives in the Fourth Form, and the two share a Fifth-Form study.

Interestingly, in the first ever book in the St Clare's series, a gypsy girl called Lotta is mentioned when the girls go on an outing to the local circus. She is a bareback rider which is precisely what Carlotta was in her circus days. Perhaps this is the first mention of her. This Lotta also appears in *Mr Pinkwhistle and the Circus*, along with her horse Black Beauty and her circus friends Jimmy, Lucky and Jumbo.

Brown, Jimmy

Owner of Sammy the Chimp, mentioned in *The Twins at St Clare's*. Interestingly, he has the same surname as Carlotta, the ex-circus girl who becomes a pupil at St Clare's after years of riding in the ring. However, it is Carlotta's mother who was of gypsy origin, so it is unlikely that Carlotta Brown and Jimmy Brown are related. Jimmy Brown also appears in his own series of stories about life in the circus, which fascinated Blyton.

Claudine

Claudine and the O'Sullivan twins are the only people Blyton deems worthy to have their names included in a title of her St Clare's books. Claudine is based on a Belgian girl who attended Blyton's school and who was 'as artful as a bag of monkeys'. She must have had a huge impact on her schooldays, even though her alter ego appears in only two books in the series. Claudine is wonderfully French, with a chic dark bob and dark eyes framing a porcelain-skinned face, entirely free of any English freckles which she so detests. She is the niece of Mam'zelle and, as a result has the French teacher wrapped firmly around her little finger. If Claudine is examined from a negative perspective, she is unscrupulous, cunning, dishonourable, manipulative and mischievous. If, however, her positive attributes are counted, she is found to be friendly, fun, kind-hearted, clever and selfless.

Claudine's antics include locking the bad-tempered new matron into a cupboard for a few hours so that the rest of her form can enjoy their midnight feast without being disturbed; throwing herself headlong into the swimming pool in order to soak Angela Favorleigh's mother who had been rude to her aunt; and organising with her younger sister Antoinette that the fire bell should be rung during a boring sports meeting so that the girls can avoid listening to high-handed Mirabel lecturing them on their hockey and lacrosse skills. Claudine may have the most extraordinary ideas, but she is always likeable because she really only behaves in the way she does in order to amuse or help. She loathes the water and sports, and as a result does not fare well with Mirabel who considers Claudine disgraceful and a very bad influence on the younger girls as she refuses to practise her catching and throwing.

Claudine and Antoinette have several other sisters – Jeanne, Louise and Marie are mentioned – and all are as French and as unaffected as can be. Claudine seems to drift happily through her days at St Clare's doing exactly as she pleases, always neatly presented, always polite and always ready to do the most unexpected things. At the end of *Fifth Formers at St Clare's*, however, we see Claudine at last taking on a little of the English sense of honour that she has been so dismissive of previously. She encourages Antoinette to go to Miss Theobald and own up that it was she who rang the fire bell in the sports meeting, as she feels bad that the blame is being shifted onto another girl. Claudine presses a hand to her chest and looks at Miss Theobald with slight discomfort as she confesses that she has 'caught' the English sense of honour at last. 'Oh! Is it catching?' asks Antoinette in great alarm. 'I don't want to have it for it seems an uncomfortable thing to have. See how it makes you behave, Claudine!'

Miss Cornwallis

Head of the Fifth Form at St Clare's.

Miss Ellis

Head of the Fourth Form and no known relation of Bobby Ellis, Miss Ellis takes on the usual format of St Clare's form mistresses in that she stands no silliness and controls the girls very effectively, except for Claudine who manages to get out of all the things that she does not want to do.

Ellis, Roberta

'Don't Care' Bobby is freckled, crinkly-eyed and always laughing. She joins the school in *Summer Term at St Clare's*, with Carlotta Brown and Prudence

Mam'zelle jumped back – her hand covered with soot.

Arnold. She and Janet Robins form a great friendship, based on their love of fun and practical jokes. These include a squeaking biscuit, which when pressed sounds like a cat mewing in the classroom, prompting a lengthy search for the mystery creature; and setting the clock forward once Miss Roberts has left the room, so that the lesson may end early. Bobby simply refuses to dedicate any time to her work when she first arrives at the school, spending her time scheming and plotting new tricks to play on the teachers for the general entertainment of the class.

She is shocked and disappointed when Miss Theobald takes her aside and tells her that she is, in her own way, a terrible cheat, because she is cheating herself and her parents in not trying her best in a school such as St Clare's where she has the opportunity to do so well. Bobby decides to take a long, hard look at herself, and does not like what she sees. From that moment on she turns over a new leaf and starts working extremely hard, much to the amazement of the class who suddenly discover that Roberta has excellent brains after all.

Elward, Doris

Natural-born actress, yet absolute dunce at academic work, Doris Elward is a constant source of entertainment to the girls of St Clare's with her marvellous ability to mimic anyone she chooses. An unsurpassed impersonation of Mam'zelle makes her the heroine of the First Form concert. Famed for her lack of ability to pronounce the French 'R'. Causes mayhem when she 'acts out' a French poem in class as it is the only way that it will stay in her memory (*Fifth Formers at St Clare's*). Doris forms an unusual friendship with brainy Pam Boardman whom she admires deeply. She makes Pam laugh, Pam helps her with her work. They share a study in the Fifth Form.

Erica

An appallingly spiteful and vindictive young lady who features in *The O'Sullivan Twins* and causes trouble on a daily basis, Erica's form-mates have little time for her, due to her reputation for malicious behaviour. She was sent down a year to the First Form from the Second, and proves to be just as dreadful with those a year younger than herself. One of her most disgusting displays of sneaky, dishonest behaviour comes when she spies on Tessie, Susan Howes, Hetty, Winnie Thomas, Janet Rollins and Pat and Isabel O'Sullivan as they enjoy a midnight feast. She knocks softly on Mam'zelle's door, waking up the French teacher so that the latter is able to hear the noises of the girls enjoying their fried sausages and night-time fun. Erica's spite is aimed directly at Pat O'Sullivan after Pat is rude to the unpleasant girl, and Erica unstitches her knitting, ruins her Nature notes and generally makes Pat's life a misery. She is delighted that the blame for all this passes conveniently on to another girl, Margery Fenworthy, but is shocked and dismayed when it is Margery who rescues her from a fire in the san. Erica's conscience comes 'very much alive', and she sees quite how terrible she has been. She confesses her sins to Lucy Oriell, and Lucy suggests to Miss Theobald that Erica might be allowed to start again somewhere new. Erica leaves St Clare's a much wiser, less selfish person, who has been given the chance to show some good in the future.

Fanshaw, Elsie

'The spiteful type', Elsie Fanshaw appears in *Second Form at St Clare's* as she and one other girl, Anna Johnson, remain behind when the rest of her year group move up into the Third Form. Elsie finds life hard with the likes of the O'Sullivan twins, Carlotta and Hilary to contend with, and is determined to exercise authority over those who have not been in the Second Form as long as she. Elsie and Anna are made joint Head Girls of the Second Form because they have been left behind, and Miss Theobald hopes that the position may do the two girls some good. Alas, Elsie Fanshaw proves a most unpopular Head Girl, because of her catty ways, and before long she is demoted and Anna takes full responsibility for the job. Elsie is furious that she no longer has the right to call meetings and make decisions and makes herself even more unpopular, wandering around like a 'wet dishcloth' and striking a pose of glowering rage whenever a fit of spite sweeps over her. She eavesdrops on a conversation held by her classmates discussing Carlotta's birthday feast and is determined to spoil the party for them all. The Second Formers realise what she is up to and things start going very wrong for Elsie. She is given another chance in the end and is moved up to the Third Form to start afresh. Blyton's most unpleasant characters often have names beginning with 'E'. They include Elsie Fanshaw, Erica and Eileen Paterson.

Favorleigh, Angela (The Honourable)

Floats into St Clare's in Blyton's penultimate book on life at the school, *Claudine at St Clare's*. Angela is very beautiful, with soft golden hair like a princess from a fairy tale, and is very quickly taken under the angelic wing of Alison O'Sullivan who thinks that Angela is the prettiest girl that has ever come to St Clare's. But the rest of the girls are very quick to realise that beauty is only skin deep, and that Angela is actually an extremely ugly character, despite her lovely outward appearance. She is a terrible snob, and looks down on girls like Claudine and Eileen Paterson feeling that they are 'charity girls' because they have relations at the school and therefore are not paying the full fees. She is arrogant and boastful, constantly reminding the girls of her rich background, wealthy parents and luxurious possessions. She mocks those whom she knows she has power over, and scorns those who call her spoilt. Alison is her only friend, but even Alison finally realises how dreadful Angela and her parents really are (*see also* Lady Favorleigh).

Angela's behaviour appears to take a turn for the better at the end of the summer term, when her father lectures her, and Alison steps in to try and improve her attitude. However, by *Fifth Formers at St Clare's*, she is back to her old habits and in the worst possible way. She takes great pleasure in the Fifth Form privilege of calling for the younger girls to do little jobs for them, such as make toast or light a fire. She knows that many of the junior school think that she is wonderful and beautiful, and she revels in seeing them fawning over her. It goes too far with a little First Former called Jane Teal, who is in and out of Angela's favour in a fashion that she finds impossible to cope with. In the end, it is little Antoinette, the chic younger sister of Claudine, who gets the better of Angela, just as efficiently as Claudine deals with Angela's mother. Angela learns that in the end beauty is no match for good brains, a merry heart and a kind nature.

Life at St Clare's is hard for her, as she realises the mistakes that she has made, but as she enters the Sixth Form, we are left feeling that, at last, she may have chosen to mend her ways.

Lady Favorleigh

Angela's 'wonderful' mother appears in *Claudine at St Clare's* and comes into direct contact with the French girl in a rather unfortunate event that remains in the minds of many of the pupils for a long time to come.

Lady Favorleigh arrives at the school for half term and her whining tones can be heard all over the school all day long. She is certainly dressed in the best clothes, and looks as beautiful as Angela promised, but she complains about everything she sees, from the water in the swimming pool, to the taste of the cakes at tea. The girls note these things and feel defensive towards St Clare's, and furious that this woman is spoiling things for everyone else. The final insult is directed towards Mam'zelle, who is proudly showing the parents her niece Claudine's beautifully embroidered cushion-cover. Angela's mother turns her nose up at the handiwork, and remarks in rather too loud tones that she hopes Angela is not taught by Mam'zelle whom she describes as 'that dreadful woman who looks so terribly dowdy'. One girl who overhears this is Claudine herself, who hatches a plan that works just as she hopes. During the swimming matches, Claudine hurls herself off the balcony where she is sitting and into the water below, soaking Angela's mother from head to foot. Lady Favorleigh is then forced to change into some sensible clothes of Miss Theobald which make her look ridiculous. Needless to say, she gets what she deserves, and even Angela feels that her mother has gone too far with her silly behaviour and constant whining. Blyton is forever hammering home the theory that parents are the making of the child, and Angela unfortunately has too much of her mother in her, which may not be entirely her fault. If her mother had been jolly and sensible, like Pat and Isabel O'Sullivan's, then she might have enjoyed St Clare's much more.

Fenworthy, Margery

Originally labelled 'a bad-tempered creature with some sort of past', Margery arrives at St Clare's in a cloud of hatred and fury, breathing threats and causing uproar with her outspoken rudeness to girls and staff alike. Her appalling attitude results in her being accused of playing horrible tricks on Pat O'Sullivan, including unstitching her knitting and destroying her nature drawings. During half term, Alison, Pat and Isabel O'Sullivan bump into an old friend of theirs from Redroofs, the school they attended before St Clare's. This girl, Pamela Holding, exclaims in amazement when she hears that Margery is at St Clare's, as she had been expelled from her school, and apparently six others, all because of her outrageously rude behaviour. Alison 'bleats' this news out to the other members of the First Form, who become more convinced than ever that Margery is the person responsible for the cruel 'jokes' played on Pat. However, things reach a dramatic climax when one night Margery rescues Erica from the san, where a fire is raging.

Margery becomes a heroine after this, as she breaks her leg in the course of the triumphant and brave mission. The irony thickens when Erica confesses that it was she, not Margery, who had been spiteful to Pat. Margery realises that St Clare's is not so bad after all, and confides in Lucy Oriell that she had been miserable because she felt that her mountain-climber father no longer loved her. Lucy, Pat and Isabel step in to help out, and Margery is a changed girl who moves swiftly up to the Second Form, as she is too old for the first. Margery Fenworthy is a classic case of the underdog succeeding, proving wrong those who were quick to judge her. Margery proves that she is someone very worthwhile.

Mr Fenworthy

The much admired mountain-climber father of Margery is reunited with his daughter when she proves herself to be as brave as he by recklessly plunging into the burning sanatorium in order to save trapped Erica.

'Well – go on, Margery.

Gardener

Plays a less than minor role in the St Clare's books, although we must assume that, as the gardens always look magnificent, he must be fairly good at his job. He is present on the scene of the fire in the san in *The O'Sullivan Twins*, though it is brave Margery Fenworthy who risks injury by climbing to help trapped Erica.

George, Rita

'One of the big girls' who catches Kathleen Gregory stealing money from her purse. An organiser of nature rambles.

Greene, Sadie

American girl who appears only in *Summer Term at St Clare's*. Sadie leaves the school at the end of that term, having gained nothing positive from her spell in the UK. Sadie thinks of nothing but her clothes, hairstyle and the cinema, and is swiftly befriended by Alison O'Sullivan who thinks that Sadie is too 'wunnerful' for words. Enid Blyton's portrayal of Americans is the same in both Malory Towers and St Clare's. Zerelda Brass is the token American in the Malory Towers series, and like Sadie she is absolutely clueless about everyday life in England. Both girls are as shallow as paddling pools and are made to seem extremely silly during their time at English boarding school, although, admittedly, Zerelda learns a good deal more common sense. Perhaps Malory Towers would have been a better option for Sadie?

Sadie is from a very wealthy family and is kidnapped at the end of her only term at St Clare's. Carlotta sets up a successful rescue mission involving her circus folk friends, and Sadie returns to St Clare's, bumping along on the back of Carlotta's horse, still complaining that her hair has been messed up by the adventure. Sadie leaves St Clare's promising to write to her 'best friend' Alison, but never does, proving herself to be fickle as well as vain, stupid and lazy. Blyton constantly makes reference to the one good side of Sadie's character – like Zerelda, the American girl is very 'good humoured'.

This shamelessly stereotypical portrayal of Americans seems very much to reflect Blyton's own view of the country and its people. America has glamour, but what is glamour when compared with a game of lacrosse in the fresh air, followed by a delicious tea of cream buns and ginger beer and a jolly pillow fight after dark? Oh, to be in *England*, now that Spring is here...

'Sadie says … Sadie says … Sadie says …'

Gregory, Kathleen

Plays an important role in the O'Sullivan twins' first term and then disappears into the background for the remaining five books. Shy, retiring girl who befriends Pat and Isabel when they first arrive and is then caught stealing from Rita of the Sixth Form, which explains her sudden generosity. Kathleen is an essentially 'good' character who chooses to spend the money that she has stolen on others, rather than on herself, providing a magnificent birthday cake with pink sugar roses for the First Form's midnight feast and giving lavish birthday presents to her friends. Pat and Isabel see that Kathleen's intentions were never truly bad, and go to see Miss Theobald immediately in order to sort the situation out.

Blyton writes very conscientiously on subjects such as theft and rule-breaking; hammering home the point time and time again that there is very often no black and white answer to these issues. Kathleen is a thief, but she is stealing to make others happy. She is given another chance, and ends the term by rescuing a small dog whom she names Binks, mentioned again in *Summer Term at St Clare's* when Kathleen claims that he and Carlotta Brown have a remarkably similar swimming style.

Harrison, Pamela

Shares a Sixth Form study with the formidable Belinda Towers. Blyton tended to give the older girls rather more sophisticated names than those further down the school. Pamela, Belinda and Georgina are three names which are curiously high-powered. It is hard not to imagine Pamela Harrison as a blonde, busty beach-babe.

Hetty

Second Former who appears in *The O'Sullivan Twins* and is involved in the midnight feast where sausages are cooked (*see also* Tessie and Erica).

Hill, Violet

'Cow-eyed' and rather silly member of the First Form who appears in *Fifth Formers at St Clare's* as a willing slave to Angela Favorleigh who uses her to do her mending and fetch and carry things at every opportunity (*see also* Jane Teal).

Hillman, Gladys

Kicks off her life in the *Second Form at St Clare's* with the nickname 'the misery girl', for obvious reasons. No one can make her smile and laugh, not even Doris with her ridiculous impersonations and silly dances. She refuses to join in the fun and frolics of school life, choosing to stay curled up with a book or simply writing letters in a corner. Curiously, it is the bad-tempered Mirabel Unwin who succeeds in bringing Gladys out of her shell. Mirabel discovers Gladys has a remarkable talent for acting when she overhears what she thinks must be two or three girls rehearsing lines in one of the little music practice rooms. She is curious as to who it could be, and when she peeks through the door is astonished to find quiet, introverted little Gladys Hillman alone in the room speaking lines in all manner of different voices and accents. When Mirabel reveals Gladys's acting talent to their peers, Gladys realises that St Clare's is a wonderful school and that she should give it a chance.

Mirabel and Gladys are extremely good for each other and strike up a warm friendship which lasts throughout the rest of their school days, although they do face problems when they reach the Fifth Form because Mirabel becomes very high-handed when she is made Head of Games. Gladys is the only girl who can really deal with the outspoken Mirabel and it is mentioned that, although Gladys does not often voice her opinion, when she does, it is always to speak words of great wisdom and foresight (*see also* Mirabel Unwin).

Mrs Hillman

Gladys's mother is referred to throughout *Second Form at St Clare's* as she is ill in hospital and Gladys is miserable, knowing that she is far away and cannot do anything to help. Mrs Hillman is also discussed in *Claudine at St Clare's* when Gladys pipes up that she would not care if her mother came to see her in an old hat and no stockings, she would still love her just the same. The form fall silent, knowing that Gladys has spoken some wise words about mothers, and Angela Favorleigh feels most annoyed that no one but Alison will listen to the stories of her wonderful mother with her fine clothes and beautiful jewels.

Hobart, Queenie

Breaks the window of the First Form classroom, but is sent to the san with flu shortly afterwards, so forgets to own up. As a result, the First Form trip to the circus is cancelled, because Miss Roberts presumes that it must have been one of the girls from her form, refusing to confess to the damage. Janet Robins, Pat and Isabel O'Sullivan and Kathleen Gregory all sneak out to the circus regardless and have a wonderful evening, only to learn the next day that it was second-former Queenie who broke the window with a tennis ball. When Miss Roberts is informed of this, she organises that the class may visit the circus that night, much to the dismay of the girls who have already been. However, fate lends a hand, and the four truants are laid low with bad colds from being out in the cold the night before. So they are unable to visit the circus again, thus clearing their consciences. Queenie is not mentioned again.

Holding, Pamela

Appears in *The O'Sullivan Twins* as a friend of Pat's and Isabel's from their previous school, Redroofs. Pamela bumps into the twins and Alison O'Sullivan during their half term break and helps to unravel the mystery of Margery Fenworthy's peculiar behaviour. Pamela, or Pam, is a name (like Winnie) that Blyton had a particular fondness for – Pamela Harrison, Pam (of the Secret Seven) and Pam Boardman. No Pamela has ever made a huge impact in Blyton's stories, however, despite the frequency of the name's use.

Howes, Susan

Popular girl who stays behind in the Fourth Form and joins the O'Sullivan twins and the rest of their form. Enid Blyton's 'Susan' characters are always sensible and good fun, as well as being popular and good at sport. Susan features also in *The O'Sullivan Twins* at the Great Midnight Feast (*see also* Tessie and Erica).

James, Winifred

Awe-inspiring Head Girl of St Clare's when the twins first arrive. Yet who would have thought, wonders Miss Roberts, that Winifred James, our dignified Head Girl, was once sent out of the room three times for playing noughts and crosses with her best friend?

Jane

Parlour maid only mentioned once at the beginning of *Summer Term at St Clare's*. Opens the main school door to the twins, Pat and Isabel O'Sullivan, as they arrive late back to school, having been in quarantine for measles.

Janet's Brother

Madcap who sends Janet tricks to play on the teachers. All of Blyton's slightly wild and sharp-tongued characters have older brothers who encourage them in their mischief (*see also* Alicia Johns in Malory Towers).

Miss Jenks

Head of the Second Form, Miss Jenks is not quite as sarcastic as First Form head Miss Roberts, but certainly 'all there'.

Jim

Appears in *Summer Term at St Clare's* as one of Carlotta Brown's circus friends.

Joan

Crops up very infrequently in *The Twins at St Clare's*. The one incident worth mentioning is when she participates in a night-time pillow fight with Doris Elward. One pillow splits and Joan is left groping for feathers in the dark, consequently upsetting her tooth mug, causing a fit of giggles that turn into hiccups from Kathleen Gregory, prompting further laughter from Janet Robins. Hilary Wentworth, as Head of Dorm, is not amused, knowing that she will get the blame for any misconduct after lights out.

Johns, Vera

Quiet, straight-haired girl mentioned only once in *The Twins at St Clare's* as being a member of the twins' form.

Johnson, Anna

Amiable character who features in *Second Form at St Clare's*. Fat, lazy and hopeless, she remains behind in the Second Form when the rest of her year move up. She and Elsie Fanshaw are made joint Head Girls of the Second Form, in the hope that they may be 'stirred up a little' by a position of author-ity. Much to the surprise of everyone, Anna pulls herself out of her languid state and becomes motivated and sensible, making positive decisions, calling meetings and proving to be a thoroughly good Head Girl. Anna illustrates a typical Blyton case of responsibility doing someone good and forcing Anna to snap out of her idle role and take charge with much more dynamic behaviour than she has ever shown before.

Jones, Pauline

Begins her time at St Clare's with the dubious surname of Bingham Jones. It soon becomes apparent that Pauline has great delusions of grandeur. Speaks in a haughty voice that gives her an air of snobbery and, like Angela, she despises the fact that she is attending a school with girls like Claudine and Eileen Paterson, feeling that she is far too high and mighty to share lessons with such lower-class charity girls. Pauline appears to have plenty of money and she gives extremely generous birthday presents, including a lovely new leather music case to Mirabel, but then ruins the effect by stating that the Bingham Joneses are just as wealthy as the Favorleighs (Angela's family). She is obsessively envious of Angela's beauty, something that she certainly does not possess, but is cleverer than Angela in class. Pauline makes constant reference to her family's rich friends, including the Lacey-Wrights who apparently have sixteen bathrooms in their palatial home. Pauline's form-mates feel that she is very cold and an awful snob, and she does not make friends.

The truth about Pauline's background is revealed when she breaks her leg in gym and her mother is sent for. Inevitably, it is Angela who bumps into the plain little woman struggling up the hill to St Clare's, and she is both horrified and delighted to discover that she is Mrs Jones, Pauline's mother, not Mrs Bingham Jones at all. Pauline is in a dreadful state of anxiety as she realises that the truth will be out and she will be revealed as the fraud that she is, but things do not turn out so badly for her. Miss Theobald advises her to tell the girls that she is sorry, sort things out with her mother, and to realise that riches are not important, and that no one will like her more for them. Pauline returns in *Fifth Formers at St Clare's* where she shares a study with the unfortunate Alma Pudden.

Miss Lewis

History teacher at St Clare's whose lessons are interesting and fun. Hilary Wentworth has a particular interest in History.

Longden, Anne-Marie

Poet and struggling intellectual, Anne-Marie is a new girl in *Fifth Formers at St Clare's* and is immediately squashed by the majority of her form-mates who feel that her work is decidedly lacking in real depth of feeling and emotion.

She is pretentious and serious, but perhaps Blyton is too harsh on this girl, who wrote the lines; 'Down the long lanes of the future / My tear-bedimmed eyes are peering.'

It seems that the St Clare's girls are not fond of this form of self-expression, and Anne-Marie decides that she will be remembered only long after her death, like the great poets before her. To make matters worse for the girl, she is forced to share a study with Felicity Ray, a girl who is a confirmed genius at music. The other girls all appreciate Felicity's gift and respect her for it. Anne-Marie is therefore completely overshadowed by this musical girl who also has no time for her writing. Anne-Marie has great respect and admiration for one teacher, Miss Willcox, for whose affection she fights with Alison O'Sullivan. Unfortunately for Anne-Marie, Miss Willcox has little time for her, and is scornful and dismissive of her work. But Anne-Marie has the final laugh, out-witting Miss Willcox in a most ingenious fashion. She submits a poem by the famous poet Matthew Arnold under her own name, and when Miss Willcox labels it the 'worst poem in the class' she triumphantly declares that Miss Willcox is in fact being rude about the work of a renowned great writer.

Anne-Marie also puts her brains into action to stage an Oscar-winning sleep-walking performance in imitation of Felicity whose genius is illustrated by her peculiar night-time behaviour. She floats convincingly down the corridors of the school one night muttering a poem under her breath, with Mam'zelle in hot pursuit. But when she drifts into the First Form dormitory, she is rudely awoken when the irrepressible Antoinette realises that she is acting and throws a jug of icy cold water over her. Anne-Marie never gets the respect she really wants, and eventually decides to give up on her poems, until she can write something that really means something.

Lorna

Passes a note in class in *The Twins at St Clare's*. No other references.

Mam'zelle

Mam'zelle's first name is Mathilde; her surname is never mentioned. She is plump, loud-voiced and completely alien to the values held by the so-strange English girls. Gullible to the point of farce, she falls for numerous tricks played on her by the girls, yet is saved from fury by her great sense of humour. She is nicknamed 'Mam'zelle Abominable!' by Pat and Isabel O'Sullivan because she considers their work abominable when they first arrive. Mam'zelle takes a leading role in the aptly named chapter 'A Most Surprising Night' in *Fifth Formers at St Clare's* when she scampers around the school shoving

Mam'zelle stared in horror at the enormous blot.

various girls into cupboards, presuming them to be burglars. The hilarity of this behaviour lies in the absurdity of Mam'zelle's thinking – she is expecting great praise for saving the school from these terrible intruders, only to find that they are not who she thinks they are. She is disappointed, amazed and confused to find Mirabel Unwin, Jane Teal and Alma Pudden emerging from imprisonment the next morning. (For further details of what they were doing wandering the school in the middle of the night, *see* Mirabel Unwin, Jane Teal and Alma Pudden.)

Mam'zelle is the teacher who appears most frequently in St Clare's, particularly when her nieces, Claudine and Antoinette, arrive at the school. Angela Favorleigh's mother looks down on Mam'zelle in disgust, dismissing her as 'dowdy', which upsets the girls very much for they are extremely fond of their well-meaning French mistress. However, it is not long before Claudine seeks revenge on the woman who dares to be rude about her aunt.

Blyton frequently mentions the French loathing of swimming, sports and any form of outdoor activity.

Pad-pad-pad went her feet, and every now and again Mam'zelle set her pince-nez firmly on her nose for they had an irritating way of jumping off when she ran. Pad-pad-pad – the chase was on!　　FIFTH FORMERS AT ST CLARE'S

Mary

Mentioned only once, playing in a lacrosse match in *The O'Sullivan Twins*.

Matron

Plump, brisk figure who deals out 'revolting' medicine from huge bottles, Matron also possesses great kindness of heart which gains her the immense liking of all the girls, except those who are furious that they will never be able to feign illness with her. She is replaced for one term by Mrs Paterson, who could not be less suited to the role that she has to fulfil. Fortunately for the girls, Matron returns towards the end of term to sort out the problems that have arisen in her absence. (*See also* Eileen Paterson, Edgar Paterson, Mrs Paterson and Pauline Jones.) Matron has to deal with a handful of girls who persist in trying to get out of games and swimming lessons. Most of the time her remedy is a good spell outside running around in the fresh air. She is immensely suspicious of characters such as Claudine who will try anything to stay indoors.

Naylor, Sheila

Arrogant and haughty when she is initially introduced to St Clare's, Sheila Naylor is in reality rather bad-mannered, even forgetting to wash her neck at times. Janet Robins remarks that she talks like 'the daughter of the dustman', and indeed it is later revealed by Winifred James, Head Girl, that Sheila's parents had made their money very recently and that her mother is the daughter of a gardener. It transpires that Sheila's conceit is merely a smoke-screen for the shy, insecure girl underneath who is in need of a little friendliness. As soon as she is given the chance, she rises to the occasion and performs the lead part in the First Form play, gaining the respect and liking of all the girls.

Blyton wrote from her own experience, about very middle-class characters from respectable homes, nearly all of whom had cooks, maids and housekeepers. As soon as a character ventured out of this social milieu, trouble arose in some form or other. Sheila Naylor is a perfect example. (*See also* Pauline Jones and Eileen Paterson.) Despite this, the main moral running throughout the whole of Blyton's writings is that kindness, friendliness and good sense are everything, regardless of background.

Oriell, Lucy

Top hole, clever, amusing, pretty and overridingly *good* character who features heavily in *The O'Sullivan Twins*. Wonderfully artistic girl, the daughter of the famous portrait painter Max Oriell, from whom she inherits her mass of black curls and shining eyes. Lucy has an impeccable academic record, and is admired and liked by everyone, almost to the point where it is possible to feel that she is *too* perfect. Receives a terrible shock when she is told that her father has been in a car accident and will be unable to use his right hand again. This means the end of his career as a painter and, potentially, the end of Lucy's time at St Clare's, as the family will be unable to pay the school fees. Lucy's great friend and mentor Margery Fenworthy seeks to put things right with the help of Miss Theobald and Miss Walker. They suggest to Lucy that she take the scholarship paper to allow her to stay on at the school that she loves so much. Lucy accepts this idea with a face glowing with happiness once again. Inevitably, she wins the scholarship and moves up into the Second Form the next term with Margery at her side. It is mentioned that she is determined to be made Head Girl of St Clare's one day, but it is never apparent that she achieves this goal.

Oriell, Max

Portrait artist father of Lucy Oriell. Max Oriell earns substantial amounts of money as a painter, but is no good at saving, resulting in poverty when he injures his painting hand in a car accident. His bravery is clear – Lucy states that he intends to start a new career using his other hand.

O'Sullivan, Alison

The 'pretty little feather-head' cousin of Pat and Isabel O'Sullivan, Alison is given to having huge crushes on highly unsuitable characters, and is invariably hurt by them as a result of her blindness to their faults. During her time at St Clare's she attaches herself to Sadie Greene, the American girl (*Summer Term at St Clare's*), Miss Quentin, the Drama teacher (*Second Form at St Clare's*) and to Miss Willcox, the English teacher (*Fifth Formers at St Clare's*). She becomes best friends with the Honourable Angela Favorleigh but eventually realises that Angela is spiteful and unkind underneath her beautiful face.

Although Alison is a weak and easily led character, she is kind and has a definite sense of honour which she can see is painfully lacking in Angela. St Clare's certainly makes Alison into a more sensible girl, but she simply cannot resist the charms of the beautiful people.

O'Sullivan, Patricia and Isabel

With her twin sister Isabel never far from her side, Patricia (Pat) O'Sullivan is a leading character in the first two St Clare's books, then takes on a less prominent role as Blyton chooses to focus her attention on more cosmopolitan classmates. She and Isabel begin their lives with very defiant attitudes, furious that they are not allowed to attend the luxurious Ringmere School where their tennis-playing pals Mary and Frances Waters have been sent. Their high and mighty ways provoke the appropriate nickname of 'The Stuck-Up Twins' which stays with them until they decide that they should settle down and start acting sensibly. Patricia is certainly the leader of the two, as is illustrated by her rebellious behaviour towards Belinda Towers in the twins' first term. Pat is not afraid to cheek the older girl, and refuses to clean her muddy shoes and lay the fire. Isabel is more passive, choosing to obey Belinda who is the intimidating Captain of Sports. The twins remain extremely close throughout their school days, eventually sharing a study in the Fifth Form and being made joint Head Girls of the school after Mam'zelle's suggestion that St Clare's needs two head girls to cope with the pressure of the job. They are both good sportswomen, and represent St Clare's in hockey and lacrosse.

'Oh, the silly donkey, she's taken my french prep.'

Pat and Isabel are at their most dynamic and entertaining during their first term when they are behaving disgracefully. It is almost as if Blyton tires of them once they have abandoned their mischievous ways and they blend into one another, barely distinguishable in the later books. Their cousin Alison is introduced in *The O'Sullivan Twins* and takes on a larger role than Pat and Isabel as life at St Clare's progresses. Both girls possess dark, wavy hair, and as Pat so frankly states in *The O'Sullivan Twins*: 'We can't help knowing that we're good at nearly everything, besides being pretty and quite amusing.' This actually sums the twins up extremely accurately.

O'Sullivan, Sarah

Kind mother of Alison O'Sullivan, and aunt of Pat and Isabel O'Sullivan. Sarah O'Sullivan seems to be a good deal more intelligent and sensible than her daughter, and does not allow her to spend too much time with Angela Favorleigh. Thinks very highly of Claudine, who joins Alison and her mother for a half-term outing in Claudine's first term. She is probably the parent who purchases Claudine's beautifully embroidered cushion-cover for quite a large amount of money – though Claudine never reveals the name of the buyer.

Paterson, Edgar

Weak-faced and uninspiring brother of Eileen.

Paterson, Eileen

Eileen is at St Clare's for only one term, when her mother takes on a temporary job as matron at the school, filling in while Matron is away ill. She is not well liked, as she is a sneak, and goes to her mother to report girls who have torn their sheets or clothes. She has one obsession in life, her brother Edgar (Eddie), whom she meets illegally outside the school grounds on a regular basis. He is out of work and looking for a job, but it is clear that he and his sister are both very afraid of their demanding mother, finding her unkind and intimidating. Eileen ends up taking money from her mother and giving it to Eddie who needs it to survive while he is looking for work. Unfortunately, the thieving gets out of hand, and their mother demands that when the thief is caught, she should be expelled. She stares in horror at Eileen and Eddie when they are brought before her and are revealed as the culprits. Miss Theobald has many bad but truthful things to say to the white-faced woman who has treated her children with such harshness that they are too scared to come to her for help and advice. All three of them leave the school together, and gradually it becomes apparent that things have been sorted out. Eileen writes a letter to Alison O'Sullivan apologising for her thieving, and informing her that she intends to get a job as a secretary in the office where her brother works. Eileen herself confesses that she was never right for St Clare's and yet she hopes that nobody thinks too badly of her. She ends her letter by saying, 'You can't imagine how difficult it was for me sometimes.'

Mrs Paterson

Replaces Matron at St Clare's for one term only and is most unsuccessful in her duties as she is cold, unfriendly and spiteful in her starched white apron (*see* Eileen Paterson).

Pudden, Alma

Living up to her name in the most revolting way, Alma is fat, pasty and pudding-faced, constantly stuffing food into her mouth, and guzzling sweets whenever she can. Sent down from the Sixth Form to join the *Fifth Formers at St Clare's* she proves to be unpopular and unpleasant. Her only pleasure and interest in life is food which leads her into all sorts of trouble, particularly when she uncovers the secret cupboard containing food for a Second Form midnight feast. Alma cannot resist 'pilfering' from the cupboard when she is hungry, taking a bottle of ginger beer, a packet of biscuits or a jar of sweets. She is furious when Alison O'Sullivan suggests that Claudine should keep the key to the store cupboard somewhere on her person to prevent the thief from striking again, and starts to play mean tricks on Alison to pay her back for ruining her fun. She manages to get her hands on the key once again and it so happens that she is caught on the night of the Second Form feast, groping around for a tin of some kind, by Mam'zelle who mistakes her for a burglar, and shoves the alarmed Alma into the store cupboard and locks the door.

It is later revealed that Alma actually has an illness that makes her constantly hungry, and makes her look pasty and unhealthy. When the girls realise that Alma cannot help her greed, they become more friendly towards her, but she is not a very amiable kind of character, with little to say of any interest.

Mr and Mrs Ray

The parents of the talented Felicity Ray, who appears in *Fifth Formers at St Clare's*, refuse to treat her like a normal child, and encourage her to do nothing but practise for a difficult music exam. As a result, Felicity drives herself to the edge of a nervous breakdown and Miss Theobald advises her parents to stop making Felicity so worried about the exam, and let her concentrate on being a normal girl. Interestingly, Enid Blyton herself was pressured into taking up a career in music, and eventually confessed to her father that she wanted to write instead. It is easy to imagine, therefore, that her sympathies lay with Felicity.

Rita

Third Form girl, mentioned only once in *Fifth Formers at St Clare's*.

Miss Roberts

Young, good-looking and tall, with simple dress sense, Miss Roberts is the crisp, efficient and no-nonsense Head of the First Formers at St Clare's who has learned to size up the girls' characters extremely quickly and accurately. She is the form teacher Blyton focuses on more than any other, as the first three books in the St Clare's series are all based on life in the First Form where Miss Roberts is very much in control.

Robins, Janet

Chatterbox jester of the first two books in the series, Janet Robins is slightly outshone by the appearance of Roberta Ellis in *Summer Term at St Clare's*. Blyton discovered a winning formula when she introduced naughty girls to her school stories for they provide her with the perfect story line through their numerous tricks played on various easy-prey teachers. The gullible Mam'zelle falls for the most ridiculous of jokes, including an inflatable balloon placed under a tablecloth which causes her plate to dance around in front of her. Janet's own behaviour gets more than slightly out of hand when she puts beetles and earwigs in Mam'zelle's glasses' case, and pretends that she cannot see them when Mam'zelle cries out in amazement. Mam'zelle is whisked off to the san for a rest, causing Janet to realise that her joke has gone too far, and that she must apologise at once.

Janet does not appear as such a central character in the last three books in the series, but is none the less a very important member of the form, and a great friend of the twins. Sharp-witted yet fair.

Sally

Member of the First Form who appears in *Fifth Formers at St Clare's* when the First Form are asked to join the Second Form's midnight feast with amusing and surprising results.

Sammy

Chimpanzee in the circus visited by the St Clare's girls in *The Twins at St Clare's*.

Specialist from London

The doctor puts in a cameo appearance in *Fifth Formers at St Clare's* when he is called to examine Felicity Ray. He diagnoses the child as being on the verge of a nervous breakdown, and states that she must not play any more music for a year, and must try to live a normal life, as far as possible.

Teal, Jane

Blyton paints a frightening picture of the hierarchy of the school system through the character of Jane Teal who appears in *Fifth Formers at St Clare's* and undergoes a complete emotional and physical crisis. Jane is a little First

Former whose loyalties are hopelessly divided between the marvellous Captain of Sports, Mirabel Unwin, and the most beautiful girl in the school, Angela Favorleigh. Mirabel wants Jane to practise extra hard on the playing fields, and Angela wants the undivided attention of the little girl to do all of the jobs that Angela hates. Jane tries to please both her idols, doing Angela's mending, and playing games whenever she can, but it soon takes its toll. Angela becomes irritated by Jane's continued admiration for Mirabel, and calls for another First Former, Violet Hill, to take over from Jane. Jane is heartbroken, and everything in her life appears to go to pieces, particularly when Mirabel thinks it is she who rang the fire bell at an important sports meeting.

She decides that she must run away from school and, surprisingly enough, she selects the same night that there are going to be several other people up and about. She falls into a terrible, delirious fever, and thinks that she has opened the door of the school but, in fact, she is trapping herself in a cupboard, much to Mam'zelle's satisfaction, as she feels that this must be another one of the burglars she has seen around the school. When she is found in the morning, she is sent to the san where Mirabel comes to visit her and apologises for her behaviour.

Blyton is entirely successful in her efforts to portray the terror and elation experienced by the younger girl as she looks up to the Fifth Formers with such awe and respect. In the end it is obvious that Angela and Mirabel are to blame for Jane's nervous state, as much as Jane herself who could not see when she had gone too far to try and please the two girls.

Tessie

Mischievous and lively girl in the Second Form when the twins and their contemporaries are in the First. A joker with a keenness for rebellion, she organises a midnight feast for her birthday which includes frying sausages over a little stove lent to her by Gladys from the school kitchens. Unfortunately, the feast is ruined by the spiteful behaviour of Erica who awakens Mam'zelle to the extraordinary smells and sounds of the midnight revellers. Best friend of Winnie Thomas.

Miss Theobald

Headmistress of St Clare's who commands respect, admiration and hard work from pupils and teachers alike in a fashion close to royalty. In the course of six books she deals calmly and efficiently with the most extraordinary of circumstances, including the kidnapping of the American girl Sadie Greene, the taming of gypsy Carlotta, two cases of thieving among girls, a fire in the

She was looking up the answers one by one.

sanatorium, a virtual nervous breakdown of a girl who plays an imaginary violin in her sleep, and numerous characters who have very peculiar ideas about what is right and wrong. She is described as deep-voiced, with a lovely smile, and is never flustered; frequently mentioned as looking 'thoughtful' when chaos is raging all around her. It is hardly surprising, all things considered, that she is grey-haired.

Thomas, Annie

Sports Captain who passes on the job to Mirabel Unwin in *Fifth Formers at St Clare's*.

Thomas, Winnie

Best friend of chirpy Second Former Tessie, Winnie is involved in the mid-night feast where sausages are cooked (*see* Tessie and Erica). Blyton had a great fondness for the name Winnie, calling no fewer than four of the girls in her school stories by this name.

Towers, Belinda

Head of Sports when the twins first arrive at St Clare's, Belinda and her room-mate, Pamela Harrison, send for Pat and Isabel O'Sullivan to clean their muddy boots and boil their kettle for cocoa. The twins are outraged by the mere notion of having to perform such menial tasks, but are forced into sub-mission by the terrifying Belinda. Belinda is made Head Girl when Winifred James leaves, which is a popular decision as she is already familiar with the girls thanks to her interest in the school sports. A girl of great physical strength, willing to help out anyone in a spot of trouble.

Unwin, Hilary and Joan

Younger brother and sister of Mirabel Unwin are mentioned only in *Second Form at St Clare's* because Mirabel is jealous of the attention they get from her parents, and resents them horribly.

Unwin, Mirabel

Strides into St Clare's in the Second Form and quickly shows herself as being rude, outspoken and arrogant. Furious at being sent away to boarding school, she has every intention of being sent home at half term, so makes life as difficult as possible for everyone else. Her frequent rudeness to staff results in her being sent out of the room in disgrace which she discovers is actually just a nuisance, as no one thinks that she is clever or funny. She refuses to read her lines correctly in Miss Quentin's Drama lesson, and Carlotta leaps in to deal with the situation in her typically Continental fashion, boxing Mirabel's ears very quickly and smartly. Most of the girls feel that this is just the sort of punishment that Mirabel needs, but Mirabel refuses to change her ways, claiming that this outburst of violence from Carlotta will only make her worse. The girls decide to play a series of tricks on Mirabel to attempt to show her how much they resent her. They sew up the sleeves of her coat, put pebbles in her shoes, give her an apple-pie bed, spill ink on her Maths prep and empty the vases of the flowers she is supposed to be looking after. Most of these tricks are carried out by spiteful Elsie Fanshaw and Alison O'Sullivan, who is furious that Mirabel should dare to disrupt her beloved Miss Quentin's class.

But Mirabel is not as bad as everyone thinks. After she refuses to snitch on the girls when she is late for games, Hilary Wentworth decides that it is time she is given a proper chance. To everyone's amazement, Gladys Hillman speaks up and tells the class that Mirabel's great talent is playing the violin and the piano, for she had heard her playing one night, and had been very moved by Mirabel's uncharacteristically sensitive playing. Naturally, once this great talent is unveiled, Mirabel finds herself enjoying life at St Clare's, making friends fast, particularly with Gladys, who eventually persuades her that she should not go home at half term, but should stay on and enjoy herself at school. In the end, this is exactly what Mirabel does.

Mirabel is also a focal point of *Fifth Formers at St Clare's* when she is made Sports Captain of the entire school. Her behaviour becomes aggressive and demanding as she obsesses over lacrosse and hockey. She is looked up to by many of the younger girls, but she makes life hard for them through her lack of understanding, and is frequently likened to a bulldozer, simply mowing down everyone in her way. Mirabel learns a bitter lesson when she realises that she is expecting too much of the younger girls and they rebel against her.

Her final humiliation comes when she is caught sneaking around after dark to discover whether the First Form are having a midnight feast which will ruin their chances of doing well in their lacrosse match the next day. Mam'zelle mistakes Mirabel's large pyjama-clad form for a burglar and locks her into a cupboard where she stays until next morning (*see* Mam'zelle and Jane Teal). Mirabel consequently fails her Fifth Form exam because of the pressure she has put herself under, and feels that she has disgraced herself through her own silly behaviour and refusal to listen to others. But all is not lost. When the girls realise that she is sorry for what she has done, they welcome her back as their Games Captain, and all is forgiven.

Mr and Mrs Unwin

Mirabel's parents, who appear in *Second Form at St Clare's*, send their daughter away to the school because of her persistent stubbornness and bad behaviour.

Miss Walker

Described by Blyton as a 'merry soul' who runs a very 'go-as-you-please' Art class enjoyed by all the girls. She acquires a friend in Margery Fenworthy when they decide to help Lucy Oriell who needs to work hard for the scholarship exam in order to stay on at St Clare's.

Waters, Mary and Frances

Mary and Frances attended Redroofs School with Pat and Isabel O'Sullivan, and go on to become pupils of the very grand and luxurious Ringmere School where they will no doubt become even more spoilt than they are already. These two sisters are introduced on the first page of the first St Clare's book when they are relaxing after a game of tennis with the twins, and they make no subsequent appearances. Redroofs is condemned by over-talkative Janet Robins as 'The school for snobs!' She goes on to mention that her cousin went there and 'Didn't she fancy herself when she came home! Expected to be waited on hand and foot and couldn't even bear to sew a button on a shoe!'

Wentworth, Hilary

Initially mentioned as being 'cheeky-looking' with curly golden hair. In fact, her character emerges as anything but cheeky, as she is one of the most responsible, hardworking and reliable girls that St Clare's produces. Firm but fair, Hilary Wentworth has a wonderful ability to 'tackle' difficult girls who need her help to reveal the true strength of their characters. Her undisputed leadership qualities would have made her the obvious choice for Head Girl of the entire school, but Blyton chooses to ship Hilary off to India to be with her parents, leaving a convenient gap for the O'Sullivan twins to fill. Hilary is never given centre stage in the St Clare's stories, but is constantly referred to as a key figure in the overall structure of the form. She is proof that it is possible to be popular and influential without being considered dull.

Miss Willcox

English teacher who arrives at St Clare's in the final book in the series. She is clearly vain and self-important, with a very high opinion of her own writing, but is able to keep the girls interested in lessons and undoubtedly 'knows her stuff'. It is uncovered that her first name is Deirdre, and Alison O'Sullivan and Anne-Marie Longden are constantly teased for being 'Deirdre Fans', as they think that the teacher is wonderfully exotic with her vague, soulful eyes, floaty scarves and gold hair pins. Miss Willcox is made to look ridiculous, however, when Anne-Marie decides to trick her in class as she persistently scorns Anne-Marie's poetry. (Anne-Marie later discovers that Miss Willcox's real name is in fact Doris.)

Williams, Molly

First Former in *Fifth Formers at St Clare's* who is good at games, and Mirabel chooses her to play in a match.

Miss Wilton

The seldom-mentioned Games teacher at St Clare's. Blyton chose to focus more on the Sports Captains who were Sixth Form girls than on the members of the Games staff.

MALORY TOWERS

First Term at Malory Towers (1946)
The Second Form at Malory Towers (1947)
Third Year at Malory Towers (1948)
Upper Fourth at Malory Towers (1949)
In the Fifth at Malory Towers (1950)
Last Term at Malory Towers (1951)

Malory Towers is the girls' boarding school attended most famously by Darrell Rivers, Alicia Johns and Gwendoline Mary Lacey. It is clearly stated that the school is set in Cornwall which accounts for the magnificent swimming pool cut out of the rocks with spectacular views of the expanse of ocean beyond, but the exact location is left vague. The school works within a House system like most boarding schools today, except the Houses are known as 'Towers' (North, South, East and West) with the majority of Blyton's best-loved characters from North Tower. Pupils at Malory Towers excel in both sporting and academic activity under the wise leadership of Miss Grayling, the impressive Headmistress who is able to draw out the very best from nearly all of the girls who attend the school. There are exceptions, but as a general rule the girls flourish in the healthy Cornish air and work and play hard throughout the seven years that the school is their second home.

Barker, Deirdre

Meek and mouse-like First Form friend of the Second Former Josephine Jones, Deirdre is mentioned in *Last Term at Malory Towers* as Jo's side-kick and only real pal who is enthralled by Jo's tales of wealth and the amazing packages of food that she receives on a regular basis. She is persuaded to run away with Jo who holds the philosophy that when the going gets tough, the tough get going, and the two girls take refuge in a shack near the school. Much to Deirdre's distress, the two girls are caught and sent back to the school and straight to Miss Grayling. Deirdre is terrified of expulsion, as her father is a sailor and would never dream of running away from anything, and Miss Grayling can see that she is truly sorry and will never be so easily led again. Deirdre stays at Malory Towers, but a less favourable option awaits Jo (*see* Josephine Jones).

Batten, Connie and Ruth

Connie and her twin sister Ruth, who appear in *Upper Fourth at Malory Towers*, are polar opposites in behaviour and appearance. Connie is rather stout and extremely bossy, while her sister is small and very low-key by comparison. Dubbed the Bisto Twins by the ever-sharp Alicia Johns, the two girls seem to enjoy their lives at Malory Towers, although it is rare to hear Ruth saying anything, as any question directed towards her is immediately answered by her sister. The other girls find this peculiar and very irritating, especially as Ruth appears to be an intelligent girl who does well in class. The truth about the two girls is revealed when petty tricks are played on Connie, involving the cutting of her tennis racquet handle and the slashing of her fine new riding whip. Ruth appears to be very upset by these incidents, and offers Connie her own possessions, but it is the forthright and clear-headed Darrell Rivers who puts two and two together and realises that it is Ruth who is playing all the mean tricks on her twin.

Ruth breaks down and confesses everything to Darrell, sobbing that she hates the way Connie always speaks for her, and also confides that Connie wants Ruth to fail her School Certificate exam on purpose, so that the two girls can be left behind in the Fourth Form together, as Connie herself has no hope of passing. Darrell is shocked and disgusted by Connie's behaviour and makes up her mind that Ruth most certainly should go up into the Fifth Form, and Connie should stay down, giving both girls the chance to stand on their own feet for a while. At the start of *In the Fifth at Malory Towers* Connie is mentioned as barging into Ruth's dormitory on a number of occasions, but is soon sent away. She forms a rather bizarre friendship with a most unsavoury character called Bridget (*see* Bridget and Moira).

Bill (Wilhelmina)

Wilhelmina, or 'Bill' as she prefers to be known, makes dramatic horseback entrances up the drive of Malory Towers at the beginning of every term. She has seven brothers and is the only girl in the family which has made her into something of a tomboy with her short-cropped dark hair, freckled, weather-beaten face and love of outdoor life. Bill is outspoken and open-faced and the girls take an immediate liking to her, despite the fact that the only thing she talks about is her beloved horse, Thunder. Much to the annoyance of Miss Peters, the Third Form teacher, Bill is distracted and dreamy in class as she is constantly thinking about Thunder and the many horses that she has left behind at home. Bill even has a habit of rocking to and fro on her chair in class, imagining that she is aboard her great steed, which sends Miss Peters into a state of high irritation. Bill's obsession with Thunder leads her into trouble when she is caught down at the stables when she is not supposed to be there, and she is banned from spending time with the creature. Much to her distress, he becomes ill with colic, and ironically it is Miss Peters who comes to the rescue of the animal in a dramatic midnight quest to find a vet (*see* Miss Peters).

Bill finds a firm friend in the equally horse-mad Clarissa Carter who arrives in *Upper Fourth at Malory Towers* and the two spend hours riding and talking about the equine events that have dominated their lives (*see* Clarissa Carter). Bill and Clarissa leave Malory Towers to set up their own riding school, the success of which is beyond doubt.

Brass, Zerelda

Gorgeous-looking but ridiculous American who finds herself at a peculiar English boarding school in *Third Year at Malory Towers*, and is not prepared for what lies in store. Zerelda Brass lives up to her glamorous name, with a heavily made-up face and a thick mass of brass-coloured hair piled up on top of her head. She travels down to the school with the Rivers family and exasperates Darrell by falling asleep in the car, just as Darrell is chatting away about her favourite subject, Malory Towers. Although Zerelda is fifteen, she looks a good deal older, and for the girls at the school she is the most extraordinary-looking girl they have ever seen. She speaks in a slow American drawl and is immediately adored by Gwendoline Lacey who admires her arresting looks and interest in the cinema. Zerelda soon finds that her ways are very different from those of the English girls, as she is not up to their academic standard and is constantly being told to take her hair down from its sophisticated style and plait it neatly into two braids. She is an amiable type of girl who is very good-natured and claims that everything is 'wunnerful', much to the amusement of the girls who love to imitate her ways. She announces that she wants to be an actress and that this is her great talent, but is shocked and disappointed when the girls roar with laughter over her 'sensitive' portrayal of Juliet, as Zerelda's accent simply does not lend itself to Shakespeare. Zerelda then realises that perhaps she is not as talented at acting as she had once thought, and at last decides to be sensible, and stops trying to act like Marilyn Monroe in favour of behaving like the funny English girls she had once mocked.

Zerelda forms an unexpected friendship with Mavis, the failed opera singer, in the last few weeks of term, as the pair both learn that pride comes before a fall. Alicia privately decides that Zerelda does have a real talent – for making people laugh – but keeps her views to herself for fear of making Zerelda bigheaded once again. Zerelda is not mentioned in the subsequent three books in

Darrell and Bill tried to hide.

the series, but as she is older than the other girls, she is moved up a year ahead of them all.

Bridget

Unpleasant younger sister of the bossy, dictatorial Moira, Bridget forms a friendship with Connie Batten, one of the twins from the Upper Fourth, and the two girls are mentioned when they happen to hear the terrible screeching singing voice of Maureen Little coming out of one of the practice rooms. Bridget begins to imitate the Fifth Former and makes such a row herself that her sister Moira hears it and comes running into the room to tell her to shut up. Bridget is rude and cheeky to her older sister and Moira simply will not stand for it. She runs off and reports her sibling to Miss Williams, head of the Fourth Form, and a bitter animosity develops between the two girls.

Carter, the Honourable Clarissa

Never are similes of ugly ducklings and swans so pertinent in Blyton's writing as they are in the character of the Honourable Clarissa Carter. Clarissa first appears in *Upper Fourth at Malory Towers* as a very plain girl with wire on her front teeth and thick-rimmed glasses completely destroying her face and obscuring her eyes. She is at once befriended by Gwendoline Mary Lacey who notes the 'Hon.' in Clarissa's title and is almost paralytic with excitement at the prospect of making a very grand friend indeed. Clarissa is introverted and shy and therefore does not contribute much to life in the Fourth Form, except for the occasion when the Fourth Formers set off on a picnic, and she visits her old governess who provides Clarissa and Gwendoline with a huge tea which they decide to finish in the form of a midnight feast with the help of the other girls.

Clarissa has a weak heart which prevents her from participating in any form of games, as she experiences terrible palpitations. Much to the disgust of the rest of her form, Gwendoline Mary decides that a weak heart would be the ideal ticket to allow her too to escape from the games and swimming that she so detests. Although Clarissa is initially taken in by Gwen's Oscar-winning 'breathless' performances, she soon wises up to the girl's fat fibs when she has tea with the Lacey family during half term. The disgraceful untruths that Gwen is filling her mother with lead Clarissa to conclude that a weak heart is another one of Gwen's selfish fantasies. Gwen is sent to a doctor who suggests that Gwen take *more* exercise to get her weight down and get rid of her spots.

Clarissa finds her true ally in the company of horse-mad Bill. By *Last Term at Malory Towers* she is galloping up the school drive on her pretty little horse,

Merrylegs, wire removed from her teeth and glasses discarded to reveal beautiful swamp-green eyes. Clarissa and Bill start up their own riding school when they leave Malory Towers.

Catherine

Holier-than-thou Catherine flashes her beaming smile in *In the Fifth at Malory Towers* and is immediately dubbed 'Saint Catherine' by her sceptical form-mates who find her quite revoltingly sweet. Catherine stays behind a year when the rest of her class is moved up to the Sixth Form, and nobody is particularly pleased to see her. Catherine revels in doing jobs for others, including darning Gwendoline's stockings and running off to water the flowers in the classroom. She is scorned and disliked for her pious attitude and silly comments and eventually gives up trying to be helpful as she receives nothing but rude comments and sarcasm in return. She feels sore and bitter about this, but does move into the Sixth Form with one ally, the quiet and gentle Mary Lou who is grateful to Catherine for praising her performance in the Fifth Form pantomime and for fussing over her dress and listening to her practise her lines.

Chartelowe, Amanda

Amanda arrives at Malory Towers in the last book in the series and certainly features heavily throughout it. Mam'zelle makes the genuine mistake of calling her Amanda Shout-a-Lot in front of her peers, which causes much amusement as Amanda is a 'great hefty girl about five foot ten inches tall' with an exceptionally booming voice. She arrives at Malory Towers at this late stage as her last school, Trenigon Towers, is burnt down in a fire, just as Maureen Little's is a few terms previously. She does not endear herself to the other girls as she is thick-skinned, with a very high opinion of her sporting abilities. Alicia suggests in a voice heavy with sarcasm that perhaps Amanda may consider entering the Olympic Games, and Amanda states that yes, she hopes to. As *Last Term at Malory Towers* was published in 1951 it is likely that Amanda was hoping to participate in the 1952 games in Helsinki.

Pride certainly comes before a fall for the strapping young Amanda, as she has a great shock in store for her. She volunteers to coach Alicia's scamp of a Second Former cousin, June, in tennis and swimming and finds that she has met her match in sheer strength of character. The two are not well suited – they are too alike perhaps – and, after a few weeks of Amanda's admittedly very beneficial coaching, June storms off and refuses to listen to her bossy voice any longer. Amanda is annoyed and upset, as she feels that June has the potential to be the best sportswoman in the whole school if she is properly trained. The final frontier is crossed when Amanda chooses to swim in the sea one morning, strictly against the school rules, and is swept away by the strong current. One girl is up at that early hour, and one girl comes to Amanda's rescue in a tiny rowing boat, risking her own life to save the struggling swimmer. That girl is June, who is labelled a heroine for her brave deed. Alas, Amanda's ligaments are badly torn and she has to give up all hopes of competing in the Olympics, but the event has taught her a great lesson. She respects the ocean and the power of the elements as she never had before, and decides to dedicate her time to coaching the younger girls at Malory Towers, so stays on another term when the other girls in her year have left.

Doctor

Assesses the condition of Gwendoline Mary Lacey who has been attempting to avoid all games by feigning a weak heart. Sends Gwen to a specialist, as required by Mrs Lacey, and this medical expert does not mince his words. His frank diagnosis to the doctor is that Gwen is quite able to take the School Certificate exam, but is fat and spotty and needs to spend more time running around outside.

Doris and Fanny

All we hear about Doris and her sister Fanny is that they are both very spiteful girls, described by the ever-eloquent Alicia Johns as 'frightfully pi', meaning pious and religious in the wrong way. Alicia was once sneaking across to West Tower for a midnight feast when she was spotted by Doris who lay in wait for her return. But Alicia boasts that there was no way that she would be caught by one of the 'Pi Sisters', and she relates the tale of how she locked Doris in a boot cupboard for the remainder of the night.

Mam'zelle Dupont

One of the two conflicting French teachers at Malory Towers, Mam'zelle Dupont is small, dumpy and hapless, falling regularly for the tricks played on her and instigated by Alicia Johns and Betty Hill. Instantly mimicable, because of her characteristically French mannerisms, she provides amusement and hilarity in every one of the six books. Mam'zelle is a pushover when it comes to the pretty, well-mannered girls such as Daphne Millicent Turner, who wins Mam'zelle's heart with her enchanting smile and successfully avoids any extra French prep, despite being appallingly bad at the subject. She is also very fond of those who she feels work hard at their French, such as Darrell and Sally, but she despairs of stupid girls like Gwendoline Mary Lacey and Zerelda Brass.

Like Mam'zelle in the St Clare's books, Mam'zelle is passionate about her family, and the class find that the longer they can distract her by discussing the birth of her new nephew (*First Term at Malory Towers*) or her *chère* Josephine, the longer they can put off learning French verbs and vocabulary. The first 'treek' that we read about comes when Mam'zelle's 'dear girls' decide to spice up their lesson by pretending that Alicia has gone deaf. Rather like the Saucepan Man in The Enchanted Wood series, Alicia seems quite unable to hear what Mam'zelle is saying, and repeats what she thinks has been said, which is, of course, completely wrong: 'Have you ear-ache?' queries Mam'zelle, and Alicia's smooth reply is, 'A rake? I don't want a rake, thank you, Mam'zelle … I am not gardening today.'

In *In the Fifth at Malory Towers* Mam'zelle gets her revenge for all the jokes that have been played on her when she confiscates a pamphlet of tricks from the irrepressible young June of the Second Form. She glances through the booklet and finds herself entranced by the idea of playing her own 'treek' on the girls who had fooled her so many times. In glee, she sends off for a set of trick teeth which will make her look quite horrendous when she flashes a smile. Her opportunity comes at a lacrosse match at the end of term when she spends the afternoon grinning like the wolf in *Red Riding Hood* with her terrible fake teeth in front of pupils and staff alike, including Miss Grayling and some prospective parents. Everyone agrees that Mam'zelle's revenge was well worth the years of waiting. Her character is based on a French teacher Blyton herself was taught by at school, who possessed all of Mam'zelle's distinctive traits.

Eileen

Girl from West Tower who is a friend of Betty Hill, Eileen is encouraged to join in the North Tower midnight feast in *Upper Fourth at Malory Towers*.

Emily

The quiet, shy Emily appears in *First Term at Malory Towers* and is renowned for being very 'clever with the needle', always to be found sewing something beautiful in the corner of the room. Emily is invited out by Darrell Rivers for half term as she is the only one left who has no one to go out for tea with and Darrell's warm-hearted nature immediately goes out to the gauche little girl. Emily opens up considerably to Darrell's mother, and they discuss embroidery at great length, horrifying Darrell with suggestions of inspiring in her an interest in darning.

Miss Grayling

Low-voiced and magnificent, the Headmistress of Malory Towers features in all six books in the series. She is described as having startling blue eyes, grey hair framing a wrinkle-free complexion and a firm mouth. Darrell Rivers finds that her knees feel shaky and she finds herself going red in the presence of such a powerful and composed woman which surely is the sign of an excellent Head. When Darrell has her first meeting with Miss Grayling, the Head's words leave a great impression on her, and she remembers them always. In Darrell's final term at the school, she chooses to take the new girls along to the Head's room simply so that she can see these new children, aged twelve, taking in the words that had once been spoken to her. Miss Grayling views Darrell as one of the school's great successes, despite the many lessons that have to be learnt along the way. There is only one person in Darrell's form who has failed throughout her time at the school, and that is Gwendoline Mary Lacey, who Miss Grayling wisely predicts will eventually have to suffer for her years of silliness and selfishness. Her words ring spookily true.

Miss Greening

Elocution coach who puts in a brief appearance in *In the Fifth at Malory Towers* as it is suggested that the girls may ask for her help in the production of their end-of-term pantomime, *Cinderella*.

Miss Hibbert

English teacher who features in *Third Year at Malory Towers* as she is casting *Romeo and Juliet*, Miss Hibbert has to witness the extraordinary performance by Zerelda Brass. 'Miss Hibbert,' it is said, 'did not look like a producer of plays.' She is small and neat with slightly wavy hair, thick glasses and a lovely speaking voice and is highly efficient at knowing how to pick the right girl for the part. She is astounded by Zerelda's diabolical rendition of Shakespeare's beautiful lines and tells the girl that she is quite appalling, angered even further by the fact that she imagines Zerelda is trying to make the other girls laugh. When the lesson is over she speaks 'unexpectedly kindly' to Zerelda, warns her that she is not suited to becoming a great actress, and suggests that she try and behave like a sensible schoolgirl, like those around her.

Hilda

Head of the First Form when Darrell Rivers is in the Upper Fourth, Hilda is mentioned in connection with the behaviour of June Johns, the naughty scamp of the first year.

Hill, Betty

Partner in crime and merry best pal of Alicia Johns, Betty Hill is a character who is never given as large a part in the Malory Towers books as might be expected of someone as amusing and popular as she most certainly is. At best, she is the sidekick of a girl who requires a best friend with a good deal of imagination and a flair for fun. Betty also has Alicia's malicious tongue, as is seen in *Upper Fourth at Malory Towers* when she revels in teasing Darrell about the 'glint' in her eye that implies Darrell may soon lose her temper. 'I glint, thou glintest, he glints, *she* glints... We glint, you glint, they glint,' chants Betty, much to the conscientious Darrell's irritation.

Betty and Alicia together are a difficult combination to cope with, as they are egged on by each other's devil-may-care attitudes. Alicia encourages Betty to join in the North Tower midnight feast in *Upper Fourth at Malory Towers*, which is very mischievous indeed as Betty is in West Tower, a different House altogether, which means that Darrell, as Head Girl of the whole year, will be in terrible trouble if they are caught. It is mentioned that Alicia, Betty, Sally and Darrell all go to St Andrews University together when they leave Malory Towers. What high jinks Betty and Alicia get up to in this establishment of higher education, we shall never know.

Hope, Daphne

Baby sister of Sally Hope, Daphne is the cause of Sally's jealousy in *First Term at Malory Towers*. Daphne appears again at the beginning of *Second Form at Malory Towers* as she wails and cries, watching her beloved big sister set off for school.

Mr and Mrs Hope

Sally Hope's strained relationship with her parents comes under close scrutiny at the end of *First Term at Malory Towers* when Darrell Rivers demands to know why Sally is so silent and queer about her family. Mr Hope is described as being a big, burly man, and his wife is small and delicate, and both parents are terribly worried when they hear that Sally has been ill with appendicitis.

Betty stuck some pellets to the ceiling.

Sally's younger sister, Daphne, is the cause of her anxiety, as Sally feels that with a younger sister around there is never any time for attention to be given to her.

Hope, Sally

Reliable, dependable and steady little Sally Hope is the best friend and *confidante* of the rather more inspiring Darrell Rivers. Sally is one of the central characters of all six books, arriving as a new girl at the same time as Darrell, and leaving at the end of the Sixth Form to attend St Andrews University with Darrell, Alicia Johns and Betty Hill. Sally is loyal and trustworthy, but also has the vices of jealousy and stubbornness. Her possessive nature is illustrated when she first arrives at Malory Towers and refuses to speak to anyone until Darrell forces her to explain why she is always so introverted. The sorry truth is revealed, and Sally confesses that she is furious at being sent away to boarding school because she is jealous of her new baby sister, Daphne, who is stealing all of her parents' attention. Darrell helps Sally to see that she is being ridiculous, and that having a younger brother or sister is a lovely thing. Before the end of term, Darrell and Sally are the best of friends, and remain so throughout their days at the school.

Sally and Alicia are very wary of each other, as each of them is vying for Darrell's attention. Sally is made Head Girl of the Second Form, much to Alicia's aggravation, and relations between them do not improve when Sally is away for the first half of the Third Form and Alicia steps into her place as Darrell's friend, since Betty Hill is also ill. Generally, however, Sally is a well-liked and successful member of the school who is eventually made Head of Games in her final year.

Irene

Musical and mathematical genius, a familiar face in all six books, Irene is scatterbrained and hopelessly disorganised, living in a cloud of music and creative activity. She is given to emitting explosive snorts in class when she is amused, particularly when a trick is being played on Mam'zelle, much to Alicia's annoyance. Her best friend Belinda Morris arrives in the Second Form, is as gifted as Irene and just as ridiculous. Irene is very well-liked, for all her vagueness, and leaves Malory Towers to pursue a career in music in which she will no doubt be extremely successful. She has her first chance to have her tunes set to lyrics and performed in *In the Fifth at Malory Towers* when she co-writes the songs for *Cinderella* with Darrell Rivers.

Miss James

Member of staff in charge of the Fifth Form at Malory Towers, commonly known as Jimmy. It is mentioned that she changes from sweet to sour 'in the twinkling of an eye'. It is Miss James who commissions the girls to produce some kind of Fifth Form entertainment. The girls choose to put on the pantomime *Cinderella*.

Janet

A shy, retiring girl who stays down in the Fifth Form with Catherine and Moira when the rest of her form move into the Sixth, Janet appears in *In the Fifth at Malory Towers* and is a great help with the production of *Cinderella* as she is very good at sewing and making the costumes. She is referred to as Jane in *Last Term at Malory Towers*, which may have been what the girls called her, once they got to know her, or this may have been a mistake on Blyton's part.

Johns, Alicia

Malory Towers' very own Queen of Satire features in all six books and, through Alicia's sharp wit, magnetic personality and brilliant mind, Blyton comes close to producing the Jennifer Saunders of her generation. She is the jester and comedienne of her year group, playing endless tricks and never missing the opportunity to spit out a wise-crack, usually at the expense of the weak-minded and less intelligent such as Gwendoline Lacey. Alicia is one of Blyton's most developed characters, from her introduction as a fun-loving, carefree, natural leader, sensitive as radar to any criticism, to her final assessment as a more balanced eighteen-year-old, still with a wild streak in her personality.

> *'She wants a lesson,' said Alicia. 'My word – if she comes and offers to show me how to juggle I'll juggle her! I'll juggle her all down the corridor and back again and down into the garden and on to the rocks and into the pool!'*
>
> IN THE FIFTH AT MALORY TOWERS

Alicia holds Darrell in very high regard, although her real best friend is Betty Hill, who is as wicked as she, but in a different House to Alicia, West Tower. Darrell is initially very impressed by Alicia's capricious attitude and longs to be her friend, but later discovers that Alicia's sharp tongue can be unkind and inconsiderate to others and so chooses Sally Hope as her companion instead. As a result there is always tension between Sally and Alicia who are both extremely jealous and possessive by nature. Alicia does, however, provide constant diversion in class with her trickery and jokes, whether she is feigning deafness, using 'pinging' balloons on Mam'zelle or simply being rude to Gwendoline Lacey who is no match for Alicia's smooth sarcasm. When Gwen announces that she is to attend a Swiss finishing school when she leaves Malory Towers, Alicia's malicious reply is: 'Let's hope it finishes you off nicely.'

But even Alicia has a lesson to learn, and this comes in *Upper Fourth at Malory Towers* when she suddenly finds herself unable to concentrate on her work for the difficult School Certificate exam. Her usually quick brain feels slow and fuzzy, and she finds herself envious of the speed at which the others seem to be writing. She faints over her work, and is sent straight to the san, where it is revealed that she has measles, and will be unable to sit the exam that term. Alicia is rather dashed by this news, and humbled by the unusual experience of not finding things coming as easily as they normally do. She makes a full recovery and plays the part of the Demon King to great applause in the Fifth Form pantomime *Cinderella*. Alicia is part of a large family with three brothers who are all as wicked as she, and are often the ones who provide her with the tricks to play on teachers. It is her brother Sam who sends her sneezing pellets to try out on Mam'zelle. Alicia's dare-devil young cousin June enters Malory Towers when Alicia reaches the Upper Fourth, and provides new excitement and tricks for her form.

Alicia leaves Malory Towers to attend St Andrews University with Darrell, Sally and Betty. Miss Potts feels that Alicia and Betty will revel in the parties and dances and will not do a scrap of work once they are there. One can only hope that this is exactly what does happen.

Johns, June

Cousin of Alicia Johns, June is as snide and malicious as her elder cousin, and as amusing and clever, which makes her a popular if untrustworthy member of her year group. June is introduced in *Upper Fourth at Malory Towers* and Darrell Rivers finds her temper severely tested by the arrogant and devil-may-care attitude of this First Former.

June takes Felicity Rivers under her control, much to Darrell's extreme suspicion, and it is all Darrell can do to stop herself from telling the young rascal where to go. Trouble is brewing when June sneaks on the Upper Fourth midnight feast in a very underhand manner and succeeds in having Darrell demoted from her position as Head of Form when she loses her cool with June and shakes her off a piano stool in fury. June has many a lesson to learn and shows just how dangerous she can be in *In the Fifth at Malory Towers* when she is found to be the person responsible for the disgusting poison pen notes received by Moira and Felicity who have both made June angry through their reactions to her defiant behaviour and cutting comments. June is threatened with expulsion but, ironically, it is Moira who saves her from this fate by going to Miss Grayling on behalf of the naughty girl.

June comes under close scrutiny again in *Last Term at Malory Towers* when she is singled out by Olympic-standard games player Amanda Chartelowe for special training, as Amanda feels that June will be the best tennis player and swimmer in the whole school if she is given the proper coaching. June and Amanda have a severe personality clash, but in the end are reconciled when June becomes a heroine for rowing out to save the drowning Amanda from the clutches of the strong current in the bay. June is a better individual by the time the Malory Towers series ends, and is proud to carry on the tradition of the school bequeathed to her by her cousin Alicia.

Johns, Sam

Alicia's scamp of an older brother is mentioned throughout the series as he is constantly sending Alicia various tricks to be played on members of staff. Alicia has three brothers and is the only girl in her family. It is also mentioned that June dared to cheek Sam in the holidays and is allowed to choose between a punishment of being spanked with a hairbrush or running twenty times around the paddock every morning. Being June, she chooses the latter.

Jones, Charlie

Father of the unattractive and gutless Josephine (Jo) Jones, 'Cheeky' Charlie Jones is a most unappealing character himself. He features only in *Last Term at Malory Towers* where he begins the term by nearly knocking the Rivers family car into a hedge with his reckless driving, and yelling to his daughter that she need not do any work as long as she has fun. His performance at half term is hardly much better, as he trumpets his opinions about the school and his daughter around the grounds. Miss Grayling confesses to a Dr and Mrs Leyton that taking on Jo has been an 'experiment that has not worked out'. Indeed, this is proven at the end of the term when Jo is caught stealing money from Matron and Charlie Jones confesses that he has been a bad father to her.

Jones, Josephine

Rebel without a clue, Josephine (Jo) Jones is a Second Former when Darrell and her contemporaries are in their final term. Jo appears in *Last Term at Malory Towers* and is a rather unfortunate girl as she is spoilt by her blatantly *nouveaux riches* parents who revel in her bad behaviour. It has to be said that Jo's lack of manners and general silliness can be blamed on the loud voice and uncouth attitude of her father, 'Cheeky' Charlie Jones, who is overheard saying to his daughter, 'Mind you're bottom of the form as I always was,' as he bids her farewell at the start of the new term. Jo is always supplied with ridiculous amounts of money which fails to impress the likes of June Johns and Felicity Rivers, who believe that it does not matter how much money you have, but only what you are like as a person.

Jo befriends a shy and easily led First Former called Deirdre, whom she chatters away to about her family and boasts to about her possessions. But she proves to be a despicable and weak person herself when she refuses to own up that she has been with Deirdre an hour after prep without permission, and as a result the whole of her form go without swimming for three days. Eventually, everything becomes too much for the cowardly Jo and she decides to run away, taking Deirdre with her, to a local shack. Inevitably, they are spotted by the sharp eyes of Bill and Clarissa on horseback, and are hauled back to school. Shockingly, Jo is expelled, and her father confesses that he is to blame for her silly behaviour, prompting Miss Grayling to think: 'How important parents are! Really, I think someone should start a school for parents too!'

Mrs Jones

Mother of Josephine Jones and wife of 'Cheeky' Charlie Jones, Mrs Jones appears briefly in *Last Term at Malory Towers* and is described as dripping with diamonds, and as being slightly ashamed of her husband's loud voice. Clearly a disastrous mother to Josephine who is a most unfortunate child.

Katherine

Mentioned as being the Head of Dorm in Darrell Rivers' first term at Malory Towers, Katherine does not play a major role in the books.

Lacey, Gwendoline Mary

Gwen is introduced at the beginning of every new term by the virtuoso display that she puts on when she bids farewell to her mother and long-suffering governess, Miss Winter. The goodbyes invariably take a very long time, and are so routine by the time the girls reach the Fifth Form that they are able to perform an exact imitation from the windows looking on to the scene below, complete with handkerchiefs and sniffing. Gwendoline is spoilt and silly, and is not even blessed with the pretty face that Blyton tends to attribute to girls of this nature. She is described as overweight and spotty in *Upper Fourth at Malory Towers*, a book that sees Gwen at her most deceitful and appalling as she tries to pretend that she has a weak heart, simply to earn sympathy and an excuse not to do games. She detests all sports and is academically very slow. She also is a dreadful snob, only ever choosing to befriend those whom she sees as beautiful or wealthy, such as Daphne Millicent Turner, Zerelda Brass, and the Honourable Clarissa Carter. Unfortunately for Gwendoline, none of these very precarious friendships lasts longer than a term, as either the girls realise how dreadful Gwen is, or she herself decides that they are not as rich as she had initially thought.

She is not given the kind heart of the equally frivolous Alison O'Sullivan in the St Clare's series, nor is she given the good sense to see how awful she really is until the closing chapters of *Last Term at Malory Towers*, when Gwen receives a terrible shock that she will live with for the rest of her life. Miss Grayling predicts that something will happen to Gwen to put things into their right perspective, and she is right. Gwen is told that her father is severely ill and may die, which leaves Gwen knocked sideways with guilt as she has been rude and offensive to him for weeks because he did not want her to attend the expensive Swiss finishing school she was so keen to go to. One of Blyton's most powerful passages describes the severity of the situation: 'Gwen felt as if someone had taken her heart right out of her body. She sat down blindly on a chair and stared at Miss Winter.' The girl is forced to leave the school in a great hurry, hoping and praying that her father will live, and knowing that it is her punishment for years of selfishness and unkindness.

It is not too late, and Gwen's father does pull through, but will be an invalid for the rest of his life, requiring Gwen to look after him. This dashes any hopes of her finishing school. Gwen writes a letter to Darrell in which she confesses to how weak and pathetic she has been at Malory Towers, begging for some kind words and communication from the girls who have suffered her silliness so long. Darrell realises that Gwen has learned a bitter lesson, and will never be so foolish again.

Mr Lacey

Mr Lacey has the ill-luck of having a tiresome and silly wife and a spoilt, lazy daughter called Gwendoline. His harsh words of advice to the girl seem to fall

Splash! In went Gwendoline.

on deaf ears: 'You were bad and foolish last term and you suffered for it. You will suffer for it again if I hear bad reports of you...' (*In the Fifth at Malory Towers*), and the general feeling is that Mr Lacey is the only person in Gwendoline's life with any sense at all. He suffers a terrible illness in Gwen's last term at the school, and will remain an invalid all his life, relying on the help of his only daughter. This is Gwendoline's terrible punishment.

Mrs Lacey

Floatily dressed, hypersensitive and neurotic, Mrs Lacey is a terrible influence on her unattractive daughter Gwendoline Mary with her whining and snobbery, and a bad wife to the altogether more sensible Mr Lacey. She falls repeatedly for Gwen's lies about how well she is doing at her lessons and in games, and fails to see how weak and two-faced her darling daughter really is. Mrs Lacey is a constant source of amusement to the other girls as she weeps mistily at the separation from her daughter at the beginning of every term.

Mr Lemming

A piano tuner makes a guest appearance in *Second Form at Malory Towers* and is the unexpected second target for Alicia Johns' invisible chalk trick that leaves victims with a smear of pink on the seat of their trousers.

Miss Lennie

Quiet and mild-tempered, the sewing mistress helps with the costumes in the pantomime staged in *In the Fifth at Malory Towers*.

Little, Maureen

Fluffy and untidy-looking with rabbit teeth and a silly giggle, Maureen Little does not make a welcome contribution to Fifth Form life. She talks incessantly about herself and her life at her wonderful old school, Mazeley Manor, which was burned down, resulting in her late appearance at Malory Towers. Maureen reminds the girls of Gwendoline Lacey so much that when Gwen arrives back at school a few days late, the two girls are shoved together and Gwen receives a terrifying taste of her own medicine. Gwen finds Maureen self-centred, silly and exhausting, with her persistent gabbling about herself, and is horrified by the fact that the girls in her form feel that she and Maureen go so well together. Maureen is made to feel very little indeed when the Fifth Formers decide that her boasting has become too unbearable, and ask her to write some songs and design some costumes and scenery for the pantomime, simply so that they can laugh at her efforts. Maureen produces some very tuneless songs and weak drawings and the girls revel in telling her that they are so bad that they are funny. This seems to bring the girl down a peg or two, although it is a harsh way to learn her lesson. Malory Towers has no time for the likes of Maureen Little and Gwendoline Mary, and pride most certainly comes before a fall.

Louella

Only ever mentioned in *In the Fifth at Malory Towers*, Louella is chosen to play the part of the Fairy Godmother in *Cinderella*. It is a popular choice as she is tall and slim with long golden curls, and is a member of South Tower, so the girls from that House are pleased to have her representing them.

Lucy

Mentioned in *Third Year at Malory Towers* as being the current Head of the Fourth Form. Lucy and the rest of her year find themselves in trouble when Zerelda Brass joins them, as she is continually receiving order marks from the teachers which count against the whole form.

Miss Lucy

Old nanny of the Honourable Clarissa Carter. Miss Lucy is visited on a hot summer afternoon in *Upper Fourth at Malory Towers* by Clarissa and the perpetually scrounging Gwendoline Mary Lacey. Miss Lucy provides the girls with a delicious spread for tea and, as she thought that all twenty of their year group would also be present, she provides huge amounts of sandwiches, cakes, biscuits, lemonade and chocolate. It is Miss Lucy who suggests that the two girls take back the remainder of the food for a midnight feast, which they think is a fine idea. The feast takes place by the cool waters of the swimming pool, but is unfortunately ruined by the careless behaviour of selfish girls from other towers and forms.

MacDonald, Jean

Noted as being very good with money and at looking after the form charities and societies, Jean is a shrewd Scots girl with no time at all for the frills and fancies of the likes of Gwendoline Mary Lacey. Jean 'never went into ecstasies about anything' and is scornful of Mam'zelle and her emotional displays of enthusiasm, coupled with her melodramatic hand gestures. Jean has only a small part to play in *First Term at Malory Towers* as she is not a very inspiring character, usually being the voice of decorum and level-headed sensibility.

Mary Lou

A timid little mouse of a girl who blossoms into someone Miss Grayling describes as 'one of Malory Towers' successes', Mary Lou begins her days at the school living in fear of everything, from spiders to other girls, swimming and the dark. Afraid of offending people, she is often too nervous to tell others to leave her alone, and she is badly used in the Second Form by beautiful but deceptive Daphne Millicent Turner who constantly persuades Mary Lou to help her with her French prep.

It is a curious irony that it is Mary Lou who manages to find herself in situations that require sudden and unexpected acts of previously untapped bravery and courage. This is seen particularly in *First Term at Malory Towers*, when she throws herself intrepidly into the swimming pool, fully clothed, in order to rescue Darrell who is feigning stomach cramps to assess Mary Lou's reaction to the situation; and also in *Second Form at Malory Towers*, where she sets off in the middle of a terrible storm to post a parcel for Daphne and is blown off the cliffs, where she hangs on to a tuft of grass and waits to be rescued.

Mary Lou performs the lead part of Cinderella in the Fifth Form pantomime, and goes on to become a children's nurse when she leaves Malory Towers, obviously the perfect vocation for her.

Matron

The Matron at Malory Towers is plump, strict, yet jolly. She features predominantly at the beginning of every new term when the girls are expected to hand in their health certificates which state whether they have had any illness over the holidays. Irene forgets or mislays her health certificate every term without fail, and drives Matron to despair. In *Last Term at Malory Towers* Irene plays a joke on Matron by handing her two wrong envelopes, one containing a photo of Irene in a bathing suit and another with a Recipe for Bad Memories inside. Matron has to deal with the usual selection of schoolgirl illnesses, including Mavis in the Third Form who gets soaked in a thunder storm in the middle of the night, Sally Hope with appendicitis and Alicia Johns with measles in the Upper Fourth.

Mavis

Memorable for a single refrain that becomes quite exhausting as the term wears on: 'When I am an opera singer I shall sing in Milan, I shall sing in New York, I shall sing in Paris…' Unfortunately for Mavis, very few of the girls are willing to sit and listen to her incessant boasting about her future career, wonderful though her voice undoubtedly is. Mavis is described as a lazy, conceited little girl with a discontented face and hair tied in two auburn plaits, and is referred to as a Voice and nothing else. As Jean MacDonald puts it in her usual blunt fashion: 'She doesn't see that she's only just a schoolgirl, with duties to do and work to get through and games to play.'

Mavis's obsession with her own vocal talents leads her into trouble on the same night that Wilhelmina (Bill) is awake in the stables, worried about Thunder, her ailing horse. Mavis makes up her mind that she will enter a talent competition in the local town and sneaks out of school after supper in order to wow the judges and be 'discovered'. She does not think her plan through thoroughly, however, and is banned from entering the contest as she is only a schoolgirl. She misses the last bus back to Malory Towers and is found by Miss Peters who, by happy coincidence, spots her huddled at the side of the road on her way back from alerting the vet about Thunder's condition.

Mavis catches a terrible throat infection, which destroys her beautiful voice for at least two or three years and forces her to look at herself and see that she deserved the punishment. In *In the Fifth at Malory Towers* Mavis is reintroduced as her singing voice is beginning to come back to her and she is allowed to play the part of the Prince in the pantomime. She is no longer boastful, arrogant and silly, but has developed into an altogether nicer character with much more to her than just a wonderful talent to perform. She becomes firm friends with the American Zerelda Brass who also has a hard lesson to learn about her own opinion of herself.

Merrylegs

Pretty little horse belonging to the Honourable Clarissa Carter and mentioned in *In the Fifth at Malory Towers*. Merrylegs is also the name of Jane Longfield's pony in the Mistletoe Farm series.

Moira

Remains behind in the Fifth Form when the rest of her form moves up into the Sixth. She features as one of the main characters in *In the Fifth at Malory Towers* as one of the two joint Head Girls of the Fifth, the other being the unbearably sweet Catherine. It is said that Moira looks as if 'all the troubles of the school rested on her shoulders', and, indeed, she has a good deal on her plate this term, including being director of *Cinderella*. Moira is a difficult girl because she is bossy, domineering and insensitive to those who are not strong characters like herself. As a result, half of the girls are scared of her, and the other half resent her. There is no denying that her organisational skills are superlative, but she is too proud to back down and say when she is wrong, or when one of Darrell's or Alicia's ideas would work better than hers.

Moira is the victim of the bitter poison pen letters that are sent by June in the First Form. The notes are written in block capitals and are never signed. One simply reads: 'WHAT'S A DICTATOR? ASK MOIRA, DON'T ASK ME.' Moira is thick-skinned but even she is hurt by the notes. Eventually June is caught out, and it is Moira who goes to the girl's rescue and succeeds in preventing her from being expelled which makes her an altogether more likeable girl, especially in the eyes of the First Form, and June's cousin Alicia.

Nora

Fluffy-looking girl mentioned in *Last Term at Malory Towers*, Nora is a friend of the in-crowd in the Second Form headed by June Johns and Felicity Rivers. Given to making explosive snorts in class when something amuses her, rather like Irene, and participates in the famous magnet trick, where Mam'zelle's hair pins are calmly removed by holding a tiny but powerful magnet up towards her head.

Pamela

Head of North Tower when Darrell Rivers first arrives at the school, Pamela appears only in *First Term at Malory Towers* and is very much looked up to by the younger girls, especially when the rumour circulates that she has already written a book. Blyton had a tendency to name older girls in her stories Pamela.

Miss Parker

Head teacher of the Second Form, given to having dreamy fits which the girls live for. With a name like Miss Parker, she is predictably always sticking her nose into things, sniffing out trouble, and earning herself the nickname of 'Nosy'.

Miss Peters

Head of the Third Form, Miss Peters is a loud-voiced, harsh and 'mannish' type of woman who stands no silliness and has a great love of horses. She is liked by most of the girls, except those who fear her sarcastic tongue and booming commands, such as Gwendoline Lacey and Mary Lou. Miss Peters is infuriated by Wilhelmina (Bill) who simply refuses to concentrate and spends her time staring out of the window, thinking about Thunder, her horse. The result of this is that Miss Peters refuses to let Bill see Thunder, as she feels that he is a distraction from her work. Bill is distraught, and even more so when she fears that Thunder is in need of a vet. The final showdown comes one stormy night when Bill finds out that Thunder has colic and winds herself up into a great state. Darrell rushes through the cold night to fetch Miss Peters who she knows will know what to do. Indeed, the teacher saddles her own horse and gallops off to fetch the vet for Thunder, who makes a full recovery. Bill realises that the best way she can repay Miss Peters is to start paying attention in class, much to the amazement of her peers, and the delight of Miss Peters. Their love of horses is enough to conquer the animosity between them, and they remain firm friends.

Raglett

Farmer who has called the vet over to help him deal with the birth of a calf. Miss Peters has to gallop to Raglett's Farm in order to ask the vet to come and help cure Thunder's colic (*see* Miss Peters and Bill).

Remmington, Marilyn and Miss

As in her St Clare's series, Blyton focuses much more on the girls as Games captains, rather than the staff. Miss Remmington is Head of Games at Malory Towers and is said not to bother with those who are not very good at sport, whereas Marilyn, who is the Head of Games in *First Form at Malory Towers*, always takes an interest in those who are hopeless and tries to encourage them.

Rita

Rita and her sister Pat are chosen to play the Ugly Sisters in the Fifth Form pantomime *Cinderella*. They have amusing faces, large feet and hair that flies out in a shock which suggests that they were made to play the comic duo.

Rivers, Darrell

Unrivalled focal character of Malory Towers, Darrell is one of Blyton's most appealing heroines, thanks to her very obvious character flaws as well as her effervescence and good nature. She appears in all six books, beginning at the age of twelve and progressing through the school, achieving academic and sporting success, but not without hard work. She is immensely popular with the majority of her peer group, and is famed for her hot temper which is first witnessed when she deals out some hearty slaps in the swimming pool to cowardly Gwendoline Lacey who had 'ducked' timid Mary Lou a mere few weeks into Darrell's first term at the school. Other girls on the receiving end of Darrell's 'glint' include Sally Hope, whom Darrell pushes across the room at the end of her first half term when Sally refuses to give Darrell an explanation for her peculiar behaviour; and Alicia Johns' young scamp of a cousin, June, who threatens to sneak on the Upper Fourth by relating tales of their midnight escapades to Miss Potts and is shaken off her piano stool by Darrell, who is at this point the Head Girl of the Upper Fourth year group. Darrell gradually learns to control her temper through sheer determination, although it is generally conceded that when she does deal out her fury, it is to people who deserve it. The current Head of English at St Mary's School, Wantage, states that if a girl behaved in such a fashion now she would be gated over a weekend (made to stay at school and work) or possibly sent home until the end of term. Today, Darrell would almost certainly not have made it to the prestigious position of Head of School while displaying such lack of self-control.

From *Upper Fourth at Malory Towers* onwards, Blyton introduces Darrell's bouncy younger sister Felicity to the school, providing a comfort to Darrell in that her sister will be there to carry on the good tradition. Darrell is generally portrayed as a sensible yet fun-loving individual who has the potential to be led astray by the wild cards of her year, particularly Alicia, whose tricks and inventive pranks appeal very much to Darrell. On one occasion she becomes so carried away with the excitement of using 'invisible chalk' on Mr Young, the Music Master, that she writes the word 'OY' on his stool, so that when he rises from his seat, it is plainly inscribed on his behind. Darrell realises that she is much better off remaining firm friends with stolid and reliable little Sally Hope.

By the time Darrell leaves Malory Towers she has the respect and trust of the entire school, including Miss Grayling, the Headmistress, who offers her words that will stay with her always: 'there is no one who has given back more than Darrell has ... You are one of our biggest successes.' Darrell leaves Malory Towers to attend St Andrews University in Scotland, where she hopes to pursue a career in the Arts. Her first artistic triumph is in *In the Fifth at Malory Towers* where she writes the verse and songs for the form's pantomime to great acclaim.

Darrell Rivers' rather unusual name can be attributed to Blyton's second husband whose name was Kenneth Darrell Waters. They married in 1943, two years before the first book in the series was written. Blyton clearly held Darrell in high regard, naming her after the husband she adored, and allowing her to follow in her own footsteps by implying that Darrell will eventually become a writer herself.

Rivers, Felicity

Three years younger than the heroine of the Malory Towers series, Darrell Rivers, Felicity has all the admirable qualities of her dynamic older sister and, indeed, their careers at the school seem almost uncannily paralleled. When Felicity first arrives at the school, in *Upper Fourth at Malory Towers*, she has great admiration for the unscrupulous June, cousin of Alicia, whom Darrell had such a high opinion of in her first term. She then realises that she is much better making friends with an altogether more stable character called Susan, just as Darrell feels 'steadied' by the calming presence of the ever-cool Sally Hope. Felicity is quite rightly very proud of her older sister, particularly when Darrell is made Head Girl in *Last Term at Malory Towers*, and it is more than likely that Felicity will go on to become Head Girl in her sister's footsteps. In introducing Felicity, Blyton was able to create escapades and high jinks for two different year groups, and in the final pages of Darrell's last term, she and Alicia make Felicity and June promise solemnly that they will carry on the tradition of Malory Towers for them.

Mr Rivers

Father of Darrell who appears with regularity in all six books, Mr Rivers is one of the few Blyton parents who actually develops into a well-formed and multi-layered character as he progresses through the series. Darrell inherits her notorious hot temper from her father, as he is quick to point out, and he is clearly an attractive-looking man, as Zerelda Brass comments on his 'beetling black brows' in *Third Year at Malory Towers*. He finds the three women in his life (his wife, Darrell and Felicity) to be typically female in that they seem to take an unnecessarily long time to get ready to go anywhere. He mentions that the family needs a shepherd to herd up its sheep as he waits impatiently in the car to set off back to the school for the beginning of term.

By profession Mr Rivers is a surgeon and he is called to Malory Towers at the end of Darrell's first term to try and decipher what can be wrong with Sally Hope who is suffering from terrible stomach pains (eventually diagnosed as appendicitis). Blyton's second husband, Kenneth Darrell Waters, was a doctor, and it is plain that Blyton had great admiration for the profession. Darrell sees her father as a figure of strength and authority. She knows he can make Sally better and flings herself into his comforting arms. He also speaks the words that will stay with Darrell throughout her years at the school and which are echoed by Miss Grayling's, the Headmistress: 'You will get a good deal out of your time at Malory Towers – see that you give a lot back!'

Mrs Rivers

Mother of Darrell and Felicity, Mrs Rivers is pretty and sensible, proud of her two daughters and in every way a model Blyton mother.

Ronaldson, Molly

Head of Games when Darrell Rivers and her contemporaries are in their third year, Molly is hearty, solid and, as Zerelda states, 'big as a horse'. Darrell quickly replies that she is one of the finest Games captains the school has ever known, with an absolute genius for picking the right people for the right match. Molly is something of a goddess to young Darrell at this time, as she selects her to play in one of the matches for the third team, and Darrell succeeds in scoring the winning goal. Games captains in Blyton's writings are always heroic and strong, and the subject of much admiration from the younger girls. See Mirable Unwin (St Clare's) for an example of a powerful Games captain gone mad.

Mam'zelle Rougier

The polar opposite to the fun-loving, bumbling Mam'zelle Dupont, Mam'zelle Rougier is thin, unsmiling, rather frightening and humourless. As a result, the girls are unable to cause as much distraction in class with her and tend to get on with their work in a more sensible fashion, although it is mentioned that Mam'zelle Dupont is more popular with the girls, so she naturally seems to get better results. Mam'zelle Rougier appears in all six books in the Malory Towers series, and is distinguishable by the pointed bun that she wears on the back of her head. She and Mam'zelle Dupont are not the best of friends and do their best to avoid each other, the sparks flying when they do come face to face, as is most clearly illustrated in *Second Form at Malory Towers* when Belinda Green produces some sketches of Mam'zelle Rougier stalking Mam'zelle Dupont with a dagger in her hand, looking positively evil. Unfortunately, the sketches fall into the hands of the bad-tempered French mistress who, appalled and furious at this depiction of herself, storms off to see Miss Grayling. After her initial anger dies down, Mam'zelle Rougier comes to realise that the constant squabbling between herself and Mam'zelle Dupont is sure to cause the girls to react in some way, and with the unexpected help of Mam'zelle Dupont she comes to see that the pictures are actually not as terrible as she had at first thought.

Mam'zelle Rougier is sour and stern, but just as French as her colleague, hating the water and outdoor activity – as all the French do in Blyton's work. The two teachers do share one belief, however: that the girls in this so English school are all most likely to be completely round the twist.

Suzanne

French niece of Mam'zelle Rougier, who features in *Last Term at Malory Towers*. Suzanne has a terribly weak grasp of the English language, and understands virtually nothing, punctuating her broken sentences with phrases like 'veery piggy-hoo-lear'. Unlike Claudine and Antoinette, the French nieces of Mam'zelle in the St Clare's stories, Suzanne does not take a leading role in life at Malory Towers. Perhaps Blyton decided that she was tired of working to the same formula for naughty French girls.

Thomas, Georgina

Georgina Thomas wears very glamorous pyjamas that are revealed when scatty new girl Belinda Green picks up her overnight bag by mistake and gasps in amazement at what she finds inside. Very little else about Georgina and her sophisticated nightwear is divulged to the reader, and she seems to feature only in *Second Form at Malory Towers*.

Thunder

Beautiful steed belonging to Wilhelmina (Bill). She and Thunder make their first appearance in *Third Year at Malory Towers*. Thunder is the cause of a midnight adventure when he develops colic (*see* Miss Peters and Bill).

Turner, Daphne Millicent

Daphne Millicent Turner waltzes into Blyton's writing in *Second Term at Malory Towers*, a radiant, elegant and refined young girl with a mass of golden

'A-tish-oo!' sneezed poor Mam'zelle.

curls and an irresistible smile that can charm anyone within a fifty-mile radius. Daphne uses this facial magnet to avoid countless French exercises, as Mam'zelle Dupont finds herself quite unable to resist its pathetic and watery beauty. Daphne is swiftly befriended by fickle Gwendoline Lacey, who is enraptured by Daphne and her tales of her family's wealth. Mary Lou also thinks that Daphne is wonderful, and Daphne finds that she can use Mary Lou to help her with her work whenever she wants. However, Daphne finds herself in serious trouble when Mary Lou takes her adoration of the girl too far, venturing out on a stormy night to deliver a parcel for Daphne, and is blown over a cliff. In horror, Daphne sets off to find Mary Lou, and somehow manages to rescue the girl, much to the amazement of all those who felt that Daphne was just a pretty face.

But her role as heroine is short-lived when it is revealed that Daphne's stories of her wonderful rich family are far from the truth and that she is plain Daphne Turner who has been stealing from the girls in order to cover up for the fact that she does not have any magnificent possessions herself. White-faced and trembling, Daphne confesses everything to the girls in her form, and much to her amazement, every single one of the girls, except for Gwendoline, decides to stick by her after the bravery she showed in rescuing Mary Lou. So Daphne is given another chance, and Gwendoline loses her 'rich' friend, much to the amusement of the girls.

Vet

The local vet makes an appearance in *Third Year at Malory Towers* when he is called in the middle of the night from helping deliver a calf at Raglett's Farm. Miss Peters rides up to him, requiring his assistance in the recovery of Thunder, Wilhelmina's horse who has colic. The vet leaps onto his horse and gallops to the school, stopping on the way to help Miss Peters rescue the soaking wet and bedraggled Mavis from the side of the road (*see* Mavis). He succeeds in saving Thunder from certain death, to the eternal gratitude of his owner.

Violet

One of the ten girls who make up the First Form in North Tower in Darrell Rivers' first term at Malory Towers. It is mentioned that she is so quiet that nobody ever really knows whether she is in the room or not. As a result, she is very much left out of things.

Miss Williams

Head of the Fourth Form, Miss Williams is introduced in *Third Year at Malory Towers*, as it is she who has to come face to face with Zerelda Brass who begins her career in the Fourth. Miss Williams has no time for girls attempting to wear make-up to class with their hair piled on top of their heads as if they are about to walk on to the set of a movie, so she finds Zerelda both difficult and confusing. Miss Williams features again in *Upper Fourth at Malory Towers* and is in charge of the girls taking their School Certificate exam.

Wilson, Ellen

Ellen arrives in *Second Form at Malory Towers* as a plain-looking rather unattractive girl with a constantly furrowed brow due to the worry of work. She spends all her time working and making sure she gets the results she should, which turns her into a very dull individual who snaps at others if they are making a noise and preventing her from getting on. Ellen finds herself in a dreadful state when she is sent to the san with a bad cough, so is unable to work for a few weeks. In panic, she decides that she will have to cheat in order to do well in a French test, and is caught by Darrell who lets her wild temper get the better of her and starts to pummel Ellen until the girl grows quite powerless to resist. Of course, Ellen is a cheat, but she is not the thief Alicia accuses her of being when various items of jewellery are stolen from people in the Second Form. Ellen finds that she is unable to prove her innocence until the real thief, the phoney Daphne Millicent Turner, owns up.

Winnie

A member of North Tower, Winnie joins in the famous poolside midnight feast in *Upper Fourth at Malory Towers*. Blyton often called her extras Winnie.

Miss Winter

Miss Winter appears in every book as the governess of Gwendoline Lacey. She is a meek, fawning woman who is blind to the glaringly obvious faults of Gwendoline and Mrs Lacey, her employer. It is clear that Gwen has been spoilt all her life by these two women who tell her how wonderful and clever she is, when it is perfectly plain to everyone else that she is not. It is Miss Winter who arrives at Malory Towers to break the dreadful news to Gwen about her father's illness, and even then cannot put on a brave face, dissolving into tears in front of Gwen and Miss Grayling.

Mr Young

Mr Young the Music Master is the only male teacher recorded in the series, and he features most recognisably in *Second Form at Malory Towers* when he is the victim of one of jester Alicia Johns' numerous tricks. He is described as sporting a pointed moustache and as being 'dapper in a well-brushed black suit with a too-high collar'. He is quite confounded when he sits down on his piano stool and finds that when he stands up, his behind is bright pink. This is because of the invisible chalk daubed on to the seat by Alicia which reveals itself only when it is warmed by a person sitting down on it. Further victims of this chalk include Mam'zelle Dupont and Mr Lemming, the piano tuner.

THE NAUGHTIEST GIRL
IN THE SCHOOL

The Naughtiest Girl in the School (1940)
The Naughtiest Girl Again (1942)
The Naughtiest Girl is a Monitor (1945)
Here's the Naughtiest Girl (1952)

Elizabeth Allen, the bold, bad girl, is the lead character for Blyton's writing on the life and events in a co-educational, radical boarding school where the pupils make the decisions and the teachers literally take a back seat. Elizabeth's time at Whyteleafe School is fraught with tensions and trouble, and she certainly has a very diverse range of experiences there because of her behaviour when she first arrives and the reputation she earns herself. There are only three full-length books set at Whyteleafe, in contrast to the six each set at Malory Towers and St Clare's, and in all three the attention is focused on Elizabeth from start to finish. This makes her a very accessible character, and evidently one that Blyton held in great regard, despite her obvious character flaws.

There are three complete novels in the Naughtiest Girl series and one short story *Here's the Naughtiest Girl*. The adventures of Elizabeth Allen and friends have been continued in Blyton style by successful children's author Anne Digby.

'Let's go and look after the new ones,' said Elizabeth. 'They're looking a bit lost.'

Allen, Elizabeth

Elizabeth is introduced in the opening chapter of *The Naughtiest Girl in the School* as the 'naughty, spoilt girl' who resolves to cause so much anarchy upon arriving at boarding school that she will be sent home. She kicks off with a rude remark at supper on her first night when she exclaims that she was given a guinea pig for Easter with a face just like Miss Thomas, her new form teacher. This is only the tip of the iceberg when Elizabeth's later antics are brought into consideration. She refuses to share her food with the other children, kicks over a Monitor when he tells her that it is time for her to go to bed, wears socks instead of stockings, throws things around in class, goes into the local town on her own, which is strictly forbidden, and is generally as rude as she can be. But Elizabeth soon discovers that Whyteleafe is actually a jolly fine school, with plenty of things going on that she loves and is very good at. She enjoys her time spent with the piano teacher, Mr Lewis, and revels in her riding and painting lessons, making it very difficult indeed for her to hate the school as much as she set out to. Elizabeth makes friends with a little girl called Joan Townsend who Rita, the Head Girl, tells Elizabeth is very unhappy. Before too long, the two girls are inseparable and enjoy outings and chats together, sharing their stamps and sweets. By half term, when the school has agreed that Elizabeth may leave if she still wants to, she has to confess in front of the whole school that she wants to stay on at Whyteleafe because she loves being part of the school.

Once she has made up her mind to be good, the endearing side to Elizabeth's character becomes apparent, and she is portrayed as a girl full of contradictions with a genuine desire to put things right. She remains hot-tempered and tempestuous throughout all three terms we see her

'I do hate him!' Burst out
Elizabeth angrily.

at Whyteleafe, unwittingly getting herself into trouble through the sheer strength of her personality. She seems to take the burdens of the entire school on to her own shoulders, and tries to work things out for herself, but as she is no more than twelve years old throughout, things prove harder than she may have imagined. The most difficult time she faces comes through her friendship with the brilliant but unreliable Julian Holland. The combination of these two brings its share of discord to the school, but they are both intelligent enough to see that all comes right in the end (*see* Julian Holland).

Elizabeth is constantly noted as excellent in the garden, and helps with the school gardening whenever she can. Her piano playing is sensitive and passionate, and her conversation lively and entertaining. She is a tomboy in many respects, bumping down stairs and wearing her curly brown hair cropped short, but she is, above all, very likeable, amusing and, as Julian says in *The Naughtiest Girl is a Monitor*, 'I'm certain as certain can be that she's good at heart!'

Mr Allen

Father of the Naughtiest Girl in the School, Mr Allen does not feature in the books as much as his wife, but there can be no doubt that he has a respectable, well-paid job as the family are referred to as being rich.

Mrs Allen

Mother of Elizabeth Allen who features in all four books. She spoils Elizabeth before she attends Whyteleafe because she is an only child, and therefore feels that boarding school will do her some good. Mrs Allen had earlier employed a governess for Elizabeth, called Miss Scott.

Miss Belle and Miss Best

Two Headmistresses of Whyteleafe School. Whyteleafe is unique in its system of having the school run by twelve Monitors, pupils elected by their peers to a position of honour. These Monitors are present at the school's weekly meetings and make decisions and answer requests in much the same way that teachers would in Blyton's other school stories. Miss Belle and Miss Best are therefore rather obscure figures who only participate in these meetings when they are asked to. Miss Belle, we are informed, is rather lovely-looking, and Miss Best, inevitably, is the exact opposite, and rather fierce of countenance, prompting Elizabeth Allen to give them the appropriate nicknames of The Beauty and The Beast. They are not given the influential qualities of the

Headmistresses at St Clare's and Malory Towers, Miss Theobald and Miss Grayling. It is an interesting fact that none of Enid Blyton's staff are ever married, or if they are, they always keep their maiden names.

Bess and Captain

Horses kept at Whyteleafe School and ridden regularly by the pupils, particularly by Robert Jones.

Miss Best

See Miss Belle.

Bubble and Squeak

Two of the rabbits owned by Harry Dunn in *The Naughtiest Girl in the School*.

Buckley, Arabella

Beautiful but empty-headed Arabella features in the last full-length book, *The Naughtiest Girl is a Monitor*. She is introduced to Elizabeth Allen two weeks before the beginning of term as their parents know one another and it is thought that the two girls will get along nicely and that Elizabeth will tell Arabella a little about the school she will be attending. Elizabeth does tell Arabella about life at Whyteleafe, and the girl does not like what she hears. Being spoilt and an only child, she cannot bear the thought of mixing with rough, ill-mannered boys and, even worse, handing over all her money to the school money box every week. Despite her prettiness and immaculate manners, when she arrives at Whyteleafe Arabella is not well received by anyone, except for a timid little girl called Rosemary Wing who thinks that Arabella is just like a fairy princess and agrees with everything she says.

Arabella decides that she will certainly keep some of her money to herself, and is then caught buying very expensive peppermint creams in the town. She manages to cover this up, but is trusted by nobody. Arabella does not enjoy the fact that Elizabeth, whom she dislikes intensely, is her Monitor, and that she is expected to answer to her. As soon as Elizabeth falls out of favour with a few people, for complicated reasons, Arabella leaps at the chance to show unkindness towards her. She organises a midnight feast for her own birthday and does not invite Elizabeth, and revels in the broken friendship between Elizabeth and Julian Holland. Although her attitude improves towards the end of term, she is still a rather vain and silly little girl who thinks far too much about her appearance. For more girls in this category, *see* Alison O'Sullivan, Angela Favorleigh and Sadie Greene in the St Clare's series, and Gwendoline Lacey, Daphne Millicent Turner and Zerelda Brass of Malory Towers.

Cheeky-Looking Small Boy

Nameless child who appears in *The Naughtiest Girl Again* when he issues a complaint against one of his fellow students, Fred White, who he claims is always borrowing his things and never giving them back. Rita, the respected Head Girl, tells him to think about the difference between making a complaint and telling tales.

Miss Chester

The Art teacher at Whyteleafe School, Miss Chester is mentioned in *The Naughtiest Girl in the School*. Elizabeth adores painting and drawing and is distraught when she is made to do sums instead of attending the Art class as a punishment for her disobedience.

Doris

Doris is reported at one of the weekly meetings in *The Naughtiest Girl Again* for forgetting to feed her beloved guinea pigs. This is quite rightly seen as a disgraceful offence, and Doris is told to stick a note up in her dormitory reminding her to feed and water her four-legged furry companions.

Dunn, Harry

Reported to be a cheat at one of the weekly school meetings, Harry Dunn is initially described as being a 'sly-looking boy' who is plainly in need of learning a serious lesson. Harry cheats in Arithmetic and as punishment is made to sit away from the rest of his class until he realises that cheating will never help him to improve in the subject. After Harry accepts his penalty, it is specified that he loses his devious looks and becomes open-faced and cheerful. He is the owner of several rabbits, and Elizabeth Allen begs him to give one to Joan Townsend as a surprise for her birthday. He plays the piano as if his fingers are a bunch of bananas.

Eileen

One of the older girls at Whyteleafe who is asked to look after Elizabeth Allen when she first arrives, Eileen is kindly faced with a mass of fair curls, and Elizabeth cannot help liking and respecting the older girl, despite her resolutions to hate everyone and everything when she first arrives.

Elsie

Elsie makes an almost imperceptible appearance in *The Naughtiest Girl in the School* as she breaks a light bulb when a tin opener flies out of her hand, and is granted one and ninepence out of the school money-box to pay for a new bulb. Blyton seems to have enjoyed writing about the very mundane goings-on of the weekly meetings at Whyteleafe School, as well as the electrifying events that set the whole school talking.

Follett, Martin

When he is first introduced to Whyteleafe School, in *The Naughtiest Girl is a Monitor* (the one book he appears in), Martin is described as 'pleasant', which is cause for immediate suspicion. He has an innocent face with eyes a little too close together and hair brushed neatly off his forehead. He is seen as a kind and generous boy for the majority of the term, lending people money and sweets when they 'mislay' their own. But Martin's amiable facade is soon stripped away, and the ugly truth is revealed. It is Martin who has been stealing money and sweets from people in his own class, and has seen the blame fall on to Julian Holland. But it is not ordinary malicious stealing, as Elizabeth Allen deduces while thinking hard about Martin Follett. It seems that the reason for his thieving is so that he can provide other people with good will, as it is always he who offers his own money and belongings when others have lost theirs. Martin's case is very similar to that of Kathleen Gregory in St Clare's who is given another chance by the school and turns into a much better girl. Martin is given the same treatment, as everyone realises that he was stealing to make others happy, not for himself. Elizabeth, who puzzled over his actions, shows the school that she too is prepared to try and understand this confused boy.

George

One of the younger boys, George is in the san at the end of *The Naughtiest Girl Again* and Elizabeth Allen goes to read to him to cheer him up. She has broken her wrist in a riding adventure and is feeling rather low-key and put out herself.

Green, Belinda

A rather unexceptional character, Belinda is a token schoolgirl with the right ideas about good and bad, and the conscientious attitude of someone who will never go far in a Blyton story as there is no real potency to her. She is a new girl with Elizabeth Allen and behaves sensibly and cordially from the moment she arrives at Whyteleafe, abiding by the rules, showing no flash of temper, nor hidden secrets. She is mentioned in *The Naughtiest Girl Again* when she makes a rude remark about Kathleen Peters' spots, but she never really rises above the unexceptional description that is first made of her. Elizabeth, for all her ridiculous silliness and odd conduct, is at least destined to be remembered at the school after she leaves; Belinda Green will not be.

Harris, Jennifer

Makes her debut in *The Naughtiest Girl Again* as a new girl in Elizabeth Allen's form. Her twinkling eyes and jolly face indicate that she is good fun and will be a popular member of the form. She soon reveals that she keeps little white mice as pets, and delights in letting them scamper about her person. Unfortunately, on one occasion, she fails to retrieve one from inside her shirt and a great disturbance is caused when the mouse begins to explore, resulting in Jenny being unable to control her wriggling and giggling. Another

'Aren't they sweet?' said Jennifer, letting a mouse run up her sleeve.

incident involving Jenny's pets is more serious, as malicious Kathleen Peters takes them from their cage and places them all in Miss Ranger's desk so that they provoke mayhem by escaping all over the form room. Worst of all, two of the little animals escape under the door, so Jenny finds herself mouse-less and in trouble, much to Kathleen's glee (*see also* Kathleen Peters).

Helston, Michael

Small boy rescued from drowning in a pond near Whyteleafe School by Elizabeth Allen. She realises that the boy has fallen in and cannot swim, so she jumps in after him and applies all her life-saving techniques to the young child, who is saved by her quick thinking. The boy's nurse simply stands at the side of the pond, weeping in distress and even forgetting to thank Elizabeth for her bravery. But his father, Edward Helston, writes to the school and expresses his gratitude to whoever the Whyteleafe girl was who saved his son. Julian Holland, bursting with pride at his friend's courage, announces that it was Elizabeth. Elizabeth asks that the school be given a holiday as her reward.

Holland, Julian

The awesomely brilliant and wonderfully unusual-looking Julian Holland is undoubtedly the most fanciable Blyton boy. Lamentably, he appears in only

> *Julian grinned. He really was an extraordinary boy. The others couldn't help liking him. He was so exciting. They begged and begged him to make some of his amazing noises in Miss Ranger's class, but he wouldn't.*
>
> THE NAUGHTIEST GIRL IS A MONITOR

one of her works, *The Naughtiest Girl is a Monitor*, but he is the incontestable hero of this book, eclipsing all other characters at Whyteleafe School (with the exception of Elizabeth Allen), and leaving them in comparative obscurity. Julian has the attraction of being the untidiest person anyone has ever seen, coupled with exceptional looks – goblin-green eyes and long black hair… 'that fell in a wild lock over his forehead'. Apart from his arresting appearance, he is also the most intelligent boy the school has ever known, and the most inventive, with the ability to produce amazing objects with his own hands, using the barest of materials. He volunteers to make a new wheelbarrow for the younger boys for their work in the school gardens, and succeeds in producing a wonderful vehicle for their use.

Julian takes an immediate shine to the impetuous and hot-tempered Elizabeth, and the two become best friends as Elizabeth's great pal Joan Townsend is conveniently away with measles. Julian's wonderful gift of mimicry is a regular source of entertainment to his classmates, and they are constantly suppressing giggles as Mam'zelle becomes convinced that there is a cow or a kitten in the room. Julian's outlook on life when he first arrives at school is casual and flippant. No one can make him work hard in class if he does not want to, and he makes an effort only with things that he enjoys doing. But shocks are in store for the boy and, as a result, he changes his attitude completely.

His friendship with Elizabeth comes under serious strain when she accuses him of stealing money from Rosemary Wing. Elizabeth had marked a shilling piece and placed it in her desk, waiting for the thief to strike. Much to her horror, it did vanish from its position and reappeared in Julian's creative hands when the pupils were all spinning coins in the common room. Julian is disgusted with his great friend for accusing him of such a serious crime, and the two become terrible enemies, with Julian playing unkind tricks on Elizabeth in class to get back at her. Elizabeth loses her position as a Monitor, and Julian forms a phoney friendship with haughty Arabella Buckley. All is not lost, however. Elizabeth apologises to Julian for jumping to a wrong conclusion, and he likes her all over again for her sense of humour and honesty.

Another shock is in store for the boy, however, when the mother whom he adores becomes dangerously ill. This event sparks the most significant turning point in Julian's life as he makes a solemn promise to himself in the little church by the school that he will use his good brains properly, and not just on having fun, in the future. His mother does recover from her illness and Julian feels he has been given another chance to prove his worth. Gone is his capricious and aloof disposition, and in its place is a wiser, more level-headed boy, with ambitions of becoming a surgeon. (He is still gorgeous, though.)

James, Ruth

Tubby and rather loud, a common conjunction in Blyton's work, Ruth James makes an exuberant entrance into Blyton's writing as she is in Elizabeth Allen's form when she first arrives at Whyteleafe School. Elizabeth, who has made up her mind to be naughty, decides that she certainly does not like bossy little Ruth, who seems determined to make Elizabeth uncomfortable. Blyton uses Ruth as a vehicle to squash Elizabeth's haughtiness, and once Elizabeth's behaviour improves, she is hardly mentioned again. It is as if

Blyton decides that Ruth is actually not a very congenial person after all, and eliminates her from the plot.

Mrs Jenks

Appears in *The Naughtiest Girl is a Monitor* as the rather fierce Allen family cook who takes a great shine to the beautifully mannered but rather affected Arabella Buckley when she comes to stay with the Allens in the holidays.

Mr Johns

Man in charge of the boys at Whyteleafe School, who appears in all three books. Despite the magnitude of his job, Mr Johns is never seen to be meddling in the lives of the boys. Preferring to leave them to sort things out themselves, he makes decisions only when he is asked to. This attitude is typical of the staff at Whyteleafe, who make a point of giving the children as much responsibility as they can handle.

Jones, Robert

Robert Jones enters Blyton's writing in *The Naughtiest Girl Again* where he begins his time as a sulky, unpopular bully. He makes an enemy of Elizabeth Allen, who sees him pushing one of the younger boys too high on a swing, flies into a temper and reports him at the school's weekly meeting. Robert is a stubborn and cunning boy and decides that he must outshine Elizabeth at everything, even delighting in being chosen instead of her to play in a lacrosse match. Unfortunately, it is Robert whom Elizabeth suspects is the person playing mean tricks on her and Jennifer Harris, when in fact it is Kathleen Peters. This mistake on Elizabeth's part leads to a terrible mix-up, and

'I hope this isn't telling tales,' began Robert,
'but I really *must* complain about Elizabeth Allen's behaviour to me.'

eventual apologies all round. Robert is given a great chance by the school when they decide that they would like him to look after the school horses, as he is a fine rider, and very fond of the animals. Robert and Elizabeth, both very strong characters, end up being genuinely good friends by the end of the book, frequently enjoying an early morning ride together in the crisp morning air; and Robert's bullying is more than made-up for by his enthusiasm to help the younger ones with their work and activities.

Kenneth

Appears in *The Naughtiest Girl Again* when he requests extra money at the school's weekly meeting to pay for a library fine. He is refused the money on the grounds that the school should not have to pay for his carelessness.

Leonard

Leonard breaks a window in his common room and proposes that he is allocated half a crown in order to pay for the damage, but is refused. For more information on window-breaking, *see* Queenie Hobart of St Clare's. Leonard features twice in *The Naughtiest Girl Again*, as he also makes a complaint about Fred's snoring in their dormitory which is particularly annoying for Leonard as he has to get up early to milk the school cows and really needs a good night's sleep.

Lesley, Joan

Mentioned as being in the same dormitory as Elizabeth Allen in *The Naughtiest Girl in the School*, Joan has a laughing face with red hair and freckles. Girls with freckles usually have a good sense of humour in Blyton's writings.

Mr Lewis

The Music Master at Whyteleafe School who appears in all of the books, but most notably in *The Naughtiest Girl in the School*, as it is he who has a heavy influence over Elizabeth's decision whether to leave the school at half term. Elizabeth is very fond of music and very talented at the piano, and Mr Lewis recognises this and manages to get the most out of the girl's playing. He encourages her to learn a beautiful 'Sea Piece' that Elizabeth loves, and chooses her to play a duet with the best pianist in the school, a boy named Richard.

Mam'zelle

The French teacher at Whyteleafe School is actually known as Mademoiselle in *The Naughtiest Girl in the School*, the first book in the series, but by the time she is mentioned in *The Naughtiest Girl Again*, she is the more informal Mam'zelle, a title shared by the French staff at Malory Towers and St Clare's. This woman is the usual haphazard blend of French excitement coupled with good teaching methods that get the most out of her pupils. She is not given the substance of the French mistresses from the two aforementioned schools, and certainly is not a key figure in life at Whyteleafe.

Marsden, Helen

Helen Marsden appears in *The Naughtiest Girl in the School* as the best friend of Belinda Green. The two begin chatting on the first night they arrive at Whyteleafe, discussing their old school. Helen never has a large role in the book, except that she makes an unkind comment to Joan Townsend who never receives any post, suggesting that Joan would go through the roof were a letter to arrive addressed to her.

'Ah now, this Kathleen again!' cried Mam'zelle.

Elizabeth Allen steps in with a retort that implies that Joan is not as much of an idiot as Helen is. The two are clearly not good friends.

Mary

Mary's mother is abroad, so when she writes to her every week from Whyteleafe School she needs an extra seven-pence for the letter's postage. She requests the extra money and is granted four-pence ha'penny towards her stamp. This event, hardly crucial to the book's storyline, occurs in *The Naughtiest Girl Again*.

Matron

Not unlike the Matrons found in the pages of Malory Towers and St Clare's, the Matron at Whyteleafe School is plump and capable with a merry disposition. On the one occasion that the Matron of one of Blyton's stories was not rotund of figure, she failed miserably in her job (*see* Mrs Paterson at St Clare's).

O'Sullivan, Nora

Plays a key role in the life of Elizabeth Allen when she first arrives at Whyteleafe School. Nora is tall and Irish, with dark hair and deep-blue eyes that do a good deal of glaring in Elizabeth's direction in her first few weeks, as she is Elizabeth's Monitor and responsible for making sure that the girl is acting sensibly and behaving as she should. Nora finds Elizabeth excessively infuriating when the latter places a dozen items on her chest of drawers instead of the regulation six. She also sees fit to report Elizabeth in the school's weekly meeting as she deliberately pours ink over her rug and refuses to go to bed at the prescribed time. By half term, however, the two girls are beginning to see eye to eye, and Nora starts to gain a little respect from Elizabeth that had been notably lacking earlier. Whether Nora O'Sullivan is related to the famous twins of St Clare's of the same name is never discussed.

Pamela

Poor Pamela's bed is near the big window in her dormitory, so that when the window is left open during the day her things blow outside into the garden below. She makes this complaint at the weekly meeting in *The Naughtiest Girl is a Monitor*. The problem is resolved by moving her chest of drawers away into a less vulnerable situation.

Patrick

Cousin of Elizabeth Allen's great friend Julian Holland, Patrick is the only new character to appear in *Here's the Naughtiest Girl*, which is little more than a short story. He resents his cousin's effortless ability to come top in class and loathes Elizabeth on sight, mainly because she is a friend of 'cocky' cousin Julian. Elizabeth is determined to catch him behaving badly, and when he skips a gardening meeting in favour of tennis practice, she grabs his racket and lobs it into a bush where it is rained upon. Needless to say, everything works out for the best in the end and Patrick comes to realise that Elizabeth and Julian aren't so bad after all. Green-eyed like his cousin.

Pearce, William

Boy who makes up part of the rich tapestry of Whyteleafe School even though he is only ever referred to once throughout the series. We know nothing about him except that he is 'serious-faced' and in the form below Elizabeth Allen, which would make him only ten or possibly eleven years old. He complains at the weekly school meeting that his violin practice times coincide with the nature rambles he so enjoys. The Head Boy, also called William, suggests that he discusses the problem with Mr Lewis, the Music teacher. We can only assume that this problem is solved.

Peter

In *The Naughtiest Girl in the School* Peter is reported in the third school meeting of Elizabeth Allen's first term for scribbling on the cloakroom walls. Peter is made to give up his weekly two shillings to pay for materials to scrub the offensive marks off. It is not clear as to whether this is the same Peter who is bullied by Robert Jones in *The Naughtiest Girl Again*, but it is quite likely. When Robert realises how unkind he has been to the younger boy, he wants to make up for his behaviour and offers to go riding with him, which Peter loves. Unfortunately, one afternoon Peter's horse, Tinker, gallops off with the boy. All Elizabeth can do is to charge after him and haul Tinker to a standstill, cursing herself for letting Peter ride the horse without Robert's permission.

Peters, Kathleen

Kathleen is pasty, spotty, greasy-haired and has a face set in a permanent scowl when she first arrives at Whyteleafe in the opening chapters of *The Naughtiest Girl Again*. By the end of the book, however, she is rosy-cheeked, dimpled and smiling, enjoying life to the full. Of course this transformation does not take place overnight, and it is only after some very serious events have sorted themselves out that she begins the metamorphosis.

Kathleen is initially resentful of the pretty, popular and intelligent girls in her class, particularly Elizabeth Allen and Jennifer Harris who seem to have so many friends and are good at so many things. She does not endear herself to her form-mates by her argumentative nature, and the final straw comes when she overhears Jenny mimicking her behaviour in class. Kathleen is determined, in a way that unpleasant Blyton characters always are, to ruin the happiness of those who have made fun of her. She begins to play petty, spiteful tricks on Jenny and Elizabeth, which leave the two girls baffled and hurt, and in trouble with various members of staff who do not believe them when they say that they have no idea how ink came to be spilt all over their homework or the spade from the school garden came to be covered in mud.

Kathleen enjoys herself thoroughly for a while, but then begins to realise that she is behaving in a shameful fashion, especially as someone else (Robert Jones) is getting the blame for her unkindness. Kathleen takes a long, hard look at herself, and finds herself plain, spotty and pale, dull and slow, mean, deceitful and cowardly. The time comes when she feels she simply must own up. In doing so, she is given another chance that sees her blossoming into an altogether much more attractive individual. Beauty comes from within, and radiates into Kathleen's pale face, changing her for ever.

Miss Ranger

First Form teacher, and as all the books in the series are based on Elizabeth Allen's life in the First Form, she is the teacher who is mentioned most regularly. Like most Blyton staff members she is firm and sensible, and refuses to put up with any silliness and misbehaviour. With Elizabeth in her class her patience is truly tested, for the girl produces excellent results one moment, and is catapulting rubbers off rulers the next.

Richard

A 'serious, long-fingered boy' who is the best pianist in the school and plays a duet with Elizabeth Allen in her first term, Richard is an inspiration to Elizabeth and plays (literally) a critical role in getting Elizabeth to stay on at Whyteleafe in *The Naughtiest Girl in the School*. They hold each other's

Elizabeth and Richard were once again playing duets.

musical talent in high esteem, though Richard states that he doesn't think much of Elizabeth's common sense when she is planning on quitting the school. It is mentioned in *The Naughtiest Girl Again* that Richard 'never thought twice about what he said and could be hurtful'. All the same, his words stick in Elizabeth's mind and make her realise that she should change her way of thinking. After this he is recognised as one of Elizabeth's firm friends.

Rita and William

Judicious Head Girl of Whyteleafe School, Rita shares her role with William, the equally discerning Head Boy. They appear as prominent characters in the books, tackling situations that would be reserved for the Headmistresses of Malory Towers or St Clare's. Rita is described as the nicest-looking girl Elizabeth Allen has ever seen, with the kindest eyes, who does not look angry when she catches Elizabeth on her own in the town, only understanding and wise. Rita and William deal with Elizabeth's disobedience in a way that makes her come to realise that they have been right all along, and that it is she, Elizabeth, who is losing out. Elizabeth has unlimited respect for these two Heads who are probably eighteen and very grown up compared to the fiery little eleven-year-old. Rita sees from the start that Elizabeth has the makings of a fine pupil and, by giving her a job to do in befriending the unhappy Joan Townsend, she wins Elizabeth's admiration and that is never lost.

Miss Scott

Features in the initial chapter of *The Naughtiest Girl in the School* as she is Elizabeth's governess who has had enough of her silly behaviour and defiant attitude. Elizabeth misbehaves by attaching her new school stockings to Miss Scott's skirt, so that she cannot find them to pack into her case. Miss Scott is mentioned as being very fond of Elizabeth, despite the girl's over-indulged character.

Squeak

See Bubble and Squeak.

Terry, John

Green-fingered boy who spends all his spare time in the school gardens, planting, digging and weeding. Indeed, the only words that ever come out of John's mouth are horticultural-based. Elizabeth eventually decides that he needs a new hobby to complement his obsession with flora, and suggests that he takes up riding. Though reluctant at first, John soon discovers a new passion, quelling all worries he had that he was dull to be so single-minded. Elizabeth has a great deal of time and regard for John, who is a year older than she and knows so much about plant life, which is also one of Elizabeth's great interests.

Thomas

Monitor in Elizabeth Allen's first term at Whyteleafe School, Thomas is mentioned only in *The Naughtiest Girl in the School* as the boy who hands around the school money-box in order to collect money from all the pupils. The procedure at Whyteleafe is that they all put whatever money they have into the school box, and are then all handed out two shillings a week from these takings. This means that everyone receives the same amount, preventing jealousy and theft. Whether this system works or not is debatable as there is a case of stealing in *The Naughtiest Girl is a Monitor* (*see* Martin Follett). Also, Arabella Buckley, who appears in the same book, is permanently talking of her wealth and beautiful clothes which suggests that, even if the children are given the same amount to spend, there will always be those who are unmistakably better off, with more to boast about to the others.

Miss Thomas

Miss Thomas is introduced in the opening chapters of *The Naughtiest Girl in the School* as it is she who greets Elizabeth at the railway station before their journey to Whyteleafe School. Miss Thomas is young and 'merry-looking' and popular with her pupils who are as young as eleven when they first attend the school. Elizabeth announces at supper that she has a guinea pig with a face like Miss Thomas's. It is unlikely that this is true.

Timmy

Blyton introduces a dog called Timmy in *The Naughtiest Girl in the School*. He is the pet of Elizabeth Allen who has to leave him behind at home. For a far more prestigious hound of the same name, see Timmy in The Famous Five.

Tinker

One of the horses at Whyteleafe School, Tinker has one flash of excitement when he bolts with small Peter on his back. Elizabeth Allen is on hand to rescue horse and rider from any danger. Tinker is also the name of Roderick Longfield's cocker spaniel in the Six Cousins series.

Townsend, Joan

Quiet, mouse-like pupil who is brought out of her shell by the most unlikely of candidates, the mischievous Elizabeth Allen. Joan features in *The Naughtiest Girl in the School* and *The Naughtiest Girl Again* but is conveniently away from school with measles for the whole of the next book, making room for the altogether more alluring character of Julian Holland as Elizabeth's new best friend.

Joan confesses to Elizabeth the reason for her unhappiness: her mother and father never write to her or pay her any attention, as the other children's parents do, and all she wants is to win their approval and love. Elizabeth becomes fiercely protective and loyal towards the reclusive girl, snapping at those who tease her (*see* Helen Marsden) and sharing everything that she has with the girl. Elizabeth inevitably becomes too involved in the scenario when she decides to order Joan a wonderful cake for her birthday, pretending that it is from Joan's mother and father, but clean forgets that Joan wants to write to her parents to thank them for the gift. When Joan receives a letter in return from her mother saying that she knows nothing about the cake, the trouble sets in and Joan becomes terribly ill after a long walk in a rainstorm. After a few days of worrying about what to do, Elizabeth sets to work to try and amend the situation and writes to Mrs Townsend, explaining everything. It is not long before Joan and her mother have sorted everything out for the best and Elizabeth's rash behaviour is seen as the catalyst in bringing the two back together.

Mr Warlow

Games teacher who emerges in *The Naughtiest Girl in the School* very briefly. At Whyteleafe, the girls and boys learn sport together, so the boys play lacrosse and the girls play cricket. As lacrosse is actually an extremely dangerous game, involving sticks flying around people's faces, it is surprising that at most schools it is almost exclusively a girls' sport.

White, Fred

As well as being someone who borrows things without asking, Fred is also accused of causing nightly disturbance through his snoring. He is not, therefore, an altogether successful pupil of Whyteleafe School. He is mentioned in *The Naughtiest Girl Again*.

William

See Rita and William.

Wing, Rosemary

A quiet, shy, timid, weak and rather pathetic little girl with a pretty face and rosebud mouth arrives at Whyteleafe School in the opening chapters of *The Naughtiest Girl is a Monitor*. Rosemary befriends the grand and beautiful Arabella Buckley whom she worships as the girl is rich and well mannered with immaculate clothes and golden hair. Rosemary makes a contribution to the ups and downs of school life when she issues complaints to her Monitor, Elizabeth Allen, about the fact that many of her things keep on going missing. Rosemary and Elizabeth between them instigate a plan to capture the thief, but taking matters into their own hands like this is not really the ideal solution. (*See also* Martin Follett and Julian Holland.)

TOYS AND ENCHANTMENT

ENID BLYTON'S FAIRY FOLK

THE ENCHANTED WOOD

THE WISHING CHAIR

MR PINKWHISTLE

AMELIA JANE

MR TWIDDLE

MR MEDDLE

THE THREE GOLLIWOGS

BRER RABBIT

NODDY

'What land? At the top of the Tree? A land at the top of a tree?' said Connie, puzzled.

THE FOLK OF THE FARAWAY TREE

ENID BLYTON'S FAIRY FOLK

Brownies

Brownies are a kind-hearted race who apparently 'attach themselves to human families and help them'. This is true of Blyton's lovable Mr Pinkwhistle (half-man, half-Brownie), and of Big-Ears who is the calming influence over Noddy in the Toyland adventures. Brownies are always pictured with long white beards and wrinkled faces because it is possible for them to live for hundreds of years. Big-Ears was one hundred at the time of Blyton's writing, so would now be coming up for his hundred and fiftieth birthday. It is the Brownie Long Beard who is the one-time holder of the key to the Jewel Caves, deep below the Magic Faraway Tree.

Brownies appear at the beginning of *The Enchanted Wood* and promise to be of assistance to the children if they are whistled for seven times. However, not all Brownies are good all the time as is proven by the existence of Mr Grim's School for Bad Brownies which features in *The Wishing Chair Again*. Under Mr Grim's rule is Winks, an extremely naughty Brownie whose behaviour is so mischievous that he finds himself sent back to the school after being given a chance to behave properly with Chinky the Pixie and the two children, Peter and Mollie.

Elves

Blyton's most appealing and famous elf is of course Silky, who appears as a chief character in the three books in the Enchanted Wood series. Although Blyton never mentioned that Silky had wings, illustrators frequently draw her

with wings, which she should not have if she is to qualify for the true definition of an Elf, that is being male and wingless. If she had possessed the ability to fly, a large number of the Faraway Tree adventures would have been solved much more efficiently, including the escape from the Enchanter in *The Enchanted Wood* when the Faraway Tree gang find themselves prisoners in a tall tower with only one window right at the top. Were Silky in possession of wings, there would  also have been no need for the Whizz-Away ointment that Moon-Face spreads on a table and bench.

Elves are frequently mischievous and can create havoc with humans, but they can also be helpful to them, as is the Elf who appears in *The Wishing Chair Again* and shows Peter and Mollie how to use the Fairy Ring to reach Pin Village where Mr Polish lives and has the Wishing Chair. Elves were originally thought to be the white ghosts of men, and are threaded through literature in association with the unearthly:

> And now about the cauldron sing
> Like elves and fairies in a ring
> Enchanting all that you put in.
> (Hecate in *Macbeth*, Act IV, Scene i)

Fairies

Blyton's view of Fairies seems to be very much in keeping with the traditional opinion of the little folk, complete with delicate silvery wings, high tinkling voices and soft golden hair. At the time Blyton began her writing, in the 1920s, Fairies were commonly perceived as being dew-drenched and beautiful, and were brought to life in the famous drawings of Cecily Mary Barker and the *Flower Fairies* books. This is a far cry from the manner in which Fairies began their existence, probably as early as the time of the old pagan gods, when they were viewed with fear and trepidation as creatures of unknown and frightening powers. The Victorians romanticised and altered this perception, hence the theory that fairies are the 'good folk' living happily at the bottom of your garden.

Interestingly, J.M. Barrie – author of *Peter Pan* (1904) – portrayed his fairies, and most famously Tinkerbell, as jealous, mischievous and cruel: 'they [fairies] were rather a nuisance to him [Peter], getting in his way and so on, and indeed he sometimes had to give them a good hiding.' Peter Pan goes on to describe the origin of fairies to Wendy, claiming that when the first baby laughed, the laughter broke into a thousand pieces which 'went skipping about' and that was the beginning of Fairies. The artist Blyton chose for her *Book of Fairies* was Horace Knowles, who seems to have been influenced by those who saw Fairies as a fragile yet elegant race who enchanted all they came across and a stark contrast to the fiercely ugly Dwarfs, Goblins and Giants that inhabited the same land. Blyton refers to Titania and Oberon as the King and Queen of Fairyland in her *Storytime Book*, which tells of Too-Wise the Wonderful Wizard who holds a party without gaining permission from the King and Queen with disastrous results.

Gnomes

Creepy the Gnome is among the first of the Fairy Folk encountered by Jo, Bessie and Fanny in the opening chapters of *The Enchanted Wood.* He derives his name from his habit of sneaking around in a rather dishonest fashion. Gnomes, however, are not all as sly as this, as is shown in the Blyton tale entitled *The Story of the Lost Ball* in which a Gnome called Karin makes a strange request: 'Oh please, Your Majesty, let me go and play on Hampstead Heath with the children!' The Queen decides that Karin should be allowed to live on the Heath, and it is mentioned that he is happiest of all on bank holidays when there are so many lost children that he hardly knows where to begin! This is reminiscent of *Peter Pan*, when children who fall out of their prams in Kensington Gardens are taken away if not claimed within seven days and looked after by Peter, their leader.

Goblins

The *Encyclopaedia Britannica* describes Goblins as 'Misshapen, ugly fairy folk who wandered from place to place...mischievous and often malicious... They sometimes attached themselves to a family and enjoyed terrifying them at night by banging saucepans, moving furniture and knocking on windows.' This reference to saucepans is interesting in the light of Blyton's Saucepan Man whose roots are never fully explored. However, it is unlikely that he was related to a Goblin, as he is in every way a likeable and amiable kind of fellow. Goblins appear all through Blyton's writing, and seem to have very different personalities, as can be seen by the extraordinary Polite Goblin who appears in *The Adventures of the Wishing Chair*, and astounds Mollie, Peter and Chinky the Pixie by behaving in a very over-courteous manner. This is actually a clever cover-up for his real intentions which are to steal the Wishing Chair and keep it for himself. In the same book, Peter and Mollie's mother's ring is stolen by a cowardly Goblin called Big Ears who clearly bears no relation to the Toyland Brownie of the same name. Big Ears is an inhabitant of Goblin Town where the houses are crooked and the streets are full of curious Goblin folk.

One even more unpleasant Goblin is Tricky, who attempts to trick Chinky and the all-powerful Mr Spells with his wheeling and dealing of the Wishing Chair. Another such creature appears in *The Magic Faraway Tree*, and is described as a 'strange Goblin with blue, pointed ears, and eyes that sparkled as if they had fireworks in them'. He offers Moon-Face a pill that will make him 'as high as a house' but Moon-Face declines. Red Goblins are also mentioned in the Enchanted Wood series as the scarlet trouble-makers who push the Faraway Tree dwellers down the Slippery Slip and try to take the tree for themselves.

Pixies

A Pixie called Tippet runs the shop in which the Wishing Chair is first found by Peter and Mollie, and a very bad-tempered creature he is, too. The *Encyclopaedia Britannica* mentions that they love to dance in the moonlight to the music of frogs and grass-hoppers, and frighten people by rapping on doors and windows. This is certainly in keeping with the Angry Pixie in the Faraway Tree who knocks on his window indignantly whenever curious visitors peer in.

Trolls

Trolls are the nasty creatures who damage the roots of the Magic Faraway Tree during the search for jewels in the Jewel Caves. The bad Trolls are banished to the Land of Smack as a punishment for their crimes. (*See* Woffles, Goat-Moth Caterpillars and the Know-Alls in the Enchanted Wood series.)

THE ENCHANTED WOOD

The Enchanted Wood (1939)
The Magic Faraway Tree (1943)
The Folk of the Faraway Tree (1946)

The Enchanted Wood stands right next to Jo, Bessie and Fanny's little cottage, so it is very accessible to the three children who star in the three books set in its midst. From the moment that the children arrive in the country they are convinced the wood is magical, so decide to explore it at the first opportunity, and immediately upon entering its dark, intriguing centre, they feel that unmistakable rush of thrilling excitement, also experienced by the children in C.S. Lewis's *Narnia* Chronicles when they first arrive on the other side of the wardrobe. Somehow they know that they are destined to have marvellous adventures in this magical location. It seems that the trees are constantly whispering secrets to one another in soft, leafy undertones, telling the children that they are part of the bewitchment. The Faraway Tree is the largest and most powerful tree in the Enchanted Wood, although there is no doubt that other trees contain magic and sorcery as well. It is not clear whether the Enchanted Wood is part of Fairyland, or Fairyland part of the Enchanted Wood, or whether the two places are connected at all, although Goblins, Pixies and Elves from both locations mill around like extras on a film set throughout Blyton's writing.

One of the most mesmerising images of the wood is when it is lit up at night, with lanterns hanging from the branches of the trees, and the fairy folk dancing, singing and casting spells. Blyton is at her most ingenious when writing about the events in the Enchanted Wood.

Angry Man in the Land of Goodies

A furious man catches Dick munching on his barley-sugar door knocker. In punishment, he holds him prisoner until the others are ready to leave the Land.

Angry Pixie

Pixie who spends his time in an almost permanent state of irritation, usually encouraged by people staring into his window, up the Faraway Tree. Connie finds herself in a terrible state after sneaking a look into the Angry Pixie's house, as the little man throws a bottle of ink over her and her clean frock.

Bessie

Sister to Fanny and Jo, Bessie appears in all three books and is mentioned as being the most sensible of the three children, her brother Jo and sister Fanny being the 'wild pair'. Manages to prevent Jack from falling down the hill in the Land of Nursery Rhyme through sheer plain talking. She participates in every adventure that the Faraway Tree tribe experience, and is briefly trapped in the Land of Enchantments when she is lured into dancing around a white ring by pixies who link hands with her and will not set her free. Fortunately, she is able to break out of the ring when the Saucepan Man finds the spell he had previously lost, which is strong enough to get them out of any tricky situation involving sorcery of any kind. Bessie achieves that greatest of all childhood desires – to be able to fly – when she is given a pair of delicate fairy wings in the Land of Birthdays.

There in the middle of the cake her name appeared in pink sugar letters.

Black Goblin

Goblin who inhabits the Land of Enchantments and offers various spells for sale. These include a 'Spell to turn your enemy into a spider', a 'Spell to enchant a bird to your hand' and a 'Spell to understand the whispering of the trees'.

Blackie

Pony who appears in *The Enchanted Wood* when Jo wishes for him in the Land of Birthdays, leaving Blyton's readers in a state of great distress that they do not live in this land too.

Bright-Winged Pixies

Party of Pixies found singing and dancing in a magic ring in the Land of Enchantments. They are so bewitching that when they invite Bessie to join them she finds herself hopelessly compelled to do so. To the dismay of the others, the ring that they are dancing in is made from chalk and she cannot leave it. Fortunately, the magic spell is found and Bessie is released.

Brownies

Brownies are peppered throughout so much of Blyton's work that it would require a separate book to list them all by name and character. They are introduced at the beginning of *The Enchanted Wood* as being friendly, good little folk who will appear if the children whistle seven times for them. Brownies should not be confused with Elves, Pixies, Fairies, Goblins or evil Trolls. For Blyton's most celebrated Brownies, *see* Mr Pinkwhistle (who is half-man, half-Brownie) and, of course, Big-Ears.

Mr Change-About and the Enchanter

These two preposterous characters erupt into the plot of *The Magic Faraway Tree* with explosive results. Mr Change-About refuses to remain as one character, and has the ability to change from being a sweet old man to a furious creature with a thin face. Moon-Face and the Saucepan Man manage to capture Mr Change-About in one of Saucepan's kettles, but are interrupted by an Enchanter who is distressed to see his great friend, Change-About, captured by a strange group of people. The Enchanter plays a trick on those who have trapped his pal, and succeeds in imprisoning them in a small round room with only a bench and table inside. He then sets off to find his friend, Wizard Wily, who will tell him how to deal with the intruders. Fortunately, Jo still has some of the Whizz-Away ointment that can be spread on the table and bench so that they are able to fly out of the room before the Enchanter and his ominous-sounding friend return.

Connie (Curious Connie)

Blyton's work contains two notable Connies, and both of these characters are rather overbearing and in need of having some sense knocked into them. Curious Connie appears in *The Folk of the Faraway Tree* when she comes to stay with Jo, Bessie and Fanny as her mother is ill. Connie arrives at the children's little cottage full of scepticism and incredulity about the stories that

Dick (who appears in *The Magic Faraway Tree*) has told her about the strange inhabitants of the Enchanted Wood. She soon reforms her opinion as, after a shaky start involving a quarrel with the Saucepan Man, she decides that the Faraway Tree is quite the most magical and wonderful place she has ever known. Connie is excessively spoilt and affected and, as her name suggests, finds it impossible to keep her nose out of trouble and other people's business. Her worst display of nosiness comes when she listens in to a wonderful secret in the Land of Secrets, and is punished by losing her voice until she is truly sorry. Strangely, this plot echoes the fate of Zacharias in the Nativity story, who will not believe that his wife Elizabeth is to have a baby and is struck dumb until the child's birth when he is finally released from the punishment. Blyton was clearly a believer in finding the right punishment to fit the character. (*See also* Elizabeth Allen in the Naughtiest Girl in the School series.) Connie's general attitude improves to bearable as the book progresses and, by the end, it is agreed that she is an altogether nicer, more polite individual.

Crackers

Crackers with legs run free in the Land of Birthdays in *The Enchanted Wood* and scamper up to people, wanting to be pulled.

Creepy the Gnome

Gnome who appears only at the beginning of *The Enchanted Wood* and is aptly named, thanks to his habit of creeping around where he should not be.

Crosspatch

The most cross-looking lady that Bessie and Fanny have ever come across. She travels in the same carriage as them on the clockwork train in *The Enchanted Wood* and grumbles throughout the journey. She carries a basket filled with extremely prickly rose sprays which keep scratching Fanny's legs.

Dick

A cousin of Jo, Bessie and Fanny, with a penchant for food and mischief, Dick features only in *The Magic Faraway Tree*. He arrives in the country feeling certain that it will prove to be rather dull, but is amazed by what lies in store for him. Dick finds himself in trouble in the Land of Goodies when his greed leads him to steal the door knocker made of barley-sugar. The owner of the house is furious, and makes him stay and say that he is sorry while the others go off to enjoy the delicious treats in the Land. Dick represents all the characteristics of a rather over-eager Blyton boy in his constant quest for food and has a personality that seems to lead him into adventure. He is likeable, but rather naughty, and learns a great deal of kindness during his stay with his cousins, exemplified by his attitude in the Land of Presents. Dick realises that he cannot take a present for himself, but must learn to give to others, and therefore receive gifts back through his own kindness.

They all left their umbrellas and macs behind and up into the Land of Enchantment they went. It wasn't a twilight land like the Land of Secrets, it was a land of strange colours and lights and shadows. Everything shone and shimmered and moved. Nothing stayed the same for a moment. It was beautiful and strange. THE FOLK OF THE FARAWAY TREE

Enchanter Wise-Man

Appears in the Land of Secrets in *The Folk of the Faraway Tree* and reveals the Secret of Laughter to a cross-looking Brownie.

Fanny

Central character in the three books based on the extraordinary goings-on in a magical wood. She is the youngest of the three children who discover the mysterious wood and the secrets that it holds and it is she who utters the bewitching words, 'Up the Faraway Tree / Jo, Bessie and me!'

Fanny and Bessie are typical Blyton girls, fond of dolls, pretty things, and adventure, as long as it is not going to prove too dangerous. They nearly always express disappointment when they are made to stay behind if there is a hint of trouble ahead, but are always relieved when they hear of the frightening encounters the boys have had to deal with. Fanny fulfils every little girl's dream by succeeding in obtaining a doll from the Land of Birthdays that walks, talks and is, in every way, human. She names her Peronel and is delighted when the little doll follows her around wherever she goes. Blyton's imagination is at its most graphic throughout her work on the characters and escapades in the Enchanted Wood, where everything is possible, and nothing is commonplace. Of course, the children who climb the Magic Faraway Tree are wonderfully blasé about the fact that they are surrounded by Goblins, Fairies, Sprites, Elves and talking squirrels, which makes the stories all the

It was simply lovely.
Fanny did enjoy herself.

more striking. Blyton plays on the credulity of children who are happy to believe in everything they can see and waste little time with gasps of disbelief.

Funny Cake Shop Woman

Runs the cake shop in the Land of Goodies. When somebody chooses a cake, their name appears on it written in icing sugar. (*See also* the Baker in *The Wishing Chair*.)

Furry the Polar Bear

In the Land of Ice and Snow in *The Enchanted Wood*, Jo meets Furry who is described as friendly but rather stupid. He is frustrated to find that the only word the bear can utter is 'Oooommmmph'. There is an inevitable communication breakdown, and Jo is relieved when he finally escapes from the glacial conditions in this Land.

Giants

Several giants are featured in the Land of Giants in *The Folk of the Faraway Tree*. They almost step on the children and their friends and mistake them for insects. Dangerous people to have walking around above you.

Gingerbread Man

Tasty-looking chap found working in the sausage roll shop in the Land of Goodies in *The Magic Faraway Tree*. He is flat and brown with two black currant-like eyes. He stands turning the handle on the sausage roll machine and Jo remarks that he is, 'Just like the gingerbread people that Mother makes for us.'

Goat-Moth Caterpillars

These peculiar creatures appear in *The Folk of the Faraway Tree* and are instrumental in saving the Tree from the evil Trolls who are destroying its roots while plundering hidden treasure. The caterpillars gnaw their way through to the bottom of the tree and frighten the Trolls who think that they are terrible snakes, thus making a clear path for Moon-Face and the other members of the Faraway Tree gang.

Goldilocks and the Three Bears

These old favourites find their way into Blyton's writing in *The Enchanted Wood* when the children, Silky and Moon-Face find themselves at Bears Station in need of their help. Blyton frequently took characters from well-known nursery rhymes and tales and incorporated them into her own work. Jo, Bessie and Fanny are constantly expressing delight at being faced with characters they have previously only heard about through their story books.

Golliwog in the Land of Toys

Golliwog who tells how the Saucepan Man has been caught stealing from the Sweet Shop. The poor fellow mistook the Land for the Land of Goodies and presumed he could simply help himself to whatever he fancied. He is thrown in jail for his crime and it is up to the others to rescue him.

Golliwogs on the Clockwork Train

Three golliwogs travel on the clockwork train in *The Enchanted Wood*. The tin train has several carriages, with doors and windows that cannot be opened. Entry is possible by sliding back the roof, just as you would do on a toy train. There is even a key in the side of the engine. The gollies get on at Golliwog Station and stare at the girls. Bessie is so taken aback by the resemblance to her own golliwog that she cannot resist staring back.

Green Goblin

Green-eyed and green-eared, this Goblin captures Moon-Face in the Land of Enchantments in *The Folk of the Faraway Tree*. Moon-Face forgets one of the rules of the Land – the rule of rudeness. He is rude to the Goblin and therefore finds himself completely under his control.

Haynes, Lizzie

Mother of Curious Connie in *The Folk of the Faraway Tree*, and friend of Jo, Bessie and Fanny's mother.

Mrs Hidden

See Dame Tell-You-All and Very Grand Fairy.

Horner, Jack

Jack Horner puts in a brief appearance in *The Folk of the Faraway Tree* in the Land of Nursery Rhyme and issues a warning that Miss Muffet's spider is in an especially bad mood. A cluster of other characters from other rhymes appear in this Land, including Tommy Tucker, Polly Flinders, Johnny Thin and Johnny Stout. Jack and Jill are saved from their usual fate of falling down the hill by Bessie, diplomatic as ever, pointing out that they should stop arguing or they will hurt themselves. They are so pleased with the fact that they are no longer going to face head injuries that they invite Bessie to their house for a nice brown and white striped humbug.

Ice-Cream Man

Seen pushing his cart around the Land of Dreams in *The Magic Faraway Tree*. Moon-Face opens his purse for money to buy some ice-cream but is shocked to discover it is full of marbles. He is allowed to use these instead of money and purchases ices for everyone. When they open the ice-cream packets they are disappointed to find whistles inside.

Ice-Cream Man in the Land of Treats

Character who dishes out free ice-creams in *The Folk of the Faraway Tree*. They are enormous and you can wish for any flavour you desire. Connie wishes for sardine ice-cream and is told she has to eat it before she can have another one in a more desirable flavour.

Imp

A nasty-looking Imp is mentioned in *The Folk of the Faraway Tree* climbing up the Ladder That Has No Top after Connie, the spoilt little girl who is silly enough to run away from the rest of the group.

Jack (of Bean-Stalk Fame)

Jack and his legendary Bean-Stalk feature in *The Folk of the Faraway Tree* as the Saucepan Man is an old friend of his and intends to ask his help to get into the Land of Giants, followed by the Land of Marvels. Jack, who is married now and living in a castle with his Princess wife, is all too pleased to help his old buddy and his collection of friends. Giantland is reached via the huge Bean-Stalk, which leads to numerous encounters with larger-than-life predators.

Jo

Jo is the older brother of Fanny and Bessie who all feature as the chief protagonists in the series. His sisters look to him for help and ideas and, as a general rule, he is the one whose quick thinking gets the others out of scrapes and danger. Jo has several adventures independent of the rest of the gang from the Tree, including being taken prisoner by a demanding snowman who requires him to become his slave, and being turned upside down by an angry policeman in Topsy Turvy Land. It is Jo's ingenuity that rescues the Saucepan Man from captivity in a red-painted fort in the Land of Toys, and he who supplies the Whizz-Away ointment that is spread on a table in order to escape from an Enchanter in the Land of Spells. Like Peter in the Secret Seven, Jo is the leader of the children, but he too is in awe of Moon-Face, the true head of the Faraway Tree.

Mr Jones

Barely features at all, except at the beginning of each book when Blyton points out that the children live with their mother and father in a tiny cottage, deep in the heart of the country.

Know-Alls

Sagacious people found in the Land of Know-Alls in *The Folk of the Faraway Tree*. There are five Know-Alls in total, and they are visited by Moon-Face, who desires to know how to save the dying Faraway Tree from the evil Trolls that are destroying its roots. The Know-Alls are 'so old that they had forgotten their youth, and so wise that they know everything' (except if it relates to their youth presumably). They radiate a calm, mysterious sense of wonder, and inform Moon-Face that, in order to save the Tree, he and his friends must dig right through its roots, following the passage of the Slippery Slip.

Kollamoolitoomarellipawkyrollo

See Mr Watzisname.

Magic Faraway Tree

The most important feature of the Enchanted Wood, and so full of magic that it is impossible to know what it is going to reveal next. The Faraway Tree is approximately 500 years old and, according to the Red Squirrel, should live to be at least a thousand years old. It possesses the incredible property of producing different fruits at each branch level, so that it may be growing ripe plums one moment, and prickly conkers the next. The Faraway Tree also boasts the

There were a great many people using the Faraway Tree that night.

Slippery Slip – the helter-skelter slide that runs from Moon-Face's house, right at the top of the tree, down to its base – which enables various children, Pixies, Fairies, Goblins and other creatures to travel down quickly and efficiently. The Faraway Tree is inhabited by Moon-Face, Silky, Mr Watzisname, the Angry Pixie, Dame Washalot and the Saucepan Man, plus numerous other characters who see to the well-being of the Tree and the smooth running of the Slippery Slip.

The Faraway Tree is without doubt unequalled in its ability to house various 'Lands' at its top. Throughout the three books Blyton wrote about life up the Faraway Tree, there is an astonishing turnover of these countries. They include: Rocking Land, the Land of Take-What-You-Want, the Country of Loneliness, Giant Land, the Land of Dame Slap, the Land of Seagulls, the Land of Birthdays, the Land of Spells, the Land of Dreams, the Land of Do-As-You-Please, the Land of Goodies, the Land of Magic Medicine, the Land of Tempers, the Land of Presents, the Land of Nursery Rhyme, the Land of Tea Parties, the Land of Secrets, the Land of Enchantments, the Land of Know-Alls and the Land of Treats. These places are the perfect settings for some of Blyton's most bizarre personalities, who all conveniently disappear when their particular Land moves on and another moves into its place. To reach these lands from the Faraway Tree, one has to move through a hole in the clouds and out the other side. If you do not get back through the hole in time, the Land may move off and you could be stuck in that country for ever, or at least until it next visits the Tree. An hour is still an hour to the Tree folk – there is no sense of time being intangible and enigmatic – it exists in the unequivocal way that the children have always known. Of all Blyton's creations, the Faraway Tree is perhaps the most desirable and the most enduring.

Magic Snowman

Comes face to face with Jo in the early chapters of *The Enchanted Wood* and speaks to him in a 'soft, snowy sort of voice', demanding that Jo should come and be his servant. This Snowman proves to be a rather tiresome figure, and eventually comes to a grisly end when Moon-Face makes the room so hot that he starts to melt away and Jo is freed from his powers.

Moon-Face

So called because he has a face as round, pale and glowing as the moon, Moon-Face is the undisputed head of the Faraway Tree, and appears in all three books as chief protagonist, organiser and decision-maker. He lives in a house near the top of the Faraway Tree which is the scene of many a pop, biscuit or goggle bun-munching session and also the starting point of the Slippery Slip – the slide that runs from the top of the Faraway Tree to the bottom. Moon-Face is initially introduced demanding toffee from the children whom he is soon to become fond of. Curiously, it is never a surprise to any folk in the Faraway Tree that three mysterious-looking humans have somehow found their way up the tree and into their lives. It is almost as if Moon-Face and Silky always knew that they would be visited by these people and therefore never ask any questions.

Moon-Face's incandescent countenance is at the centre of every adventure up the Faraway Tree and, as a general rule, he is full of ideas and plans for outsmarting the many creatures, spells and eccentricities that come his way. He knows that in order to rescue Jo from the Magic Snowman they must take a train to the Three Bears' house and acquire the assistance of his aforementioned furry friends. It is also Moon-Face who realises that there is a way of escaping from the Enchanter by spreading magic Whizz-Away ointment on a table and bench, enabling them to fly away aboard this strange method of

A dust-pan and brush shot in with a clatter.

transport. However, the other side of the coin is Moon-Face's terrible hot temper which leads him to be taken prisoner by a Goblin in the Land of Enchantments. Fortunately, he escapes with the help of his friends who cannot bear to see the great Moon-Face having to be anyone's servant.

Mother to Jo, Bessie and Fanny

Mother of Jo, Bessie and Fanny who features in all the books. The family move deep into the heart of the country in the opening pages of *The Enchanted Wood* and it is not long before they discover the magic that lies in the wood beyond their house. Their mother is a curiously glacial character who thinks nothing of her three children capering around in a dark wood all day, sometimes not returning until late at night, usually with ripped clothes and full of tales of peculiar people. In classic Blyton style, she is a great provider of food, giving the children biscuits, apples and chocolate cake to take with them to the Enchanted Wood, and promising them potatoes baked in their jackets on their return. She likes the Saucepan Man because he provides her with new kitchen utensils when she needs them, and thinks that Moon-Face is wonderful because when he comes to stay for a few days he helps in the garden. But like many Blyton mothers she is essentially rather a vague figure, floating in and out of the plot with no definite character traits established.

Miss Muffet

Miss Muffet appears in the Land of Nursery Rhyme in *The Folk of the Faraway Tree* as the character who has to deal with a cranky spider with flu. She is met by Moon-Face and his posse who have come to release the Saucepan Man from the aforementioned eight-legged bug. Miss Muffet tells the Spider that he needs a hot mustard bath in order to get rid of his cold, and while he is relaxing, the breakout is executed.

Miss Muffet's Spider

Most insects, like caterpillars and earwigs, in Blyton's work tend to be friend-ly, but this creature is far from amicable. Miss Muffet's Spider features in the Land of Nursery Rhyme in *The Folk of the Faraway Tree*, as he captures the Saucepan Man in his web because Saucepan had been singing a rude song about him that went:

> *Two smacks for a spider*
> *Two smacks on his nose*
> *Two whacks on his ankles*
> *Hey tiddly-toes!*

The spider is also in a bad temper because he has a terrible cold and keeps on having to pull out his handkerchief and sneeze. In the end, Moon-Face and the rest of the Faraway Tree crowd burst into the Spider's 'webby cave' and instigate a rescue mission.

Muffin Man

The Muffin Man features in the Land of Dreams in *The Magic Faraway Tree*. This is the most fanciful of all the lands visited by the Faraway Tree crew. Bessie feels that a muffin would be delicious, but when the man lifts his tray of muffins down from his head, he reveals small kittens instead. He hands one to each member of the group, and before they can express their astonish-ment, the kittens begin to grow and grow, until they are the size of large cats.

Nice-Looking Witch

Witch, given no name, who appears in *The Magic Faraway Tree* in the Land of Spells where she is knitting stockings from the green smoke swirling up from her fire. She provides Jo with some purple ointment that is rubbed on the soles of his feet, and a magic poem to put him the right way up again, after his encounter with an angry policeman in Topsy-Turvy Land. The witch is paid in gold, which she immediately throws on the fire, and begins to knit yellow stockings from the smoke that it makes.

Old Woman

Found at the top of Jack's Bean-Stalk in *The Folk of the Faraway Tree*, an 'old woman' complains about the noise that Connie is making up the Ladder That Has No Top.

Old Woman who Lives in a Shoe

Features in *The Magic Faraway Tree* as her Land is visited by the Faraway Tree folk who are distressed that this old woman has seen fit to take over Silky the Elf's little house for herself. She complains bitterly that she cannot cope with the naughty children running riot in her shoe-house, and that she has decided to give up on them and stay away. Using cunning and lateral thinking, Silky and friends succeed in persuading her that she should go back up to her own Land and see her children who are causing chaos trying on her clothes and behaving appallingly. Silky returns to her home, much to the relief of all the Faraway Tree inhabitants.

Owl

Appears as a messenger to the children from Silky the Elf. He sleeps during the day.

Peronel

Walking, talking, living doll Fanny wishes for in the Land of Birthdays. Comes complete with a bag full of clothes. She has small plump legs, a beautiful face and wears a blue dress. However, along with Silky's clock, she is never mentioned again.

Policemen in the Land of Dreams

Six men of the law appear when the Faraway Tree friends blow their whistles in Dreamland. They take the group to the swimming baths and proceed to cry, filling the pool with their tears. The policemen then turn into blue fish and swim away.

Rabbits

Generally friendly and helpful creatures, rabbits are to be found in *The Folk of the Faraway Tree* in the Land of Tea Parties, where they act as waiters, dressed in little aprons, scampering around providing everyone with food and drink in the form of such delights as dewdrop and honey sandwiches with ginger beer. (*See also* Brer Rabbit (for Blyton's most celebrated rabbit) and Woffles.)

Red Dragon

Impressive-sounding character who is mentioned when the children first meet Silky. As they knock on her door she calls that if it is the Red Dragon then he must call again next week. Unfortunately, the Dragon is never mentioned again and we do not get to learn more about him.

Red Squirrel

Without the help of this little creature, the organisation of life in the Faraway Tree would go into sharp decline. He features in all three books and stands on guard at the bottom of the Tree, waiting for individuals to shoot through the trap door at the end of the Slippery Slip and out into the wood. He then organises for the cushions that are sat on for the duration of the journey through the Tree to be sent back up through the branches on a pulley-system to Moon-Face. The Red Squirrel has no name, but is distinguished by the red jumper he is always seen to be wearing.

Roundabout Man

Pompous man whom the children meet in Roundabout Land in *The Enchanted Wood*. He is a tall, skinny chap who sings from a book in time with the hurdy-gurdy roundabout music that is constantly playing. He chants 'Hie-diddle-ho-diddle, derry-derry down' as the Land spins around like a roundabout and he is rude when the children break his rhythm. This Land only stops once in a blue moon, but luckily this lunar event *does* occur, which allows Jo, Bessie, Fanny and the rabbits to escape.

Sailor Dolls

Three dolls are found climbing up the Tree in soaking wet clothes, making their way back up to the Land of Toys. They foolishly peep in on the Angry Pixie and he pushes them into some thorns. They then find themselves on the receiving end of Dame Washalot's dirty water. Jo agrees to exchange their sailor costumes for the clothes left in the Land of Toys.

Sandman

The Sandman is traditionally associated with sleepiness, and in Blyton's writing he is to be found in the Land of Dreams in *The Magic Faraway Tree* throwing handfuls of sand into people's eyes which causes immediate drowsiness. He succeeds in sending Moon-Face, Jo, Bessie, Fanny and Dick to sleep, but Silky manages to overcome the lethargy and sets about putting things right. The Sandman's powers are eventually destroyed by the water ruining the fine dryness of his sand, so he is unable to throw it anymore.

Mrs Saucepan

The rosy-cheeked, bright-eyed mother of the Saucepan Man appears in *The Folk of the Faraway Tree* when she leaves her job as cook for Dame Slap, and decides that she will come and live in the Faraway Tree, near her friend, Dame Washalot, and start her own cake shop. Deafness clearly runs in the Saucepan family, as this old lady is terribly hard of hearing, and needs everything to be repeated several times. We never hear anything of a Mr Saucepan, nor is it explained why the Saucepan Man lets his mother spend so many years as the cook to such a formidable woman as Dame Slap.

Saucepan Man

A very distinctive character, thanks to his habit of hanging saucepans, kettles and all manner of crockery around his person, the Saucepan Man features in all three books and is the individual who has the quirkiest and most eccentric personality, which is quite an achievement when he is surrounded by Goblins, Enchanters and jumper-wearing squirrels. He is famous for his deafness, caused by the constant clatter of his utensils around his ears, and the fact that he wears a saucepan over his head. As a result, conversing with him is near impossible. He repeats what he *thinks* has been said and is invariably wrong. Despite this perpetual failure of communication, the Saucepan Man is very much loved by all in the Enchanted Wood, although Curious Connie does not find him quite as wonderful as the others when she first encounters him. The Saucepan Man also has a habit of making up farcical songs:

> *Two books for a book-worm*
> *Two butts for a goat*
> *Two winks for a winkle*
> *Who can't sing a note!*

These songs are usually greeted with shouts of laughter at their sheer silliness, although the Saucepan Man has a real talent for these verses, and actually uses them to get himself out of trouble, by signalling his whereabouts through the lyrics. Saucepan Man is known to have mood swings, as when in *The Folk of the Faraway Tree* he is convinced that nobody wants to meet his mother. The

Saucepan took the brush and dabbed a daisy nearby.

real reason for this is because she lives in the Land of Dame Slap which is a most unpleasant place to visit (*see* Dame Slap and Mrs Saucepan). Saucepan holds Silky and Moon-Face in extremely high reverence, so he is unable to be cross for long, especially when everyone agrees to meet his mother and buy her presents.

The Saucepan Man also makes an appearance in the Noddy books *Cheer Up, Little Noddy* and *Noddy Goes to the Fair*. Here he owns a donkey that Noddy looks after while his car is being mended, and is as deaf and endearing as ever. Where and when the Saucepan Man got his donkey is explained in *Noddy in Toyland*.

Sharp-Nosed Woman Selling Cushions

Eccentric sharp-nosed old lady who crops up at a crucial moment in *The Enchanted Wood*, and appears in no other books involving characters in and beyond the Great Faraway Tree. Her business as a seller of cushions is ingenious, and she certainly must have cornered the market, as she lives in Rocking Land, where standing still and upright is a virtual impossibility. Her cushions provide the necessary padding and coverage needed to sustain any amount of tumbling in this unusual land, and are used by the folk of the Faraway Tree who are not enjoying the bumpy geographical setting in which they have found themselves.

Silky

Exquisite little Elf called Silky because of her extraordinarily long, fair, soft hair that she is permanently brushing. Silky is the golden girl of all three books in the series, and shares many adventures with the children and her peculiar collection of friends. She lives in the Faraway Tree, below Moon-

Silky went down and fetched some more pop biscuits.

Face's house, and is very much loved by Jo, Bessie and Fanny. She is permanently baking 'pop biscuits' which are called so because they explode honey from their centre once they are bitten into.

Silky lives a remarkably civilised life for an Elf, and possesses very human traits (such as concern for others, illustrated when she gives Connie a towel to dry herself after a soaking from Dame Washalot) and practical thinking, which comes into force when she wets the Sandman's sand so that he is unable to send people to sleep with it. This behaviour is completely at variance with J.M. Barrie's view of Fairies or Elves who are described as being particularly nasty in *Peter Pan*, with Tinkerbell as the representative of the fairy kingdom behaving in a resentful and unkind fashion most of the time. Silky is dainty and considerate at all times, and becomes flushed with excitement when she thinks of a way to save the Faraway Tree from certain death by suggesting that caterpillars dig down into the tree, making a path for the others to follow so that they can investigate the problem: 'Silky blushed. It wasn't often that she had better ideas than Moon-Face, but this time she really had thought of something good.'

Silky's Clock

Small clock with a smiley face which Silky obtains in the Land of Take-What-You-Want in the Enchanted Wood. It has two feet which enable it to walk and it communicates by chiming. The clock plays a vital part in the children's escape from Dame Slap when she locks them in a tiny room. It drops its own key, which Moon-Face uses to open the door with a little magic powder, and later wanders about under Dame Slap's feet which allows the others to flee while she chases the heroic timepiece. The clock makes a surprise return at the end of the book when it is a guest at Bessie's birthday party in the wonderful Land of Birthdays.

Singing Cat

Creature found in the Land of Spells in *The Magic Faraway Tree* that bursts into song whenever its tail is pulled. It sings about the age-old problem of whiskers growing too long.

Dame Slap

Described as a tall woman with spectacles, white hair and a big white bonnet, Dame Slap appears in a most objectionable fashion in *The Enchanted Wood* and *The Magic Faraway Tree*. She runs a school full of Pixies who spend their time unwittingly running into terrible trouble with the Dame who deals with their misconduct by issuing resounding slaps in their direction. Moon-Face, Silky, Jo, Bessie, Fanny and Dick find themselves in Dame Slap's vicinity and, before they can escape, they are forced to sit down at desks and answer Dame Slap's absurd questions. One such interrogation runs as follows: 'If a train runs at six miles per hour and has to pass under four tunnels, put down what the guard's mother is likely to have for dinner on Sundays.'

Moon-Face is particularly outraged by the silliness of this demand, which may seem ridiculous since he himself is a man of no conventional appearance who lives in a tree and does business with a jumper-wearing squirrel. But it is this twisting of the commonplace that Blyton excels in when writing about the adventures in the Faraway Tree. Despite the unconventional lifestyles of the characters living in the Tree, there is a vein of absolute integrity running through them that makes it possible to empathise with them and their irritation at being asked such ludicrous questions as 'Why is a blackboard?' by such an unpleasant woman as Dame Slap.

Dame Slap reappears in *The Folk of the Faraway Tree* when the Saucepan Man announces that his mother works as her cook, and decides to pay her a visit. Before long, the group find themselves sitting in Dame Slap's school once again, but, fortunately, are rescued by Saucepan who had taken his mother to the Land of Tea Parties for a treat. Dame Slap then loses her cook, as Mrs Saucepan decides that she would like to come and live in the Faraway Tree and leave the Dame for ever. Dame Slap also stars in a book called *Dame Slap and Her School* which Blyton wrote in 1943.

Sir Stamp-a-Lot

Character of great ferocity who features in the Land of Tempers found at the top of the Faraway Tree. He and his cousin, Lady Yell-Around, are in a perpetual state of fury and frenzied disposition. Sir Stamp-a-Lot threatens to pull out hair, scratch ears and pinch the nose of anyone who dares to interfere with him. There is cause for interference, however, as he takes over Moon-Face's house for his own, and his cousin takes Silky's little home for herself. Luckily for Moon-Face and Silky, these two characters do not have their way for long as their behaviour is reported to the Head Man in the Land of Tempers who makes sure that they are returned to the place where they belong.

Tall Enchanter

A mystical Enchanter with a flowing cape is found in the Land of Enchantments in *The Folk of the Faraway Tree*. Silky ignores Mrs Saucepan's advice and strokes the Enchanter's cat, thus making herself his slave. The Tall Enchanter says that she will be good company for the cat and she can cook the mice he catches.

Teddies on the Clockwork Train

When the Magic Faraway Tree gang arrive at Bears Station in *The Enchanted Wood*, the children are delighted to see lots of different teddy bears walking around. They come in all shapes and sizes, colours and varieties. To communicate, they must press their stomachs and trigger their growls. A blue bear tells them where they can find the house of the Three Bears.

Dame Tell-You-All

Gentlewoman who appears in the Land of Secrets in *The Folk of the Faraway Tree* and is one of the group of extremely wise natives who live in this Land and are able to reveal any secret that you have always yearned to know. Dame Tell-You-All is visited by a tall Elf who wants to know the secret of how to fasten on her wings and fly. Other inhabitants include Witch Know-a-Lot, the Enchanter Wise-Man, Mrs Hidden and the Wizard Tall-Hat.

Topsy-Turvy Policeman

In Topsy-Turvy Land in *The Magic Faraway Tree* the policeman flies into a fury when Jo tells him how ridiculous he looks walking on his hands. As

'It's a biscuit tree!' said the children.

everyone else in Topsy-Turvy Land has a similar gait to this man of the law, it is more likely that Jo is the one who looks ridiculous. A spell is cast upon him so that, however hard he tries to remain upright, he too is forced to walk on his hands. It takes a visit to the Land of Spells to put him right again.

Train Driver in the Land of Do-As-You-Please

Driver who is only too pleased to let Jo drive his train in *The Magic Faraway Tree*. After all, it *is* the Land of Do-As-You-Please. The driver offers him some advice before he steps off, including 'Look out for the level crossing gates, in case they are shut. It would be a pity to bump into them and break them.' Unfortunately, this being a Blyton train, the driving does not go according to plan. All manner of things go wrong, with levers not working and stations being raced past. When they arrive back where they started from, the driver explains why the train wouldn't respond properly: 'Oh, I dare say it wanted to get back at me. It's a monkey sometimes.'

Tree that Sings

This remarkable foliage is found near the top of the Bean-Stalk that is ascended in *The Folk of the Faraway Tree*, and it sings a soft, whispery song about the sun and the rain. Even though the tree is singing in Tree Language, it is perfectly comprehensible to Moon-Face, Silky, the Saucepan Man, Jo, Bessie and Fanny.

Twinkle

Pixie spanked by the notorious Dame Slap for not brushing her hair in *The Enchanted Wood*, and never referred to again.

Very Grand Fairy

Fairy with wealth and beauty who appears in the Land of Secrets in *The Folk of the Faraway Tree*, prompting all kinds of speculation about what she could possibly want, as she seems to have everything. This is all too much for Curious Connie who feels that she simply must discover what the Grand Fairy is going to ask the wise Mrs Hidden. So Connie finds her way into Mrs Hidden's room and listens to the secret in glee, 'shivering with delight'. Alas for Connie, who is shortly afterwards rendered literally speechless for three days as punishment for being so inquisitive.

Dame Washalot

Obsessed with washing clothes to the point of farce, this woman appears in all three books. Has a habit of hurling her dirty soapy water down the Faraway Tree when she has finished with it, soaking anyone who does not dodge out of the way quickly enough. For Jo, Bessie and Fanny avoiding the water becomes a ritual, and part of the fun of climbing the Tree. Dame Washalot does the children a great favour when she takes on their mother's laundry when she is ill and unable to get it all done. For Dame Washalot the prospect of so much washing is enough to send her into raptures, as often she runs out of her own clothes to wash and is reduced to cleaning the leaves of the Faraway Tree. It is safe to conclude that she is addicted to washing.

It is revealed in *The Folk of the Faraway Tree* that Dame Washalot's great friend is Mrs Saucepan, the Saucepan Man's mother, who eventually comes to live near her friend in the great Tree itself.

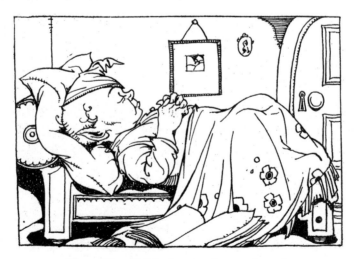

That night old Watzisname slept on the sofa.

Mr Watzisname

As his real name is Kollamoolitoomarellipawkyrollo, this particular character is known as Mr Watzisname for obvious reasons. He himself is unaware of what his real name is until he visits the Land of Know-All where he finds out. His real name fails to catch on. He is usually to be found up the Faraway Tree in his house, fast asleep and snoring with his mouth wide open. The mischievous Moon-Face once popped an acorn into his mouth as he slept, causing a frenzy of rage from Watzisname, who promptly threw Moon-Face through the clouds and into the strange Land at the top of the tree. He's a grumpy person, but one with a heart of gold.

Mr Whiskers

Brownie heading a family of fifty-one other Brownies to be found in the Enchanted Wood. Named Whiskers because of his long facial hair.

Witch's Servant

Flies into a terrible temper in the Land of Spells in *The Magic Faraway Tree* when Jo pulls the black cat's tail in order to hear it sing. The servant had only just obtained the singing spell and is angry that some of its powers are being used up by inquisitive little boys.

Witch Wily

In *The Folk of the Faraway Tree* this rather nasty character chases a Goblin up the Ladder That Has No Top and makes him too afraid to come down. The reason for this is that the Goblin splashed some Giant-Proof paint on the witch, making it impossible for her to do her shopping as no Giant would go near her to sell her any goods. Witch Wily could be a relation of Wizard Wily who features in *The Magic Faraway Tree* as the sinister-sounding friend of the Enchanter. Fortunately, escape is made from all Witches and Wizards of this name.

Wizard Mighty-One

Fearsome but greatly respected wizard who comes up the Tree towards the end of *The Enchanted Wood*, Wizard Mighty-One has green eyes like a cat and is so powerful that even Moon-Face bows before him. The Wizard comes searching for one hundred servants and takes the mischievous red Goblins who are caught in the Slippery Slip. When they try and escape he taps them with his magic wand so they are unable to run away.

Wizard Tall-Hat

Wizard Tall-Hat features in the Land of Secrets in *The Folk of the Faraway Tree* and discloses the Secret of Forgetting to a Goblin who has done a terrible thing and cannot forgive himself. The Wizard suggests that, by doing one hundred good deeds, he may learn to forget about the one bad deed he has done. Jo comments, 'It must be awful to do something wicked and not be able to forget it.' So sympathies are with the little Goblin, as Blyton demonstrates the Christian roots of her writing.

Woffles

Rabbit who acts as a mole for Moon-Face in the closing chapters of *The Folk of the Faraway Tree* when he is sent down the Tree to try and obtain information as to why the Faraway Tree appears to be dying. He returns looking upset and flustered as some strange little Brownies have pulled nearly all the hairs out of his bob-tail. Woffles and a gang of his friends dig a hole that enables them to see into the dangers lurking under the Tree's surface. They are all proud to be of assistance to the great Moon-Face.

Wooden Soldier

A figure from the Land of Toys, this soldier has no name, and is mentioned in *The Magic Faraway Tree* as he climbs down the ladder from his Land, and into the tree below. Moon-Face demands to know where he comes from, for he was expecting the Land of Goodies to be at the top of the tree, not the Land of Toys.

Woodpecker and his Cousins

Feathered friends who come to the rescue in *The Magic Faraway Tree* as they are commissioned to peck a hole through the bark of the Tree so that Moon-Face, Silky and the Saucepan Man can be retrieved from the inside where they have been trapped by Sir Stamp-a-Lot and his cousin, Lady Yell-Around. The woodpeckers are friendly and efficient and before long have made a large enough hole to enable a quick and easy breakout.

THE WISHING CHAIR

The Adventures of the Wishing Chair (1937)
The Wishing Chair Again (1950)

The Wishing Chair is the most alluring of all Blyton inventions and is most certainly a star in its own right, as without it Mollie and Peter would live perfectly normal lives during their school holidays, and Chinky the Pixie would be confined to the imagination. It is stolen by the two children from an antique shop run by a strange wizard and Tippet the Pixie in the opening chapters of the first book, as it takes flight with Peter and Mollie aboard, barging out of the shop and into the sky. From then on the Wishing Chair is a never-ending source of fascination, especially as it is not known when the Chair is next going to sprout its little red wings.

Although the Wishing Chair cannot speak, it has a distinct personality, behaving in a very irrational fashion most of the time, and even gets into a silly, over-excited mood when it ends up wedged in a chimney pot. It certainly undergoes a series of transformations: it is made invisible in order to escape the Polite Pixie, then is painted back again with the help of Witch Snipper, who does not have quite enough paint to finish the job, so there is always an invisible patch on the back of the Chair from then onwards. Its seat is deliberately ripped with scissors and ruined with ink by the children who are afraid that if it looks too smart their mother will want to keep it in the house instead of relegating it to their playroom. It is *nearly* sold to the evil Mr Twisty, is stolen by Tricky the Goblin, sold to Mr Polish of Pin village and then passed on to Mr Spells in his magnificent castle. It has its wings pecked off by a Snoogle and is raided by Grabbit Gnomes, all of whom want the Wishing Chair for themselves. Despite the incredible magic and sorcery that Blyton describes in fairyland and beyond, this Chair is the most coveted possession of all. At least it gets to rest during the term time when the children are at school.

Dame Apple-Pie

The subject of the Town Crier's cry in the market near Buttercup Field. He declares, 'Oyez! Oyez! Dame Apple-Pie has lost her spectacles! Oyez! Oyez!'

Baker

An almost edible character, the Baker is to be found in the Land of Goodies in *The Wishing Chair Again*. He lives with his wife and they are both round, plump, with eyes like currants. His shop is filled with rows upon rows of all kinds of iced cakes. When somebody chooses a cake their name appears magically upon it in white icing sugar.

Blackbird

When the gang visit the Windy Wizard in *The Adventures of the Wishing Chair* to find out how to get Thomas's face back to normal, he decides they need some of the wind that changed his face. With this spell he summons up a blackbird who was present when the mishap occurred: 'Come, birds, and bring / The breeze from your wing.'

Mr Blacky

Golliwog friend of Chinky the Pixie who appears in *The Wishing Chair Again*. Mr Blacky is a very fine fellow indeed and provides a huge army of toys to overthrow the dictatorial Mr Grim. It is mentioned that Mr Blacky is so old that his hair has turned grey. In fact, he is one hundred and fifty-three years old and has been the head of Golliwog village for nearly one hundred years. He comes from this village in Toyland and is very earnest and polite to Peter and Mollie, who are delighted to make his acquaintance.

Brownie from Greatheart's Party

Confident Brownie who is a guest at Magician Greatheart's party. At supper the guests are surprised to find nothing to eat on the long dining table. Greatheart tells them they must wish for what they would like to eat. This Brownie wishes for honey, lemonade and sugar biscuits which immediately appear beside him. The fairy sitting next to him is delighted when her wish of chocolate blancmange and ice cream is granted.

Brownie, Ho-Ho

Pupil at Mr Grim's School for Bad Brownies which can be found in *The Wishing Chair Again*. He befriends the Wishing Chair gang and leads them to the storeroom where their missing toys are kept.

Bus Crew

Chinky and the children take a bus on a journey to get home in *The Adventures of the Wishing Chair*. Mollie and Peter are amazed when they notice that the bus driver is a duck and the conductor is a rabbit.

Bus Drivers of the Dawn Bus

The first of two drivers whom the children meet on the Dawn Bus in *The Wishing Chair Again* is an odd-looking Brownie with a beard so long he ties it around his waist into a bow. He transports Fairies, Wizards, Goblins and the like and foolishly allows Chinky to drive the bus. The poor Pixie is flung out into the road as the driver tries to regain control. As the bus carries on down the road at high speed Mollie and Peter beg him to go back for Chinky. He replies: 'I don't know how to back this bus...I keep meaning to learn but I never seem to have time.' He refuses to stop before a stopping place and declares: 'Full speed ahead is my motto. I've got to get all these tired passengers back home as soon as possible.' He does eventually stop when he falls fast asleep while entering the Land of Dreams.

No ordinary navigator, the second bus driver has some significant comments to make on the subject of his job. Like the first bus driver, he drives the fairy folk around in the Dawn Bus and is quite set on his views on road safety. When Peter asks him, 'Do you like going round corners on two wheels?' he replies that, 'It saves wear and tear on the other two!' His confident statement when the bus nearly veers into a pool of water is: 'I always do that to give the passengers a fright – must give them their money's worth.' (In retrospect he sounds like a fairly standard bus driver.)

Chimney Sweep

This soot-covered little fellow frees the Wishing Chair from a chimney in *The Adventures of the Wishing Chair*. He fixes his brushes together and pushes the Chair out of the chimney much to the relief of its occupants.

Chinky

The most lovable Pixie that Blyton creates, Chinky is an extension of the two children who are the main focus of the Wishing Chair books, but with the added bonus of having magic powers, a large number of interesting relations and many a mystical story to tell. It is mentioned that Chinky is 'not quite so big as the children', and that Mollie and Peter were delighted with the novelty

of having their very own Pixie. It soon becomes plain that Chinky is a great friend to the children, being a merry, obliging fellow with a mind of his own. He has the ingenuity to turn himself into a snowflake when he falls off the Wishing Chair, so that he has a soft landing in the Buttercup Field, and helps the children to learn several important lessons about life through his stormy arguments with his mischievous friend, Winks, which involve turning each other into bad smells and puffs of green smoke.

Chinky's family appear very conventional. He has a greedy cousin called Pipkin who is always thinking and talking about food, and another cousin called Sleep-Alone who is constantly complaining that he never has any peace and quiet. His mother does not seem to worry that her son spends the majority of his time in a playroom with two *children*, who we must remember are as alien to Pixies as Pixies are to humans. Chinky lives with his mother in Fairyland when the two children are away at school, looking after the Wishing Chair for them and waiting eagerly for their return.

Cinders

The magical but jealous black cat belonging to Mr Spells, Cinders takes a great dislike to Winks the naughty Brownie, and claws him at every opportunity.

Dimple

With 'neat, silvery wings and a big dimple in her cheek when she smiled', Dimple the Elf features in *The Adventures of the Wishing Chair* as she participates in the heroic rescue of Chinky the Pixie from the dreaded Enchanter Clip-Clap. She lives in Dimple Cottage and has a servant mouse called Harriet. Provides the children with a spell to make them small enough to try and rescue Chinky without being seen (*see* Enchanter Clip-Clap).

Elves with Invitations

Two friendly Elves visit the children in the playroom and ask to borrow the Wishing Chair. They are going to Magician Greatheart's party and wish to travel by Chair. When the children agree the Elves invite them and Chinky to the party too. The following night the Elves with three Elf friends appear at the playroom in their finest clothes – flower-petal suits sewn with spider web.

Enchanter Clip-Clap

So called because the noise of thunder seems to follow him everywhere. Wears his long beard in a plait that reaches the ground and looks very peculiar as a result. He appears in *The Adventures of the Wishing Chair* as he captures poor little Chinky the Pixie, leaving Peter, Mollie and Chinky's mother, Mrs Twinkle, in a terrible state of anxiety. In order to rescue Chinky from the Magician's clutches, the three enlist the help of a young Elf called Dimple who gives them each a pill to make them as small as mice. This enables them to reach Chinky without being seen by the Magician, or so they think. The Enchanter is too clever for them, sees what they are trying to do, and sends them shooting back to their original sizes. But Chinky manages to outwit him once again by shrinking the Wishing Chair and escaping when the Great Enchanter Clip-Clap is least expecting it.

Freckles

Freckled thrush who appears in *The Adventures of the Wishing Chair* and helps instigate a search for Peter and Mollie's mother's ring that has disappeared somewhere in the garden. Freckles reports back to Chinky that the ring is nowhere to be found in the garden, leaving Chinky immediately suspicious that it must have been taken by Goblins who are not honest when they find a beautiful jewel (*see* Goblin Big-Ears).

Giant Frogs

Blunt-snouted inhabitants of the Snoogle's moat in *The Adventures of the Wishing Chair*. The children dare not escape by swimming across the water for fear that the Giant Frogs will bite them: 'Oooh!' says Mollie. 'I'm not going to jump in there!'

Giant Small-One

Weedy-voiced Giant who features in *The Wishing Chair Again*, and is constantly trying to find a spell to make him as large and powerful as his brother, the magnificent Giant Twisty. The Wishing Chair posse come face to knee-cap with Small-One as they demand to know where the Wandering Castle containing Twisty could have roamed off to.

Giant Too-Big

An extra large giant found near the Wandering Castle in *The Wishing Chair Again*, an acquaintance of Chinky who refers to him as being a 'nice fellow'.

Giant Twisty

Giant Twisty participates in almost the final Wishing Chair show-down. He lives, most inconveniently, in the Wandering Castle which lives up to its name and is never able to stay in one place for any amount of time. The older brother of the rather pathetic Giant Small-One, he captures Chinky and the Wishing Chair in his castle which drifts into the Country of Loneliness where it is possible not to be found for years on end. Peter, Mollie, Winks, Mr Spells and his cat, Cinders, set off to find the Giant and release Chinky, enlisting the help of Chinky's grouchy cousin, Sleep-Alone, who is longing to have the Wandering Castle to himself. Despite being locked behind a door with a Keep Shut Spell, the children and their friends manage to escape, using Mr Spells' intense Go Small Spell that makes them tiny enough to break out without being caught. Giant Twisty is left with no Chinky, no Wishing Chair and no Wandering Castle as Sleep-Alone has stolen it for his own use.

Gnome Doctor

The heroic and jolly-faced Gnome Doctor is majestically brought to the playroom by the Wishing Chair in *The Adventures of the Wishing Chair* after the Ugly Goblin puts Chinky under a Sleeping Spell. He has a silvery beard, a gigantic nose and a large umbrella. We know he is intelligent as he has something in common with a lot of clever Blyton characters – he wears several pairs of glasses. Peter wonders who he is and Mollie, curiously, says that he is some sort of fairy. As midnight approaches he magically produces a towel and soap from the air. After washing Chinky's face he brushes his sleeping eyes with a feather from a peacock. Next he smears his eyelids with a strange scented yellow-coloured ointment. As the clock is about to strike and all seems lost for the Pixie, the Doctor removes a black ball from the air, pours blue powder inside and throws in a match. The explosion shakes the playroom and the spell is broken as Chinky wakes up fit and well if a little hungry.

Gobbo

One of Chinky the Pixie's numerous cousins, Gobbo appears in *The Adventures of the Wishing Chair* as a resident of the village of Apple-Pie. He asks for Chinky's help to rid the village of the Wizard Ho-Ho who catches Pixies and puts horrible spells on them for his own amusement. Peter, Mollie and Chinky immediately board the Wishing Chair and head for the village where Gobbo provides them with coconut cakes and lemonade. Gobbo provides Chinky with a sleeping spell that he uses to send the evil Wizard Ho-Ho to sleep. They then fly off in the Chair to Dame Tap-Tap who Ho-Ho once threatened to turn into a ladybird and who has been waiting to punish him for years. Daily life is thus restored in Apple-Pie village.

Goblin Big-Ears

This questionable character appears in *The Adventures of the Wishing Chair* as the thief who steals Peter and Mollie's mother's diamond ring. Chinky realises that he has been about in their garden by chanting a Goblin spell that reveals blue smoke if such a creature has been present. This Big-Ears appears to have no connection to the famous Toy Town creation of the same name as he is a terrible coward and very sly, living in a little yellow cottage at the foot of the hill in Goblin Town. Goblin Big-Ears stammers in fright at the sight of the children and Chinky coming to retrieve their property and yelps that he has given the ring to the Snoogle.

Grabbit Gnomes

The appropriately named Grabbit Gnomes appear in the opening chapters of *The Adventures of the Wishing Chair* and spend their time seizing everything in their path, especially things that do not belong to them. They are enchanted by the sight of the Wishing Chair, standing luminous in the moonlight, and immediately pile on to it, yelping and screeching to one another. Chinky the

Pixie has other ideas, and ties one of the legs of the chair to a tree so that it cannot fly away, but hovers in mid-air with the zealous little Gnomes unable to escape. They are scattered in all directions when the Wishing Chair finally bumps to the ground, and never appear again.

> *Someone was leaning out of the window of a big toadstool house, pointing at the children. In a trice all the Grabbit Gnomes woke up and came pouring out of their houses. 'Robbers! What are you doing here? Robbers!'*
> THE ADVENTURES OF THE WISHING CHAIR

Mr Grim

Suitably named gentleman who runs the School for Bad Brownies. Rather like Dame Slap in *The Magic Faraway Tree*, Mr Grim spends his time scolding and spanking the naughty Brownies who long to escape but cannot help behaving badly and deserving their scoldings. He is described as 'a big, burly brownie with a tremendous beard falling to the floor, with pointed ears and shaggy eyebrows that almost hid his eyes'. Chinky and the two children find themselves sitting in Mr Grim's class where such ridiculous questions are asked as 'If I take fifty-two hairs from my beard, how many will I have left?' Mr Grim is a dishonest man, stealing Chinky's wand which flew to his school out of the playroom window with wings that sprouted from the growing ointment Mollie carelessly rubbed on it. He is eventually overthrown with the help of Mister Blacky the Golliwog and his army of toys.

Dame Handy Pandy

Neighbour of Mr Spells' mother and Mr Piggle-Pie in *The Wishing Chair Again*.

Harriet

Neatly dressed in a check cap and apron, Harriet is the mouse servant to Dimple the Elf of Dimple Cottage. Harriet appears in *The Adventures of the Wishing Chair* as she answers the door to Peter and Mollie who are trying to rescue their friend Chinky the Pixie from the Enchanter Clip-Clap.

Harriet's Aunt

Kindly aunt to Harriet the Mouse who is found in the tunnel in *The Adventures of the Wishing Chair*. Wears large spectacles and lives in a home constructed mostly from paper. She shows the children the way into the cellars so they can set about rescuing Chinky the Pixie.

Hoot

Owl summoned by Mr Spells in *The Wishing Chair Again*. The Wishing Chair flies away with Chinky hanging on upside down by his foot and it is hoped that Hoot might have seen where he flew off to. He is described as an intelligent bird who never misses anything that happens at night. Mr Spells casts a spell to make it night-time and blows through his hands to call like an owl. Hoot explains to the magician that he did indeed see Chinky and followed him to the Wandering Castle.

Uncle Jack

The children go off for the day with their uncle Jack in *The Adventures of the Wishing Chair* after a quarrel with Chinky. After a visit to the farm he buys them a lovely black puppy which is, strangely, never mentioned again.

Jane

Housemaid to the children in *The Adventures of the Wishing Chair*.

Mr Knobbles

See Mr Twisty.

Little Round Man

A man described as being 'little' and 'round' features in Buttercup Field in *The Adventures of the Wishing Chair*. He speaks in riddles and asks the children, Mollie and Peter, 'Have you seen a horse that quacks like a duck?' The children find him quite infuriating as they are looking for their good friend Chinky the Pixie who has vanished without trace.

The chair rose up very high indeed, far beyond the housetops, and flew towards the children's home.

Little Round Woman

Plump lady who can be found along with the Little Round Man in Buttercup Field in *The Adventures of the Wishing Chair*. She carries a bundle on her head and sings as she comes towards the children. When Peter asks if she has seen a Pixie (Chinky) falling from the sky she rudely answers: 'No. Have you?' Mollie replies that she has and the Little Round Woman calls her a fibber.

Maggle-Mig

Magical creature created by Winks after he steals Witch Wendle's wand in *The Wishing Chair Again*. Resembles a small feathered giraffe with a shoe on each of its four feet. Chinky is furious when it chases him, and grabs his magic wand from the toy cupboard to change the Maggle-Mig into a Snickeroo which attacks Winks. The Pixie and Brownie start to fight and end up turning one another into a puff of smoke and a bad smell respectively. Just as it seems that all is lost for them, Witch Wendle saves the day and restores both to their usual, if a little embarrassed, selves.

Magician Greatheart

Peter, Mollie and Chinky are invited to Magician Greatheart's party in *The Adventures of the Wishing Chair*, and spend a wonderful evening in the Magician's Palace, flying through the eerie moonlight on the Wishing Chair to this most exclusive of destinations. The Magician himself is 'tall and handsome with eyes that look right through people', and he certainly knows how to throw a good party. His guests are allowed to wish what they would like to eat, and Mollie requests cream buns and ginger beer while her brother opts for treacle pudding and a jug of lemonade. The Greatheart Magician presents each guest with an egg which he claims will hatch into a present by morning. Sure enough, Peter's hatches into a silver watch, and Mollie's into a bead necklace.

Magician Sly Boots

This curiously named fellow is alluded to in *The Wishing Chair Again*. Ho-Ho the Brownie explains that Mr Grim might be planning to sell the children's missing toys to this Magician. Quite why he would want them is a different matter.

Merman

It is fortunate that a Merman appears in *The Adventures of the Wishing Chair* as Peter and Mollie and Chinky the Pixie are stranded in the water, thanks to Mollie's silliness in wanting to visit the Disappearing Island, which predictably disappears as soon as they get too close. The Merman offers to pull the strange party ashore, including the soaking Wishing Chair.

Mollie

Mollie and her brother Peter are the main characters in the Wishing Chair stories. Very like Jo, Bessie and Fanny in *The Magic Faraway Tree*, they are classic Blyton children who do their best to do what is right most of the time, but find it very hard to resist an adventure, particularly those involving Giants, Enchanters and Snoogles. Mollie is lucky enough to know that her brother and their great pal Chinky the Pixie will always be there to look after her. As Chinky states: 'Both Peter and I know we have to look after you because you're a girl. We had to think of you, didn't we, Peter?' Mollie has the inevitable Blyton girl tendency to cry in times of difficulty, although it is often stated that Mollie is 'half afraid' or 'almost crying'. The irony of the situation lies in the fact that most of the girls Blyton writes about seem to show

Mollie was so disappointed that she cried into her handkerchief.

remarkable bravery in their day-to-day existence, fending off pirates or evil goblins with remarkable calm, give or take a few tears here and there. Mollie is always champing at the bit to explore new lands in the Wishing Chair, throwing caution to the wind and preparing to face anything that comes her way with gay abandon, including Grabbit Gnomes, the Windy Wizard and Mr Grim.

It is also made clear that Mollie is a fan of Blyton's writing, as she exclaims in delight when Chinky mentions that he has visited the Faraway Tree, demanding: 'Did you see Moon-Face and Silky and the old Saucepan Man? I've read the books about the Faraway Tree and always wished I could climb it!' This self-referencing is a typically Blyton device. (*See* Susie in The Secret Seven.)

Mother

Peter and Mollie's mother is quite happy for her children to spend their school holidays playing with a Pixie called Chinky and a strange chair that deposits them in a variety of mysterious lands, but this is probably because she has no idea that this is what they are doing. She is barely mentioned in the two books in the Wishing Chair series, but because of the one-dimensional nature of her character, this is no real shame.

Peter

Peter and his sister Mollie are the two children lucky enough to own a magical Wishing Chair with the power to take them wherever they choose to go. They accept the arrival of this amazing gimmick in their lives with astonishing cool, apparently feeling that it is inevitable that this wonderful piece of equipment has come their way. Peter is brave and clever and, like all good boys, makes sure that he looks after his sister at all times. He also knows exactly how to deal with adults who try to take the Wishing Chair away, including the bizarre Mr Twisty who receives a very terse reply from Peter when he suggests buying the Chair: 'Certainly not! Please go away or I'll call the gardener!' This is pretty impressive coming from a young boy, but Blyton lads with the name of Peter seem to possess a firm authority that they feel free to exercise at any time.

Peter, Mollie and their great friend Chinky the Pixie find themselves immersed in escapades of the most peculiar variety when travelling aboard the Wishing Chair. During term time they attend boarding school, which they both love, but they are always longing to return to their playroom for more excitement in the holidays.

Mr Piggle-Pie

The bad-tempered neighbour of Mrs Spells in *The Wishing Chair Again*, Mr Piggle-Pie is annoyed at the noise the Wishing Chair gang are making and shouts at them that he will get dressed and chase them. Cinders the cat warns Winks that Mr Piggle-Pie will spank him for making such a racket.

Pipkin

Plump and greedy cousin of Chinky the Pixie who lives in the Land of Goodies. Pipkin extends an invitation to Chinky, Winks the Brownie and the children (Peter and Mollie) to visit him in this enchanted place. He has a biscuit tree in his garden which is wonderful until there is hot weather when the chocolate melts all over the little Pixie asleep underneath. Pipkin is a generous and portly chap, and the group spend a splendid afternoon with him, stuffing themselves with all manner of delicious goodies. Winks is imprisoned for eating part of someone's house, but escapes by eating through the chocolate-cake prison walls.

Pixie King

Chinky the Pixie makes several references to the Pixie King when they encounter the Snoogle in *The Adventures of the Wishing Chair*. At first he threatens that he will send the Chair to fetch him. He says that the King will punish the Snoogle by taking away his castle for daring to interfere with a Pixie. He later suggests that they escape from the castle by sending a bird to fetch the King. Unfortunately there are no birds to be found in the Land of the Snoogle.

Pixies

Four all-singing, all-dancing Pixies whom Chinky summons to help reveal the whereabouts of the stolen cat, Whiskers. They appear when he claps softly three times, loudly three times, whistles like a blackbird and utters the magic words 'Looma, looma, looma loo'. Chinky sits in the Chair looking into his magic mirror as the children watch in amazement. The four Pixies hold hands and dance around Chinky and the Wishing Chair while chanting a magic spell. As they dance faster and faster their singing gets higher and higher pitched until Chinky is able to see Whiskers in his magic mirror.

Policemen

A pair of policemen chase after Winks when he causes chaos in the Land of Goodies. He is enjoying himself so much that he tries to eat the chimney from a house. It crashes to the ground and the policemen blow their whistles and arrest the naughty Brownie. Chinky and the children leave him to face his punishment. Later that evening he returns to the playroom after a hungry escape eating the chocolate-cake prison walls.

Mr Polish

Runs a furniture shop and is the father of Polly Polish. Lives in Pin, the tidiest village ever seen. (*See* Polly Polish and Small Elf Looking Rather Alarmed.)

Polish, Polly

Appears in *The Wishing Chair Again* as the daughter of Mr Polish who runs the furniture shop in Pin. Pin is the neatest village that has ever been known, with not a blade of grass out of place. Polly Polish tells Peter, Mollie and Chinky the Pixie that her father is delighted to have a complete set of six chairs, instead of the five that he has had for years. One of these chairs is the children's Wishing Chair. In order to find out which one it is, they look for a little invisible patch at the back of their chair where there was not enough paint to make it entirely detectable again after the children had been forced to make it disappear to escape the Polite Pixie.

Dame Quick-Fingers

Part of Chinky the Pixie's huge family, Dame Quick-Fingers is his great-aunt, and Chinky suggests that he and the children, Peter and Mollie, visit her in order to find a spell for growing back wings on the Wishing Chair. The Dame owns a pack of six flying dogs, lives in a snug little cottage, and is ready to provide the visitors with sticky treacle tarts while she makes up the Wing-Growing ointment necessary to install new wings on the Chair. When they grow back, much to the children's delight, the wings are big and green and yellow, not small and red as they had been previously.

Rosebud

Doll belonging to Mollie in *The Wishing Chair Again*. Mollie is naughty and bored one afternoon, and spreads some of Dame Quick Fingers' Wing-Growing ointment on to Rosebud. She is delighted to see her 'gaily flying around the room', but not so pleased when Rosebud zooms out of the window and into the garden, along with Peter's toy engine and several other playroom toys.

> *The goblin bowed politely. 'It doesn't matter at all!' he said. 'What a marvellous chair you have and how pleased I am to see you! Pray sit down and let me give you some lemonade.'*
> THE ADVENTURES OF THE WISHING CHAIR

Round-Faced Gnome

Gnome who attempts to rescue the Wishing Chair gang when they are stuck in a large red chimney in *The Adventures of the Wishing Chair* by fetching the local chimney sweep.

Sheep

A large old sheep is found knitting and running a toffee shop in the Land of Dreams experienced in *The Adventures of the Wishing Chair*. Mollie asks for a bag of toffee, but when she opens it up green peas are revealed.

Showing-Off Clock

Over-inquisitive clock belonging to Witch Snippet. It is so enthralled by the repainting of the Wishing Chair that it leaps down off the mantelpiece to observe proceedings from a closer angle. It makes this cameo appearance in *The Adventures of the Wishing Chair*.

Sleep-Alone

Cousin of Chinky the Pixie. As his name implies, his one aim in life is to have a decent night's kip without being disturbed by the plethora of sprites, elves, fairies and goblins that inhabit his world. He features in *The Wishing Chair Again*, is usually extremely grumpy and travels around in his private boat and plane, looking for suitable locations in which to nod off. He is described as being 'more like a brownie than a pixie' with a long beard winding around him like a scarf. Sleep-Alone is first stumbled upon when Chinky, Peter and Mollie are attempting to find the Land of Goodness Knows Where, and he is extremely curt with them, telling Mollie that she is 'a very stupid little girl' as she does not know that the obvious way to find the Land of Goodness Knows Where is to ask Goodness. He also threatens to drop Chinky from his aeroplane into the Land of Rubbish which suggests that family values are waning in this particular pixie/goblin tribe.

Slipperies

The Slipperies make a brief and unwelcome appearance in *The Wishing Chair Again* as they attempt to get their greasy hands on the Chair by telling the children to look out for Dame Quick Fingers' pack of flying dogs which are nowhere to be seen. Each Slippery is described as having one blue eye and one green, and none of them can look straight at the children. Their hair is slick and smooth and their mouths are perpetually smiling, as they rub their hands together in glee. They scamper away in terror when Peter threatens to whistle for the dogs and send them chasing after them.

Small Elf Looking Rather Alarmed

Elf who helps the children to find out where the Wishing Chair can be in *The Wishing Chair Again*. He shows the children how to use a Fairy Ring by gathering inside it and finding the secret button that shoots the group downwards as if they were in a lift. They travel to the immaculate village of Pin to find out where the Wishing Chair has been taken. As Mollie comments: 'If only people knew how near their gardens are to curious and wonderful places, how surprised they would be!'

Small Goblin

Goblin resting in the Silver Buttercup Field in *The Wishing Chair Again* who overhears Giant Small-One's servant revealing the whereabouts of the Wandering Castle to Twisty. Mr Spells stops him while he is walking up High Hill and he tells everyone that the Castle has gone to 'Loneliness'.

Small Pixie

Tiny Pixie stopped by Mr Spells as she runs down the High Hill in *The Wishing Chair Again*. Spells asks her where the Wandering Castle is located and she replies, 'Let me see, now – I saw it yesterday … Yes, I remember now. It's in the Silver Buttercup Field, sir.' Mr Spells explains that the local enchanters are always trying out silly new spells and the shimmering Silver Buttercup Field is the result of one of them.

Snickeroo

Animal resembling a small crocodile with horns (*see* Maggle-Mig).

Snoogle

The Snoogle appears in two chapters of *The Adventures of the Wishing Chair*, though he is a fascinating creation who deserves more focus. The Snoogle has the body of a dragon, the tail of a cat and the head of a yellow duck, yet curiously enjoys boiled eggs. Unsurprisingly, it is a rather confused creature who is actually more scared of Peter, Mollie and Chinky the Pixie than they are of its extraordinary appearance. Although he succeeds in capturing the children and Chinky in his castle, after pecking off the Wishing Chair's four red wings, it is not long before they manage to escape, as the Snoogle had obviously not counted on the Wishing Chair growing back its wings so quickly.

Mr Spells

Mr Spells features in *The Wishing Chair Again* and can be reached by travelling on the bus to Tall Hill and then the boat to The Hill. He lives in a castle in the shape of a cottage, or a cottage in the shape of a castle, and is described as 'quite a nice fellow' by the Small Elf Looking Rather Alarmed. Mr Spells buys the Wishing Chair as one of a set of six from Mr Polish, although the Wishing Chair is the only one with any magical powers, and Peter and Mollie set off to find out what he has done with it. On finding the chair in his castle/cottage, the children attempt to fly off with Chinky who has come to try and explain to Mr Spells about the confusion but is put into a deep sleep. The children get no further than the garden in the Wishing Chair, as Mr Spells succeeds in lassoing them down. Once he has heard their story, however, he decides to let them go free, and take Chinky with them.

Mr Spells puts in another appearance in *The Wishing Chair Again* when the children ask for his help to find Chinky who disappears hanging off the Wishing Chair by a rope caught up round one of his feet. He leads them to the Giant Twisty's Wandering Castle where Chinky has been taken captive, and they instigate a remarkable rescue of the little Pixie.

Mrs Spells

The children and Winks meet the mother of the remarkable Mr Spells in *The Wishing Chair Again* when they go in search of her son. A kindly old lady, she provides them with strawberryade, strawberry-shaped strawberry ice and biscuits with tiny sugar strawberries in the middle.

Spot

The Wishing Chair mysteriously mutates into a dog called Spot in the Land of Dreams visited by Mollie, Peter and Chinky the Pixie. Spot is chased by a clown who catches Chinky and turns into a policeman. At this same moment, Spot changes into a duck, and the policeman becomes a 'blue motor van that trundles itself down the street'.

Tall Wizard

This long-bearded fellow with a deep voice, like the rumbling of faraway thunder, is tall and thin with a pointed wizard's cap that makes him look even bigger. He is found in the first chapter of *The Adventures of the Wishing Chair* in Tippet's shop. In fact, judging by the way he shouts at Tippet, he is most probably the owner of the shop, and therefore the original owner of the Wishing Chair.

Dame Tap-Tap

See Gobbo.

Thomas

Features in *The Adventures of the Wishing Chair* and undergoes a grisly experience when he pulls awful faces and the wind changes. He is invited over to play soldiers with Mollie and Peter, and despite their warnings, proceeds to pull ridiculous expressions until his face is stuck with his nose wrinkled and his cheeks blown out. It is fortuitous for the silly boy that Chinky is able to think of a way to help, and he and Peter set off to see the Windy Wizard who is able to restore Thomas's face to its rather dour normality.

Tickles

When Chinky misses his dinner at Mr Grim's School he is so hungry on his return to the playroom that he goes for supper with Tickles. He explains this in a note to Mollie and Peter.

Tippet

Described as being both pixiey and gnome-like, Tippet appears in *The Adventures of the Wishing Chair*. He is crucial to the overall structure of the book as it is he who is responsible for the Chair before the two children get their hands on it. He is a grumpy-looking man who runs the antique shop where Peter and Mollie purchase their mother's birthday present. He complains to himself as he opens up various boxes, looking for a piece of paper to wrap their gift in, and reveals a red fox, a cloud of butterflies and a magical black cat instead. He is furious when the children fall into the Wishing Chair and it flies away with them, and screams at them to 'Wish it back! Wish it back!'

Town Crier

A traditional Town Crier is to be found in the Buttercup Field in *The Adventures of the Wishing Chair*. Mollie and Peter beg him to ring his bell and ask the crowd whether anyone has seen the lost pixie, Chinky. They have a great response from a number of people who have seen a large snowflake fall from the sky, but not a pixie.

Off they went, flying through the moonlight.

Tricky

There has never been any suggestion that the Bristol-based trip-hop artist took his name from this cunning little Goblin in *The Wishing Chair Again*, but it is possible. Tricky is a naughty creature, always out to make a quick buck, and steals the Wishing Chair from Peter and Mollie's playroom in order to try and sell it to Mr Polish of Pin village. He then recommends that Mr Spells buys the chair off Mr Polish, and attempts to steal the chair back for himself, to sell it on once again, as it is very valuable. A dodgy dealer of a Goblin who ends up playing musical chairs with Chinky and getting into a terrible fight.

Mrs Twinkle

Mother of Chinky the Pixie, Mrs Twinkle is an elderly Pixie who looks after Chinky when he is not with the two children, Peter and Mollie, and is a great provider of ginger buns and lemonade. The two children meet her when Chinky disappears without trace, and they plan a rescue mission to release him from the Enchanter Clip-Clap.

Mr Twisty

Sly-looking individual who appears in *The Adventures of the Wishing Chair* and makes valiant efforts to buy the chair from Peter and Mollie. He offers the children's mother two pounds for it and Mother agrees on the price and tells him to come back to collect the chair that night. Peter and Mollie are distraught until they enlist the help of Mr Knobbles, the carpenter, to make a duplicate chair that they can sell to Mr Twisty without him realising the truth. Mr Knobbles, a bald-headed Pixie with large ears and a house under the big oak tree, can make such a replica only with the help of a 'quick spell' which will enable him to work three times as fast as usual. He purchases the spell and sets to work, and has the job finished in time for the reappearance of the devious Mr Twisty, so the Wishing Chair is saved.

Ugly Goblin

Villainous creature who spitefully casts a Sleeping Spell on poor Chinky in *The Adventures of the Wishing Chair*. To make things worse the Chair decides to grow wings and fly off, leaving the children without any way of seeking help. The Ugly Goblin tiptoes into the playroom and gleefully informs Peter and Mollie that 'I meant to steal the Chair before he woke up – but you came! Now I'm going to find the Chair!' He leaves by warning that if the children don't find a way to break the spell and wake Chinky, by midnight the Pixie will vanish for ever.

Whiskers

The black cat belonging to Peter and Mollie in *The Adventures of the Wishing Chair* is kidnapped by Witch Kirri-Kirri who requires the assistance of the lovable feline in her kitchen. Chinky the Pixie explains that, 'Black cats are clever with spells.' The children and Chinky make their way to the Witch's house by train and, once hidden in her garden, make sounds like mice so that the Witch will send Whiskers out to deal with them. Whiskers is successfully caught and returns home with the children, being very wary of falling asleep on the naughty Wishing Chair again!

Windy Wizard

The Windy Wizard appears in *The Adventures of the Wishing Chair* as the only being who can restore the countenance of a foolish boy called Thomas who pulled faces when the wind changed. The Windy Wizard lives in a draught-ridden house and states that the only way to help Thomas is to possess some of the wind that changed his face. In order to acquire such an elemental force of nature the Wizard calls a blackbird that has some of the wind stored in its wings. The wind is packed into some bellows, and is let out in Thomas's distorted face which at once regains its old shape.

Winks

Perhaps the naughtiest Brownie in Mr Grim's School for Bad Brownies, Winks simply cannot help misbehaving. He was originally sent to Mr Grim for turning all of his grandmother's pigs blue, yet is a particularly endearing character. When Mr Grim is overthrown by Mister Blacky and his army, Winks returns to the playroom with Chinky and the two children. Winks is a terrible story-teller and tries to catch out the Land of Goodies by pretending that his favourite soup is pepper-flavoured, feeling sure that such a horrid flavour will not exist. It does, and the silly Brownie is forced to have a few mouthfuls. He is imprisoned in the Land of Goodies for breaking off part of someone's edible house and trying to eat it, but he breaks out of jail by gnawing his way through the chocolate-flavoured walls. When he visits the powerful Mr Spells the wizard turns Winks' hands blue in punishment for his meddling ways, so he knows how his grandmother's pigs must have felt. In the end, Winks' behaviour is so very bad that he is sent back to Mr Grim's school for the term time, but is allowed to visit the children in the playroom during the holidays. They cannot help feeling fond of the naughty little fiend.

Witch Kirri-Kirri

A very powerful Witch with her own railway station (Kirri-Kirri Station) appears in *The Adventures of the Wishing Chair* as she steals Whiskers, Peter and Mollie's beloved cat.

Witch Snippet

Resident of the Spinning House in Jiffy Wood which can stop circulating only for a brief time. The Witch has a kind face with bright-blue eyes 'the colour of forget-me-nots', and she supplies the children Peter and Mollie and Chinky the Pixie with very strong paint that has the property of restoring visibility to things that have been made invisible. The Wishing Chair has been made unobservable in order to escape from the Polite Goblin, which is understandably inconvenient for those using it as a regular form of transport. Witch Snippet is very accommodating and the Wishing Chair looks almost back to its old self when they have finished with it, except there is not quite enough paint to finish off a tiny part at the back of the chair. This area remains invisible, which comes in useful in *The Wishing Chair Again* when the children have to identify their chair among other replicas.

Witch Wendle

Appears in the final chapters of *The Wishing Chair Again* and is vital to the story because, without her help, Chinky the Pixie and Winks the naughty Brownie would remain a puff of green smoke and a bad smell respectively for the rest of their lives. Chinky and Winks are in terrible tempers and put spells on one another that the two children, Peter and Mollie, have no idea how to undo. The Wishing Chair obligingly grows its wings, and the children request to be taken to Witch Wendle, from whom the disobedient Winks has stolen a very magic wand. Witch Wendle has sparkly eyes, a smiling face, lives in a castle in the clouds and knows that to recover Chinky and Winks they must travel by Wishing Chair to the Land of Spells. It is worth mentioning that this land appears at the top of the Faraway Tree in *The Magic Faraway Tree* (1943) and to reach this land the children and the witch travel through the Village of Stupids, the Land of No-Goods and the Country of Try-Again.

Witch Wendle is successful in her mission to retrieve Chinky and Winks, and Winks is actually poured out of a teapot while the witch uses a magic chant:

> *Teapot, teapot, pour for me,*
> *A brownie naughty as can be*
> *He's not as clever as he thinks*
> *That wicked, wilful little Winks!*

It is also Witch Wendle who sends Winks back to Mr Grim's School for Bad Brownies as punishment for stealing her wand.

Witch with the Book of Goodness

In order to find the Land of Goodness Knows Where, Chinky the Pixie, Peter and Mollie refer to a book belonging to a witch in *The Wishing Chair Again*. This witch throws her book of Goodness into the middle of her kitchen floor and it begins to glow, ready to give out any information that the little group wish to know. Just as they are finding out where the Land is, they hear the sound of flapping wings, and the Wishing Chair disappears without them.

Wizard Ho-Ho

See Gobbo.

Yellow Bird

Appears in *The Adventures of the Wishing Chair* where it dives down to the ground, picks up Chinky the Pixie in its beak, and deposits him in the home of the Enchanter Clip-Clap. Curiously, a yellow bird also features in Arthur Miller's *The Crucible* as the symbol of evil and mayhem in the town of Salem. Was he a secret Blyton fan?

MR PINKWHISTLE

The Adventures of Mr Pinkwhistle (1941)
Mr Pinkwhistle Interferes (1950)
Mr Pinkwhistle's Party (1955)

MR PINKWHISTLE

Mr Pinkwhistle has the burden of being half-man and half-Brownie, which results in an identity crisis that causes a great deal of anxiety. He finds that humans will not speak to him as he is not all human, and Brownies will not speak to him as he is not all Brownie. How he came to be such a strange and conflicting mix is never revealed but, whatever Mr Pinkwhistle is, he is one of Blyton's most endearing heroes. He is described as 'kind, but fierce too when he is putting things right!' And, indeed, this is what Mr Pinkwhistle delights in. He sees it as his personal responsibility to keep his neighbourhood happy, and to make sure that any wrongdoers have their come-uppance, thus restoring perfect harmony to all.

He owns a cat called Sooty who has powers of wizardry and is a proficient conversationalist and problem-solver in his own right. Sooty is the only living creature that knows Mr Pinkwhistle's secret – the ability to make himself invisible at any time – which comes in extremely useful when he is playing tricks on naughty children. He tends to fly into a great state of indignation when he hears that people, particularly children, the elderly or the misshapen,

are suffering unhappiness of any kind, and his efforts to amend various situations usually involve teaching someone a lesson and making them realise the error of their ways. His catch phrase, 'It just doesn't seem fair!', is usually coupled with a stamping of his foot in indignation. It is certainly true that Mr Pinkwhistle's reason for existence is to help those who have been wronged, so he depends on a regular supply of naughty children and misbehaviour in order to keep his job of teaching them a lesson.

Sooty

A black and very magic cat, Sooty appears in all three books and is the one companion of Mr Pinkwhistle. Sooty does a little problem-solving of his own in the story *Mr Pinkwhistle's Cat Is Very Busy*, but generally leaves the good works to his earnest and committed master. In *The Adventures of the Wishing Chair* Chinky the Pixie mentions that 'black cats are very clever with spells', and Sooty is certainly a remarkable feline to keep the secret of Mr Pinkwhistle's strange genealogy to himself.

AMELIA JANE

Naughty Amelia Jane (1939)
Amelia Jane Again (1946)
More About Amelia Jane (1954)

Aimed at some of her youngest readers, Amelia Jane, the mischievous rag doll, featured in many of Blyton's *Sunny Stories* and was based on a doll belonging to Blyton's daughter, Gillian. The recurring theme of these books is simple – Amelia Jane loves to create anarchy in the nursery and is frequently up to tricks that exasperate the other toys greatly.

Amelia Jane

'A big, long-legged doll with an ugly face, a bright red frock, and black curls', Amelia Jane is the most famous of Blyton's dolls, and the least well behaved. But one must remember that Amelia Jane was made at home, and home-made toys, as Blyton tells us, are never as well behaved as shop toys.

In *Naughty Amelia Jane* she runs riot with Nanny's scissors, damaging the curtains and hearth rug and cutting one of Nanny's best handkerchiefs into twenty-two tiny pieces. Most appallingly of all, she snips the Pink Rabbit's tail off. Only the intervention of the Brownies prevents further destruction. The Pink Rabbit is not the only toy to suffer at the hands of Amelia Jane. The Clockwork Mouse is squirted with soda water, while Tom the Toy Soldier is wet and uncomfortable for two days after having a jug of milk poured down his neck.

The other toys get their revenge on many occasions, each time prompting Amelia Jane

'Shoes!' said Amelia Jane. 'Whatever do you mean?'

to turn over a new leaf. There are examples of Amelia Jane being good, perhaps most famously when flying a toy aeroplane to rescue the Brownies from the Goblins, and let it not be forgotten that Amelia Jane also saved the Clockwork Mouse when it inadvertently set fire to itself. But her good behaviour is always only temporary. The final word on Amelia Jane should be left to fellow nursery toy, Bear, who observes, 'When she's good she's very, very good – but when she's bad she's horrid!'

> *The pink rabbit cried all the more when he heard that. 'I don't want to be like a guinea pig,' he wept. 'I want to be like a rabbit! I hate Amelia Jane! Punish her, Tom! She is a very wicked doll!'*
> *NAUGHTY AMELIA JANE*

Cowboy Doll

Creates havoc with his long rope during a brief visit to the nursery in *Naughty Amelia Jane*. Has a most wicked face and, with Amelia Jane always there to prompt him, lassoes many of the nursery toys.

Mister Noah

Mister Noah lives in the wooden ark and has no time for Amelia Jane, refusing even to say good morning to her.

Tibbs

Tibbs has an uneasy relationship with the other toys. They object to him chewing them from time to time, while Tibbs himself is often blamed unfairly for Amelia Jane's misdemeanours.

MR TWIDDLE

Hello, Mr Twiddle (1942)
Well Really, Mr Twiddle! (1953)

*He wore the bright red kitchen tablecloth round his shoulders,
the waste-paper basket for a hat; he had a yellow duster in his
pocket instead of a handkerchief, and he carried the kitchen
poker for his stick! Really Mr Twiddle!'*

HELLO, MR TWIDDLE

Mr Twiddle

Mr Twiddle causes pandemonium during the course of two books through his
illogical, ridiculous behaviour. If he is not smoking his fountain pen and
putting his pipe into the ink stand, he is wrestling with snowmen and putting
the clock into the oven, or cleaning his teeth with glue instead of toothpaste.

His long-suffering wife is well aware of her husband's lack of common
sense and is frequently heard making comments such as 'You want brains as
well as legs, dear Twiddle!' Despite her continual sarcasm towards the man,
she makes the same old mistakes in agreeing to let Twiddle take on simple
tasks that are too much for him to cope with. Mr Twiddle feels that 'There
always seemed something to do, just as he had himself nicely settled.' He is

certainly under the thumb of his demanding wife who makes sure that he is never allowed to rest for too long. Yet Mr Twiddle remarks with great authority that 'Some folks call me a stupid man, but it isn't many who can tie a shoe-lace with one hand.' He is good-humoured and obliging despite his shortcomings, which is just as well, as he is even recorded emptying an entire box of fireworks directly onto a bonfire, much to his wife's obvious distress. Yet she is genuinely fond of Twiddle and remarks, 'You'll make me die of laughing one of these days!'

MR MEDDLE

Mr Meddle's Mischief (1940)
Mr Meddle's Muddles (1950)
Merry Mr Meddle (1954)

Mr Meddle

Mr Meddle, 'a Pixie who could not mind his own business', is rather like Mr Twiddle in that he is quite incapable of performing any task, however simple, with any degree of success. He causes unprecedented mayhem in the houses of his friends and neighbours as he tries to help them out in their daily routine and fails completely, breaking Mother Hey-Ho's best milk jug and then pouring boiling hot and freezing cold water over her as he tries to wash her hair. His organisational skills reach their zenith when he sends his friend Pippin and his wife on a train to Orange Town instead of Lemon Village, much to their obvious distress.

He is unable to resist meddling with things, hence his name, and never seems to learn from his mistakes, which is another similarity with the equally

goofy Mr Twiddle. Being a Pixie, Meddle has pointed ears which go with the air of mischief and chaos that surrounds him. Like Twiddle, Mr Meddle is an endearing character who cannot help being in the wrong place at the wrong time.

THE THREE GOLLIWOGS

The Three Golliwogs (1944)

Today, a story about toys whom nobody liked 'because of their black faces', with the names of Golly, Woggie and Nigger and the title *The Three Golliwogs*, would quite rightly be considered outrageously politically incorrect. However, at the time of Blyton's writing, language had not become so racially sensitive, as is illustrated in Agatha Christie's *Ten Little Niggers*, the title of which was changed to *Ten Little Indians* for television purposes. So it is important to keep Blyton's characters within their political and social era because, apart from anything else, she is revealing to us a great deal about the attitudes held at that time towards people of different races.

Golly, Woggie and Nigger are actually rather adorable characters, as are most of Blyton's golliwogs, unlike her Goblins who are nearly always devious and calculating. The three of them live in a cottage with pretty walls, a blue gate and honeysuckle growing up the outside. In the course of the book they throw a party and are dismayed when no one attends, assuming that it must be because people do not like them as much as the other toys. However, all is put to rights when they realise that they have got the wrong date, and their friends do arrive after all, bearing presents and food. They have two aunts, one named Coal Black and another called Keziah, who both make cameo appearances in the book. Although *The Three Golliwogs* may be considered unsuitable in the twenty-first century, it should not be taken as promoting racism, but as a light-hearted and innocent tale in which the golliwogs come out on top.

BRER RABBIT

The star of Blyton's Brer Rabbit stories, his mischievous nature is not unlike that of the naughty doll Amelia Jane. His regular victims Brer Wolf and Brer Bear are always vowing to get their revenge, and both agree that he would taste nice with onions and carrots. Brer Fox has Brer Rabbit pencilled in on his dinner menu as well, but the rabbit is far too wily a customer to get caught. For example, when Brer Wolf starts pestering him outside his house, he convinces Wolf that Old Man Wolf-Eater is staying with him, and Wolf is soon frightened away. Brer Rabbit's other master stroke is to have Benjamin Ram as a staunch ally. Mr Benjamin Ram thinks Brer Rabbit the kindest fellow in the world, and he is happy to use his considerable butting power to help him out in awkward situations.

Brer Rabbit is not, in fact, a Blyton Original. He is the brainchild of Joel Chandler Harris, who invented the character for his series of books about a cotton plantation slave called Uncle Remus, who tells wonderfully elaborate stories about strange creatures, including Brer Rabbit and Brer Fox. Uncle Remus also appeared in the Disney semi-animated movie *Song of the South* (1947, directed by Harvey Foster) where the part of Remus was played by James Bassett.

NODDY

Noddy Goes to Toyland (1949)
Hurrah for Little Noddy (1950)
Noddy and his Car (1951)
Here Comes Noddy Again (1951)
Well Done, Noddy (1951)
Noddy Goes to the Seaside (1951)
Noddy Goes to School (1952)
Noddy Gets into Trouble (1953)
Noddy and the Magic Rubber (1954)
You Funny Little Noddy (1955)
Noddy Meets Father Christmas (1955)
Noddy and Tessie Bear (1956)
Be Brave, Little Noddy! (1956)
Noddy and the Bumpy Dog (1957)
Do Look Out, Noddy! (1957)
You're a Good Friend, Noddy (1958)
Noddy Has an Adventure (1958)
Noddy Goes to Sea (1959)
Noddy and the Bunkey (1959)
Cheer Up, Little Noddy! (1960)
Noddy Goes to the Fair (1960)
Mr Plod and Little Noddy (1961)
Noddy and the Tootles (1962)
Noddy and the Aeroplane (1964)

'There have been lots of books written about me.'
NODDY MEETS FATHER CHRISTMAS

Unwitting focus of years of controversy and outrage, Noddy is the best loved and most celebrated of all Blyton's characters. There are twenty-four books in the Noddy series, a further one hundred short stories about his various escapades in Toyland and endless merchandise based on his life that continues to sell all over the world. Indeed, Noddy himself appears to be aware of his phenomenal appeal as he casually states in *Noddy Meets Father Christmas*: 'There have been lots of books written about me.' His appeal is indisputable, and his charm apparently limitless. He has battled through decades of contention and now gasps for breath at the start of the twenty-first century, head still nodding and bell still ringing out for all to hear. In a recent debate at the Oxford Union on the subject of whether Blyton's books are still suitable for today's child, Noddy emerged victorious. He combines every child's dream of having a car, their own house and their own money, with a moral lesson to be learned in every story – even if the lesson is never to open your door to a Bunkey (half-bunny, half-monkey).

Angela Goldenhair

Lovely resident of Toyland who loses her scarf in *Noddy and his Car* and vents her fury on Noddy who is entirely blameless, for once. The scarf is later retrieved from the head of Sally Sly who works on the Toyland Farm.

Big-Ears

The most famous brownie of all time, Big-Ears is single-handedly responsible for propelling Noddy into Toyland and helping him set up home next to the Tubby Bear family. Big-Ears himself resides in Toadstool House in the Dark Wood, with Whiskers his cat, and fills his days helping Noddy out of scrapes and cycling around on his little red bicycle. Big-Ears is the voice of reason and sensibility to the impetuous Noddy, telling him not to be so silly when Noddy befriends the altogether unsuitable Bunkey, and warning him that he is getting a swollen head because he has too high an opinion of himself.

Big-Ears has reason to be authoritative as he states that he is a grand one hundred years of age, and has seen many things come and go in Toyland.

Noddy is like a son to the brownie, who loves him dearly, despite the little nodding man's obvious flaws. Although Big-Ears came under serious condemnation in the 1950s and 1960s from libraries and schools, his charisma remains unaltered and he is still as widely read and loved today as he ever was in the past. To be a brownie called Big-Ears may not be as insulting as the name would be if applied to a human.

Bumpy Dog

Unable to resist bumping people, the Bumpy Dog appears in Toyland in *Noddy and the Bumpy Dog* and does not leave the town. Noddy is extremely fond of the dog, despite his naughty behaviour, but is relieved when he is taken off his hands to live with the altogether more patient Tessie Bear.

Bunkey

An animal which claims to be a cross between a bunny rabbit and a monkey, hence his name, appears in Toyland, attaches himself to Noddy and proceeds to cause all kinds of trouble, including pouring gravy on the feet of Mr Tubby Bear. Everyone in Toytown is amazed by the peculiar nature of the Bunkey, despite their own unconventional personalities, and the whole town marvels at the astonishing combination of the two animals. However, at the end of the book *Noddy and the Bunkey*, it is revealed that he is in fact just a plain old monkey after all, wearing a hat with rabbit ears sticking out of the top to create a rabbit effect. The whole of Toytown has been taken in by his cunning disguise.

Miss Bunny

Noddy's skills as a songwriter and lyricist come into play when he writes a song about Miss Bunny. The residents of Toyland are so impressed that he invents songs about many of his other friends, and the songs become his trademark. Miss Bunny considers him very clever indeed.

Donkey Belonging to Mr Saucepan Man

Mr Saucepan Man, a favourite character from the Enchanted Wood series, makes a cameo appearance in Toytown, fuelling suspicions that he is one of Blyton's favourite characters. He appears with a donkey in tow who had certainly never been mentioned up the Faraway Tree. The donkey is left in Noddy's care for a while, and Noddy learns to love the animal in *Cheer Up, Little Noddy!* When Saucepan reappears in Toyland, no doubt on his way back from seeing his friends Silky and Moon-Face, Noddy is distressed by the donkey's lack of concern on leaving him. However, one book later, the donkey and Mr Saucepan Man reappear at a fair, and the donkey shows sufficient glee at seeing his good friend Noddy once again.

Miss Fluffy Cat

Friendly and fluffy feline resident of Toytown who revels in visits to the shops in Noddy's taxi.

Little-Ears

The frequently ailing cousin of Big-Ears, Little-Ears seems to have quite the opposite appearance to his distinguished relation. He lives quite a distance from the other characters and Big-Ears sometimes disappears for days on end to look after him.

Mr Marvel Monkey

Monkeys are troublesome characters at the best of times, but Mr Marvel Monkey takes things a step further when he arrives in Toytown. He manages to lure Noddy into thinking that he is living a dull life and needs a break, much to the dismay and fury of the ever-steady Big-Ears, and the two set off together to find adventure. Marvel Monkey is a show-off and rather tiresome, but it seems that Noddy is eager for a break from the monotony of his life and, indeed, becomes quite indignant with Big-Ears who is upset that his best friend is fraternising with a silly monkey like Marvel. Unfortunately for Noddy, Big-Ears is right about Marvel, and the monkey gets into terrible trouble when he is revealed as a fraud and a thief. Noddy seems to be something of a monkey magnet, as he is visited by the Bunkey, Mr Marvel

Monkey and Bert Monkey in the course of the twenty-four books in his series.

Mary Mouse

Mary Mouse and her six children are mentioned in the first book in the Noddy series, but she also appears in her own series of twenty-four books for a younger audience. Her story begins when she is sent away from her home by her mother, who banishes her because she is simply too meticulous and neat, and starts a new life as the cook and housekeeper in the Doll's House belonging to Mummy and Daddy Doll. Here she cooks and cleans and looks after the children (Pip, Melia and Roundy) and the dog Jumpy, thus creating the theme of harmonious family life that Blyton focuses on throughout the Mary Mouse books.

Mary eventually marries a delightful mouse called Whiskers, the Doll's House gardener, and the two bring up a family of six, three boys called Squeaky, Frisky and Scampy, and three girls called Woffly, Patter and Tiny. In typical Blyton fashion, the boys are rowdy and adventurous, spending their days on their scooters and terrorising the girls who prefer to play quietly with their doll mice out of harm's way.

When paper was scarce during the war, Blyton's publisher used up spare paper cut off the bottom of more orthodox-sized books for printing the Mary Mouse stories, which accounts for their unusual long narrow format with drawings across every page and text below. The books sold remarkably well, helped by the parallel between Mary Mouse's home and those of the readers.

Mr Milko

Friendly milkman and great conversationalist, Mr Milko is one of Toytown's most vital characters, delivering his wares every morning in time for the residents to make their cups of tea and cocoa. He accepts no form of payment from Noddy, other than the fun of tapping him on the wooden head and ringing his bell which causes Mr Milko great amusement. None of the residents of Toytown have ever encountered a toy with a head on a spring before, so Noddy is the subject of much entertainment.

Monkey, Bert

Bert Monkey scampers into Toyland in possession of an astonishing invisible rubber which has the power to rub out literally anything that one chooses. Inevitably, the rubber goes missing, and it is up to Noddy and Bert to find it again, in case it falls into the wrong hands. Noddy has little time for Bert Monkey whom he considers a pest and a pain and tells him so too, particularly as he spends his time knocking things over with his tail. When the rubber is found again, after it has been passed into and out of the hands of Noah's son, Shem, Noddy delights in rubbing out Bert Monkey's tail so that it cannot cause any more trouble. Perhaps this was rather too drastic a measure to have taken, but Noddy can be harsh when he feels that a lesson needs to be learned.

Mr and Mrs Noah

Residents of Toyland, the Noah family live in their ark and spend their days trying to control the ridiculous number of animals they have on board their floating home. Mr and Mrs Noah are good friends of Noddy in Toytown, and he makes their acquaintance on the first day he arrives in his new home, as he stumbles across one of the lions from their ark who is frightening Tessie Bear. Noddy also meets Mr and Mrs Noah's son, Shem, when he is searching for a missing magic rubber that Shem has given away in return for an ice-cream.

Noddy

Noddy is first introduced as a nameless, possessionless wooden boy with a head on a spring that is perpetually nodding, hair made from cat's fur and bright-blue beady eyes. He runs away from his creator, Mr Carver, to find himself a home and some friends. As luck would have it, he chances upon that most famous of all brownies, Big-Ears, who takes Noddy under his wing and puts him on a train to Toytown, Toyland. It is Big-Ears who is responsible for the way that we view Noddy today as it is he who gives Noddy his name and takes him to buy some suitable clothing, consisting of the familiar red shoes with their blue laces, bright-blue flares, red shirt, yellow belt and tie and blue hat with the jingling bell on top. Big-Ears also assists Noddy in the building of his House for One, made from a handy instruction kit labelled 'Build Your Own Home'. Noddy is the subject of as much debate in Toyland as he is in the real world, as on his first night in his new house PC Plod demands that he go to court the next day where the judges will assess whether he is in fact a real toy. Thanks to his kind-hearted behaviour towards a little doll he is allowed to stay in Toyland, and a decision is reached that he *is* a toy.

Noddy does not spend his days in Toytown sitting idle or hopping from the Land of Goodies to the Land of Do-As-You-Please while munching on honey-flavoured cakes, like the Faraway Tree folk. He seeks immediate employment, and finds himself working as a cleaner for a family of dolls and as a mechanic in the local garage run by Mr Sparks. An act of heroism involving the recovery of several vehicles stolen from the garage by a gang of goblins in the middle of the night results in a present for Noddy of his very own blue and yellow car, which he decides to use as a taxi. Again, his driving is a contentious subject as PC Plod feels that Noddy is a liability and drives too fast, and indeed his car does end up being repaired and re-serviced countless times in the books. Mrs Noah from the Toytown Noah's Ark comments, 'You work very hard and you are a very good driver, even though you do knock down lamp-posts sometimes,' to which Noddy curtly replies with all the prowess of a young Michael Schumacher, 'Well, they shouldn't get in my way.'

Noddy is very much a child, despite his independence, and is no stranger to tears and tantrums when he is not getting his own way, or things are not going right for him. He is frequently wailing that 'nobody likes me any more' and expects the whole of Toytown to come to a grinding halt if he is feeling unhappy. Perhaps it is through creating a very obviously flawed, infantile hero, with all the indignation of youth, that Blyton gains the respect of her young audience who surely empathise with Noddy when he is chided for being too boastful or told off for making friends with unsuitable personalities.

Noddy's day-to-day existence consists of driving his friends and acquaintances around Toytown in his taxi for a standard charge of sixpence per journey, and running into adventure along the way. His best friend is Big-Ears the brownie who is always ready to deal out help and advice to the 'little nodding man', and his neighbours are the Tubby Bear family who live in a rather grand house in comparison to his. Through the twenty-four books based in Toytown, Noddy befriends such diverse characters as the Bumpy Dog, Mr Saucepan Man and Bert the naughty monkey, as well as making voyages out of the confines of Toytown to the seaside and the Dark Woods where the goblins live. Noddy also attends school for the duration of one book and learns that he is not as clever as he had previously thought, which stops his head from (literally) swelling any more. He has the talent of being an accomplished songwriter and singer who is able to think of a verse and tune to fit any occasion or person, much to the admiration of those around him.

Noddy came under severe criticism from parents, librarians and teachers at the height of his popularity with children. Indeed, one critic, Colin Welch, most famously described him as 'the most egocentric, joyless, snivelling and pious anti-hero in the history of fiction'. The complaints about Noddy branded his relationship with Big-Ears as 'suspect' and suggested that children were so ensnared by Blyton's writing that it became impossible for them to move on to other authors. Further criticism was levelled at Blyton, accusing her of racism following the appearance of a 'bad' golliwog in Toyland. Blyton counterbalanced this by saying that her writing about one bad golliwog meant nothing as she had written several 'good' golliwogs into her stories as well. In the end, Noddy was banned from many libraries, but the final say came from the children who naturally 'did not give a "parp parp" for librarians and all those big words', as Roy Nash pointed out in an article in the *Daily Mail* in 1964 about the banning of Noddy.

Mr Plod

Toytown's resident bobby who spends his days restoring harmony to a town which is by all reckonings astonishingly human in its crime figures, and accusing Noddy of reckless driving. Like all policemen, Mr Plod relies on corruption for his job to exist at all, which is not a problem in Toytown where disreputable goblins are to be found stealing cars and causing chaos on the streets, and the only taxi driver in the town (Noddy) is far more likely to hit a lamp-post than drive past it.

Like Hilary Wentworth in the St Clare's series, Mr Plod is firm but fair, if a little slow at times. Noddy and the residents of Toytown are greatly distressed when Mr Plod is made to go into hospital in *Mr Plod and Little Noddy* after falling off a ladder and damaging his head. Indeed, Miss Kitten demands to know, 'Who is going to stop Mickey Monkey and his friends from being rude to people and making faces at them?' It seems that, for all that Mr Plod has a rather tiresome job that can land his fellow toys in trouble, he does have the respect and admiration of the masses. He is proof that a policeman's job is not easy, but can be very rewarding. He has a great fondness for a cup of steaming cocoa at the end of a busy day.

Sally Sly

There is no better adjective to describe Sally, who works on the Toyland farm, than Sly. She is always snooping around and causing trouble, and steals a scarf belonging to Angela Goldenhair in *Noddy and his Car*, but does not succeed in getting away with her petty theft. She needs a constant eye to be kept on her and her mischievous ways.

Skittles

Toyland appears to be full of Skittles who enjoy being crashed into by cars, as is shown in *Noddy Meets Father Christmas* when the Skittles are sent flying all over the place. Sally Skittle is the Mother of all Skittles, and is often found using Noddy's taxi service around Toytown.

Sly and Gobbo

Sly and Gobbo are the two troublesome goblins who live in the Dark Woods outside Toytown. As a rule, Blyton's goblins are not pleasant people, unlike pixies, elves and fairies who are generally good beings. Noddy has his fair share of trouble with Sly and Gobbo, and learns to be wary of their wicked ways.

Mr Sparks

Owner of the Toytown garage where Noddy's little car seems to spend most of its time, Mr Sparks is a kindly-looking doll who employs Noddy when he first arrives in Toyland to help out at his garage.

Mr Straw

Toytown's resident farmers, Mr and Mrs Straw, supply the town with the milk that is collected by Milko the Milkman and distributed around Toytown.

Mr Teddy

Brother of Mr Tubby Bear, Mr Teddy is the slightly less plump of the two, who appears in Toyland on a number of occasions. Mr Teddy Bear loses his hat in the third book in the series, *Noddy and his Car*, and it is found by Noddy on the naughty head of a monkey. Crime and theft are rife in Toytown, so it is lucky that the residents can rely on Mr Plod to put things to rights.

Miss Tessie Bear

Miss Tessie Bear and Noddy are great friends and are often out adventuring together. As a result, she is often the subject of Noddy's songs, much to her delight. Tessie Bear takes on the responsibility of the notorious Bumpy Dog, whom she loves, when Noddy is unable to cope with him any longer.

Mr Tootle and His Little Toots

With no warning, Mr Tootle and his little Toots appear in Toytown and, like every arrival, they are drawn to Noddy's house. Mr Toots possesses the extraordinary gift of being able to make people dance, and then runs away with Noddy's car, leaving him in the company of a horse. Luckily, by the end of the book, Noddy's dear little car is recovered and the Tootles family disappear once again with their trusty steed.

Master Tubby Bear

Rather inclined to be naughty, Master Tubby Bear is the son of Mr and Mrs Tubby Bear. He puts glue in his father's shoe in *Noddy and the Tootles* and needs to prove to his parents that he is not going to do such a thing again. Kindly Noddy is ready to give people a second chance, most of the time, and is prepared to help Master Tubby, whom he is genuinely fond of.

Mr Tubby Bear

Next-door neighbours to Noddy in Toytown, the Tubby Bears live in a plush house in comparison to Noddy's modest House for One. Mr Tubby Bear is a rather austere figure of fatherhood who is always ready to help Noddy out, indeed, he lends a paw to the construction of Noddy's home when he first arrives in Toyland.

Mrs Tubby Bear

Mrs Tubby Bear of the Tubby Bear family wears 'lovely clothes...a full red skirt and a pretty green shawl', implying that the Tubby Bears are well off, especially when their house is mentioned as being 'rather grand'. Mrs Tubby Bear spends her time trying to organise her two children, who are more often than not in some scrape or other, and using Noddy's ever-ready taxi service to whizz into town and purchase clothes and food.

Wobbly Man

Friendly and plump, the Wobbly Man wobbles wherever he goes which makes daily tasks a challenge to say the least. He is to be found living in Toyland and always calls out a cheerful hello to Noddy when he passes by. It is mentioned in *Well Done, Noddy* that the Wobbly Man cannot plant beans in his garden, because he wobbles too much to complete the job properly.

FARM STORIES

CHERRY TREE FARM AND WILLOW FARM
SIX COUSINS

'Good gracious! Can this be Cyril?' asked Jane in pretended astonishment. 'He's quite good-looking now we can see his face!'

'Time he did get a haircut,' growled Mr Longfield. 'I was thinking of taking the shears to it soon.'

SIX COUSINS AT MISTLETOE FARM

CHERRY TREE FARM AND
WILLOW FARM

The Children of Cherry Tree Farm (1940)
The Children of Willow Farm (1942)
Adventures on Willow Farm (1942)

The 'Cherry Tree' and 'Willow' farm stories are less glamorous than the Six Cousins books, and progress at a gentler pace with more of an educational feel to them. The books are introduced with the news that Rory, Benjy, Sheila and Penny are to spend some time on their aunt and uncle's farm as they have been ill and the doctor suggests they need good, country air in their lungs. The visit to the legendary Cherry Tree Farm is a great success and their parents are so pleased with their plump, healthy children that they decide to buy a farm for themselves, Willow Farm. Needless to say, this news delights the children who had been living in mortal fear of being sent off to boarding school.

Blyton deals with a large number of farming issues including lambing, treating ill animals, keeping hens and hay-making. Although the characters are perhaps not as strong as on Mistletoe Farm, the books have a lyrical, poetic quality to them which shows Blyton's great love and understanding of country living and country folk. These books are a vital slice of history, for farming methods and values have changed so much since the time of their writing that much of what Willow Farm is about seems to come from another world – a world where the wireless takes time to warm up, and children can ride donkeys to school and keep pet squirrels. There is no mention of what part of the country Willow Farm is situated in, although at one point Christmas Common is mentioned. Christmas Common is to be found in Oxfordshire, in the heart of the Chiltern Hills.

Bee Man

A 'funny little fellow with a wrinkled face like an old, old apple and eyes as black as ripe pear-pips' comes to introduce the bees and their hives to Willow Farm. Informs the children that there is no point in running away from bees as they can outrun the fastest train. Squeaky-voiced.

Bellow

Aptly named bull. Resident of Cherry Tree Farm. Not fond of strangers.

Benjy

Dreamy eleven-year-old who has a 'way with animals'. Benjy is lucky enough to own a pet squirrel, Scamper, who sits on his shoulder and waits for him in the trees outside while he is taught at school. 'Animals always loved the boy and he was never afraid of them' with the exception, perhaps, of Stamper the bull whom Benjy never warms to. Indeed, his instincts are proved right, and Stamper is eventually sold back to his original owner. Saves the day when he runs to fetch Tammylan from the hillside to help the ailing carthorse Darling. When the big horse is saved, it is mentioned as being 'just as good as a chapter out of a book!' How true.

Aunt Bess

Lives at Cherry Tree Farm with her husband Tim. Willingly takes on Rory, Sheila, Benjy and Penny when they are ill and in need of country air. Provides them with plenty of good clean living and delicious food.

Bill

When the children wake up at Willow Farm, the first person they see is Bill re-thatching the roof. With a face 'burnt brown as an oak apple', Bill is regularly on the scene to work with anything in the medium of dried grass. His wife is mentioned when hay-making begins as she loves the chaff from the hay to fill her mattresses. Bill utters the immortal words, 'It won't fall, it would have fallen before if it was going to,' just seconds before the tree that he is sawing away collapses.

Blossom

Red and white cow belonging to Willow Farm.

Bray

See Hee-Haw

'Well, you come and watch me do a bit of thatching.'

Brownie

Naughty little hen belonging to Aunt Bess and Cherry Tree Farm. Decides to lay her eggs in a hedge.

Mr By-Himself

Cat on Willow Farm. The name for this creature must surely have been taken from the Just So Story 'The Cat that Walked by Himself' by Rudyard Kipling.

Canter

See Hee-Haw.

Captain

Carthorse at Willow Farm. A gentle giant.

Darky

Purchased with Patchy for Willow Farm. Little brown horse with gentle eyes. Knows the milk-round like the back of her hoof.

Darling

Sweet-tempered, dark brown carthorse from Willow Farm. Has patient eyes and long-sweeping lashes and never minds how much of a load she is asked to carry. Contracts colic one night and has her life saved by Tammylan and his alternative herbal medicine.

Davey

Wise, blue-eyed shepherd on Willow Farm. With his grey hair, smiley face and excellent knowledge of sheep, Davey and his three dogs are a great asset to the hardworking farm. Considers Penny 'too cheap to be Penny', so renames her 'Tupenny'. It is Davey who gives Penny the responsibility of rearing her first pet lamb, Skippetty. Believes that however much he knows about the country, his dogs know more.

Dopey

'Walking dustbin' of a goat belonging to Penny. Utterly undisciplined and rather silly, Dopey is none the less a lovable character. Eats everything in sight, including Harriet's cushion, Penny's father's newspaper and Rory's homework. 'Rory was very angry and tried to rescue half a page of French verbs from the kid's mouth.' How would Mam'zelle Dupont (*see* Malory Towers) have reacted to this very elaborate excuse for not handing in prep on time?

Fanny

Fifteen-year-old niece of Harriet the cook. Fanny is initially so shy that it is hard to get her to say anything at all, but she blossoms where poultry is concerned, proving herself to be a great help to Sheila with the hens and ducks. 'A real country girl, liking everything to do with farm life.'

Mr Farley

Original owner and breeder of Stamper the bull, bought by the children's father for Willow Farm. 'We did well to choose him, he's settling down fine,' claims the farmer, but he speaks too soon as the bull flies into a rage and starts showing the whites of his eyes. Mr Farley is eventually asked if he would like the bull back for half the price that he sold him for.

Everyone watches, mouths open in amazement, as the 'little man with an enormous voice and hands as big as hams' stands up to the bovine fiend and calms him down again before leading him away. Blue-eyed, like many of Blyton's country folk.

Father

Purchases Willow Farm and sets about making the best of country life, having previously lived and worked in London. Life on Willow Farm is evidently well suited to the man who farms well and marvels at how his children have grown since moving to the country. When Rory decides to take farming matters into his own hands and sets fire to one of the fields, his father blames himself for forgetting that his son is 'only a lad of fourteen'.

Harriet

Cook at Willow Farm. A former dairy maid, Harriet and her niece Fanny provide large meals and sound advice.

Hee-Haw

Donkey belonging to Penny. Lives at Willow Farm with Sheila's donkey, Canter, Benjy's Bray and Rory's Neddy.

Hoppitty

See Jumpitty.

Jim

Herdsman on Willow Farm. 'A tiny man with very broad shoulders and long arms', Jim is excessively strong and capable, although he does suffer concussion when dealing with a fallen tree. Never too busy to talk to Penny, he works well with Bill the Thatcher. Does the milk-round with Patchy and Darky who pull the cart.

John

The children's father (*see* Father). Makes the occasional howling error, for example when buying a mad bull.

Jumpitty

Jumpitty and Hoppitty are the two lambs hand-reared by Penny in *Adventures on Willow Farm*. Jumpitty has a black nose; Hoppitty does not. They spend their days following Penny around as did her previous lamb, Skippetty. No doubt when these two are fully grown they will be less appealing to the excited little girl.

Mark

Accident-prone friend of the children who comes to stay at Willow Farm on more than one occasion. Enjoys life on the farm immensely, although he is initially unimpressed by having to ride donkeys, clean the hen house and wake up at the crack of dawn. Causes mayhem when he leaves a gate open, and

Captain, Darling, Patchy and Darky escape. Fortunately, all the horses are recovered safely, but Mark feels very stupid indeed. When he's not slipping over and covering himself in hen food, Mark is good company, and the children enjoy having him around. Is confused when Penny tells him that the piglets have been born and that they did not come out of an egg. 'Penny wondered how to explain to him about kittens and puppies and calves and lambs and piglets.' Loves his food, claiming that he could eat 'as much as that old sow there'.

Mother

A typical Blyton mother. Considerate, kindly, sweet-tempered and sensible. Lives for her husband and family. Finds the move from London to Willow Farm most agreeable.

Nancy

Collie belonging to Davey the shepherd at Willow Farm. 'We depend on our dogs more than anything else,' says Davey as Nancy and her canine pals round up the 'stupid' sheep.

Ned

Cowman at Cherry Tree Farm. Shows the children how to milk the cows, and is amused when Penny complains that Daisy 'smacks her' with her tail.

Neddy

See Hee-Haw.

Patchy

Horse bought to pull the milk cart at Willow Farm. Brown and white with long legs, he is not the most beautiful animal, but healthy and good-tempered.

Paul Pry

Bullock on Willow Farm, so called because of his nosey ways. Enjoys making the odd house-call, and takes a great shine to Harriet the cook.

Penny

Eight years old with a penchant for hiding in cupboards and nesting-boxes, Penny is the youngest of the family and always wishing that she was that little bit older. Is beside herself with delight when she is given her own pet lamb, Skippetty, in *The Children of Willow Farm*, though is less impressed when he quickly grows up into a sheep. Always trying her hardest and taking a keen interest in the farm, it comes as no surprise that everyone has a soft spot for young Penny. Likes talking to the bees, which she has been told will bring good luck to the household. Later is given two more lambs, the aptly named Hoppitty and Jumpitty, and a goat – the destructive gourmet, Dopey.

Polly

Pony from Cherry Tree Farm who collects the children when they first arrive at the station.

Prickles

Hedgehog befriended by Penny during her stay at Cherry Tree Farm. Penny grows very fond of her 'quaint pet', but is not amused by his need to hibernate in winter.

Rascal

Collie belonging to Davey the shepherd. Together with Tinker and Nancy, they are an invaluable part of the farm. It is Rascal who warns Davey that one of his ewes is stuck in the fence and unable to tend to her lambs. 'Sharp as needles they are, and think for themselves just as much as you do!' claims Davey.

Rory

The oldest of the four children, Rory is an impressive fourteen years old by the time the family move to Willow Farm. His time at Cherry Tree Farm changes him from townie to strong, responsible young man. 'Who would have thought you were the same boy as the ill-grown, pale, weedy Rory of last year?', his father marvels, rather tactlessly. A boy who 'when he felt things, felt them very deeply', Rory is desperate for a dog of his own and is devastated when Benjy finds an elderly dog run over by the roadside. Even Tammylan is unable to save the creature, and Rory vows that he will never have a dog after this. However, he is moved to change his mind by the collie puppy True, who turns out to be one of the farm's greatest assets. Rory has one moment of madness when he 'gets too big for his boots' and sets fire to one of his father's fields. Although the field was due to be burnt, Rory and Mark have no control over the flames and they spread out of control. Much to their relief, they are saved by a sudden shower of rain, but Rory never forgets his silly behaviour and is much the wiser for the experience.

Scamper

Squirrel belonging to Benjy. Enjoys sitting on his shoulder and eating nuts. Likes to hang out with his fellow squirrels too, but is never far away from the boy he adores. Scamper is looked after by Tammylan when Benjy leaves Cherry Tree Farm, but returns again when the family move into Willow Farm.

Shadow

Faithful collie belonging to Cherry Tree Farm. Often to be found lying at the feet of Uncle Tim.

Shadow, the collie, lay at Uncle Tim's feet. A big white cat washed herself by the fire. Auntie Bess darned a stocking and Uncle Tim listened to the children's chatter.
THE CHILDREN OF CHERRY TREE FARM

Sheila

Thirteen years old and the second oldest child at Willow Farm. A marvel with poultry, Sheila adores her hens, and takes great pride in knowing each one individually. Has plenty of help from Fanny and Penny, but everyone knows that it is Sheila who painstakingly fills in the 'egg book', recording every single egg that is laid. 'I do like doing something real like this,' she claims. Enjoys translating animal noises into English.

Skippetty

Lamb belonging to Penny. Introduced in *The Children of Willow Farm*, Skippetty is white with a black face and a great deal of attitude. As Harriet

'The old mother-pig is there too.'

states, 'I've never known such a creature for poking its nose into things.' Hand-reared by Penny, he follows her everywhere, though the line is drawn when he turns up at her school. Eats everything, including Jim's cheese lunches. Penny is disappointed when Skippetty grows up into a sheep, considering it 'very sad' that he is no longer a sweet, frolicking lamb.

Smithy

Blacksmith who re-shoes the horses from Willow Farm. A big man with a beard and plenty of black, curly hair, he offers Benjy career advice. 'Don't be a smith, young sir! You'll not make any money at that!'

Stamper

Bad-tempered bull bought for Willow Farm but sent back to his original owner because of his anger issues. When Stamper leaves the farm it is mentioned that 'nobody missed him'.

Taffy

Farmhand at Cherry Tree Farm. Has the enviable task of leading Bellow the bull up and down the lane. When Rory shows his interest in having a go, Taffy puts forward the theory that it would be the bull leading Rory, not the other way round.

Tammylan

'Wild man' who features heavily in the children's countryside adventures. Tammylan befriends Rory, Benjy, Sheila and Penny in *The Children of Cherry Tree Farm* and is never far away from Willow Farm. 'As natural as the animals he loved so much, as gay as the birds, as wise as the hills around him', Tammylan is a Blyton all-round Good Guy, with no other side to him like Twigg the poacher in the Mistletoe Farm series. If an animal is injured or ill, you can be sure that Tammylan will have the natural cure; his achievements include saving Darling the carthorse from colic with his unconventional medicine. Lives in a cave with little more than a home-made blanket and a wooden chair as possessions. Twinkle-eyed. Naturally.

Uncle Tim

Lives with his wife Bess at Cherry Tree Farm.

Tinker

Mongrel belonging to Davey the shepherd at Willow Farm. Works well with Nancy and Rascal the collies. (For other dogs called Tinker, *see* the Mistletoe Farm and The Famous Five series.)

Thomas, Dick

All we know about this unfortunate boy is that at some point he finds a bird with a broken wing and tortures it. Legend has it that Tammylan shakes the boy to within an inch of his life to punish him for this cruel deed.

SIX COUSINS

Six Cousins at Mistletoe Farm (1948)
Six Cousins Again (1950)

Blyton wrote extensively on the subject of farming and nature, and never with more bounce and wit than in the Six Cousins series. Through only two books, we follow the 'six cousins' who are thrown together when three of them (Melisande, Cyril and Roderick Longfield) have their smart London home, Three Towers, destroyed by fire and move to Mistletoe Farm to join Jack, Jane and Susan Longfield for an eight-month stay. Building on the contrasting characters, Blyton 'rubs corners off' them all and gives the town cousins a love of the country and the country cousins a taste for good clothes and poetry. By the end of *Six Cousins at Mistletoe Farm* the town cousins receive the news that they shall be moving to nearby Holly Farm where their father will tackle a new career in farming, and their elegant mother will have to fulfil the role of farmer's wife. *Six Cousins Again* deals with the move and the troubles that face the family in their first year on Holly Farm and contains some of Blyton's most sharply observed writing, most notably concerning Rose Longfield who finds farm life hard to cope with.

Blyton wrote the first book in the series as her daughter Imogen recovered from scarlet fever, and allowed Imogen to name the animals. Particular attention is given to the Icelandic pony, Boodi, and Crackers the silky-eared cocker spaniel.

Benedict

Real name Raymond Jones. 'Hermit' who befriends Cyril after asking him the question 'What's the day of the week?' when he spots the artistic-looking lad walking the bull. Benedict dresses in a long gown tied with a rope, talks of Milton and Homer, and bombards Cyril with questions about local farms and farm life which flatters Cyril into thinking that Benedict is genuinely interested in his life. Unfortunately, Benedict's motives are entirely dishonest, as he turns out to be the neighbourhood thief. The inspector reveals that Benedict is a well-educated man who likes to pose as a cultured scholar. In fact, he used to be a good musician who played first violin in a dance band. Cyril is shocked and disappointed when he realises how he has been taken in by the man.

'Hey! What's the day of the week?'

Surprisingly, he is never caught by the police, so we must assume that Benedict and his thieving ways have moved on to the next county. Likes wandering about at night, muttering to himself. (For another character who enjoys putting on this sort of performance, *see* Anne-Marie Longden in St Clare's.)

Boodi

Dark-brown, Icelandic pony with curious habits, belonging to Susan Longfield. Has a wicked look in his eye and enjoys squeezing his rider's leg against a hedge in an attempt to unseat them. Acquired by Mr Longfield in payment of a bad debt. It is mentioned that Jack and Jane could not understand why Susan loved Boodi when there were 'lovely ponies like Merrylegs and Darkie to rave over'. Behaves badly when Roderick rides him, to Susan's secret delight. 'It was nice to think that Boodi kept his best behaviour for his little mistress alone!'

Crackers

Black cocker spaniel belonging to Susan Longfield. Very much part of the family and dearly loved by Roderick Longfield, who is comforted by Crackers when he suffers from nightmares about the fire that has destroyed his home. Blyton's fondness for this breed of dog is clear throughout her writing and she must have agreed with Tommy Lane, who tells Roderick, 'Ah, you can't beat they spaniels!'

'Roderick lay and pictured Crackers' funny, mournful face.'

Darkie

Pony owned by Jack Longfield. Darkie is used to survey the land at Mistletoe Farm as well as to take Jack to his school.

Dorcas

Faithful cook at Mistletoe Farm, much loved by everyone. Elderly and with a bright-red face, she moves about 'surprisingly briskly' for such a large woman. Loves Mrs Longfield and all of her children, and becomes increasingly fond of Roderick as his time at the farm progresses. Always to be found in the kitchen preparing something delicious. Dislikes Rose Longfield in whom she sees no beauty of character. 'You'll look in vain for that kind of beauty in Mrs David's face,' she announces. Rose Longfield in return sees a spiteful old woman in Dorcas, not noticing 'the worn old hands clasped together...the thin grey hair so neatly brushed back for Sunday afternoon'. It is this disregard for the adorable, hard-working Dorcas that makes Rose Longfield an even more unpleasant character. Nicknamed 'Dorkie' by Susan and Roderick, she is a vital part of the tapestry that makes up life at Mistletoe Farm. Much missed by Roderick when his family move to Holly Farm.

Ellen

Thin, 'sour-puss' cook at Holly Farm. Encourages the gypsies by becoming very silly over having her tea-leaves read at the back door and disobeys orders to send them away. Is rude and unpleasant to Twigg the poacher whom she considers to be nothing more than scum, and is disapproving of Roderick who she thinks is far too greedy. Eventually runs away from Holly Farm after she wrongly accuses Sally the scullery maid of stealing. As a general rule, if you're thin, you are a dishonest piece of work where Blyton is concerned. On the other hand, plumpness and truthfulness seem to go hand in hand.

Hazel

Shepherd on Mistletoe Farm. Lives a quiet country existence, spending his days under the hawthorn hedge and tending to his sheep. Is most amused by Sam Twigg. Has twinkling eyes. Old.

Lane, Tommy

Friend of Twigg the poacher, Tommy Lane provides Roderick with his first ever dog, Tinker. Roderick collects the young pup from Tommy's cottage where the talk is of nothing but badgers, pheasants, owls, hares, foxes, weasels, otters and moles. 'Sitting there with his new pup pressed into his neck listening to the country wisdom of the two old men was a memory that was to remain with Roderick for the rest of his life.'

Long, Richard

Good-looking, fun-loving friend of Jack's, a few years older than him at school. Charms everyone he meets with his knowledge of horses and glamour. Is rather taken with Melisande, 'not that he had much time for girls, but when he noticed them he liked them to look pretty'. Is less impressed by Jane, who reminds him of his Aunt Judith who is nothing more than a horsey bore. However, he invites both Jane and Melisande to a party and is amazed by the change in Jane who has clean hair and is wearing a pretty dress. 'You're different Jane! Quite different!' he announces, tactfully. Richard is mentioned in *Six Cousins Again* as he is invited to the party at Holly Farm which is cancelled at the last minute.

Longfield, Cyril

Older brother of Melisande and Roderick. Cyril is affected and foolhardy with long hair and a whimsical view on life but naturally enough much of this is eliminated after a few months on Mistletoe Farm. 'An awful ass', decides Jane, for Cyril likes dressing in bows and sandals and spouts poetry at random. Jack despairs of his 'artsy-fartsy' cousin and dreads going to school with him as he knows that he will be mocked. One day, as he sits watching old Hazel the shepherd talking to Susan and Roderick, he twigs that poetry is nothing unless it 'means something real'. He recites a few lines of verse that are taken up by his Aunt Linnie, much to Jack's astonishment, and a close friendship based on a mutual love of poetry and music begins between the two. Cyril falls in with a bad lot when he befriends the 'hermit' Benedict with whom he is deeply impressed. When Benedict turns out to be a fraud, Cyril feels angry and foolish but we know that he will never make the same mistakes again. By the time we meet Cyril in *Six Cousins Again* he is a changed boy who experiences great frustration with his mother when she tells him that he should finish his schooling and go to university and keep his hair long. 'I'm not very keen on the kind of fellows who wear their hair long now,' he says. We can only imagine what Cyril will make of the hippie movement some twenty years on.

Longfield, David

Brother to Peter Longfield and husband to the beautiful Rose. Is introduced to us as 'charming as ever but weak as water', but proves to be made of sterner stuff, choosing to make the best of his new farming career and putting his best foot forward. Clearly madly in love with his wife, he is dismayed when she does not take to life on the farm, and remarks rather hurtfully after feasting on Linnie's Christmas dinner that 'it's a pity you can't cook like this, Rose!' There is drama at the end of *Six Cousins Again* when his three children are asked to decide whom they want to live with – their father on Holly Farm or their mother in London. It is not often that Blyton tore families in two in her writing, and there are echoes in this particular chapter of the difficult times she suffered when her own parents argued. How good it must have felt when Blyton resolved the Longfield family dispute at last – as Rose decides to 'stick by her man' and become the country wife he so desperately wants.

Longfield, Jack

Jane's twin and Susan's older brother, Jack is 'slow and silent, but what a temper he had!' This tall, curly-haired fifteen-year-old is not amused by the arrival of the three town cousins and is livid at the prospect of sharing what little space he has with his cousin Cyril, with whom he has absolutely nothing in common. Obsessed with Mistletoe Farm ('it's in my very bones'), he intends to follow in the large footsteps of his father and become a farmer himself when he leaves school. Character develops significantly when he forms a friendship with Twigg the poacher and sneaks out of his bedroom at night to scour the countryside for badgers. Is highly suspicious of Cyril's friend Benedict, and with good reason.

Longfield, Jane

Jack Longfield's twin sister, and Susan's older sister. Jane is introduced as being 'quick, talkative and impatient'. Smells strongly of horse, has dirty fingernails, rarely brushes her teeth, never washes her jodhpurs and leaves her room in a tip. Inevitably comes under fire from Melisande when she arrives at Mistletoe Farm, but is reluctant to change her ways. Richard Long thinks that she is 'an awful lump of a girl' who will turn out 'just like Aunt Judith, loud voice, big hands, always knocking things over'. After several rows with various members of the family and a severe talking-to from her twin, she puts her mind to improving her appearance and the results are so astonishing that Richard fails to recognise her at his party. 'What a difference it made when people looked after themselves, even a little!' thinks Jane, gazing at herself in wonderment. She remains horse-mad, and spends most of her time grooming Merrylegs, her pony.

Longfield, Linnie

One of the few Blyton adults who is given more than a one-dimensional role in her stories, Linnie Longfield plays an important part in the unravelling of the Mistletoe Farm adventures. 'Plump with soft, curling hair and eyes that twinkled', she holds the family together with her excellent baking, deft butter-making and sense of fair play. When the three town cousins come to stay at the farm it is Aunt Linnie who cheerfully and selflessly takes on the extra mouths to feed, despite the protests coming from all around. Any danger of Linnie becoming 'holier than thou' and just that little bit too perfect is cleverly offset by her sister-in-law Rose Longfield who is horribly jealous of Linnie and refuses to see the good in her. Blyton captures the irrational emotion beautifully: 'Linnie was too good to be true, she knew how to do everything, she was a paragon of all the virtues!' But despite Rose's belief that Linnie has 'never had a thought outside her eternal cooking and washing and her hens and her butter', it is clear that there is another side to Linnie: the side that enjoys quoting poetry with Cyril and listening to symphonies on the radio. It is of course Linnie who finally makes Rose see that she is behaving badly, and forces her to realise that only by confronting her fears will they ever diminish. It is strange perhaps that Blyton herself was unable to confront many of her own problems, blocking from her mind her parents' broken marriage and her father's death. In her writing, it seems, she was able to tackle life's hurdles with greater success.

Longfield, Melisande

Fifteen-year-old sister to Cyril and Roderick. Arrives at Mistletoe Farm in great distress with an amazing ability to 'turn on the tap' whenever she wants. 'She cries if she so much as has to carry up a pail of hot water,' observes Dorcas, with obvious scorn. (For another character with this talent, *see* Gwendoline Lacey in Malory Towers.) Is the polar opposite to her untidy cousin Jane and, used to London, parties and shopping, is appalled by the simple living that she finds at Mistletoe Farm. Melisande starts to realise after a while that some of the jobs on the farm are actually quite enjoyable, and spends less time worrying about how she looks and more time helping her aunt with her duties. This is not to say that Melisande lets herself go – she is always immaculately turned out in neat, clean shorts and a well-pressed blouse. Her finest hour comes when the handsome Richard Long is invited to Mistletoe Farm. He spots Melisande on his way to the farm and offers her a lift on his horse, Lordly One, thinking that 'Melisande was not only a pretty girl but a most amusing one too.' Melisande slightly reverts back to her old ways at the beginning of *Six Cousins Again* with much talk of parties and dresses, but by the end has proved herself to be a sensible girl with the right attitude to country living. Earns the nickname of 'Smellisande' from her cousin Susan, who claims that she 'reeks' of perfume.

Longfield, Peter

'Burly' farmer and father of Jack, Jane and Susan. Does not speak much, but when he does it provokes a reaction. Well respected in the neighbourhood, and well liked by Twigg the poacher. Has lived at Mistletoe Farm since he was a boy, as did his father and grandfather before him, but is prepared to put sentiment and tradition aside if his wife Linnie should choose to live at the more modern, efficient Holly Farm.

Longfield, Roderick

Character who changes the most after his spell at Mistletoe Farm. Roderick arrives as nothing more than a little 'mother's boy' who has been affected worse than either of his elder siblings by the fire that has destroyed his previous home. He is initially described as a 'pretty, girlish boy, too plump and with rather a stupid look on his pale face'. What a difference a few months in the country can make! Susan befriends Roderick and before long he is enjoying life on the farm and is sleeping without nightmares thanks to the calming presence of Crackers on the end of his bed. Develops a massive appetite (surprise surprise) and is most unimpressed by his mother's idea of tea at Holly Farm and demands to know where the ham, eggs, sausage rolls, pickles, fruit cake and cream cheese are. Longs for a dog of his own to the extent that he invents an imaginary cocker spaniel called Tinker, and falls out with his mother when she refuses to let the dream become reality. Grows up hugely in the course of the two books, turning from a weedy little boy into a sensible young man quite capable of cheerfully taking on many of the farm tasks.

Longfield, Rose

Pretty, spoilt and difficult wife of David Longfield and mother to Melisande, Cyril and Roderick. When the family home is destroyed in a fire Rose suffers from terrible shock, crying for days on end and retiring to a nursing home for eight months. She is visited by her sister-in-law Linnie who is angry to see her 'looking perfectly well' in bed. Rose refuses to see to her duties and only emerges once in *Six Cousins at Mistletoe Farm* when she visits her children for the day and is shocked by how robust, plump and rosy-cheeked they have become. Tells Melisande in no uncertain terms that she has ballooned: 'Really dear, you are quite fat, quite coarse-looking. I did so hope you would take after me!' A selfish woman who neglects her family in their hour of need, Rose Longfield has no intention of putting herself out when her husband buys Holly Farm, and refuses to do any farm jobs, professing to be unable to make butter and to dislike dogs. Merrily organises a huge birthday party at vast expense which has to be cancelled at the last minute as her husband finally tells her she is overstepping the mark. Is haunted constantly by the saintly face of her sister in law Linnie who runs Mistletoe Farm so perfectly, yet it is Linnie who puts Rose on the right track with some good, plain talking. We are given only a tiny glimpse into the new, reformed Rose Longfield in the final pages of *Six Cousins Again*, and can but hope that after turning over a new leaf she will stick to this new way of life.

Longfield, Susan

Eleven-year-old daughter of Peter and Linnie Longfield and younger sister to twins Jack and Jane. Susan has the uncanny knack of hitting the nail on the head with her observations, and is 'devastatingly honest'. Followed everywhere by the 'faithful black shadow' of Crackers her cocker spaniel. Adores her pony, Boodi, and is the only cousin who remains unchanged after the departure of Melisande, Roderick and Cyril, but then, who would want her to change?

Susan rode there on Boodi.

Lordly-One

Magnificent steed belonging to Richard Long. When Richard spots Melisande struggling up the hill to Mistletoe Farm weighed down with shopping baskets, he offers her and her groceries a lift on his legendary mount. Melisande is most impressed.

Merrylegs

Pony belonging to Jane Longfield. Adored by his owner, who spends far more time grooming Merrylegs than she does herself, and more time cleaning his stall than her own bedroom.

Mr Potts

Canine friend of Sam Twigg. Golden spaniel who loves to play with Susan Longfield's dog, Crackers. Named after the local policeman so that Twigg can call for his dog in a most amusing way. 'Here Potty! Come to heel now!' (For another golden spaniel, *see* Scamper in The Secret Seven.)

Lordly-One took them both easily.

Mr Potts

Useless policeman who fails to detect the thieving ways of Benedict the Hermit, choosing instead to blame Sam Twigg for any local crime. Mr Potts is most impressed by Benedict who refers to him as 'sergeant'. In *Six Cousins Again*, Mr Potts again points the finger of blame at Sam Twigg when things go missing at Holly Farm and animals are being poisoned. Of course, Twigg is not to blame, but Mr Potts is so convinced of his guilt that he has him arrested. Despite his stupidity, Potts retains a certain vulnerable charm, as does PC Plod in the Noddy stories. Rides a bicycle.

Sally

Sweet-natured girl of about seventeen who happens to be the niece of Dorcas from Mistletoe Farm. Plump and apple-cheeked with a mop of dark hair, Sally arrives to help at Holly Farm but finds that she has taken on more than she had bargained for. Sparks fly between herself and Ellen who looks down her nose at honest, hard-working Sally, and even accuses the poor girl of thieving from her. No wonder Sally decides she has had enough and leaves the farm. All is not lost, as her new job does not go as planned, and by the end of

Six Cousins Again she is back at Holly Farm, very much on her own terms. Churns butter beautifully and respects the hunger of a young lad like Roderick, surreptitiously supplying him with hunks of bread and cheese when not enough food is provided at tea time.

Twigg, Sam

Poacher with a heart of gold and a humorous expression. Features in both books in the series and is well liked by all at Mistletoe Farm, despite his dodgy ways. Wears a baggy coat and leather gaiters with 'astonishingly small' feet poking out of them. Twigg is very fond of the Longfield family, and is dismayed when he is accused of thieving from Holly Farm. Jack sets about proving Twigg's innocence and in the process they find out who the real thief is. Has golden spaniel named after the local policeman, Mr Potts. Expert on the country and the natural world, Twigg invites Jack to go looking for badgers at night and recommends that Roderick have one of Tommy Lane's cocker spaniel puppies. 'A most entertaining companion', with forthright views on the female species: 'Women! They can't hold their tongues for one minute!'

FURTHER READING

Enid Blyton: A Biography   Barbara Stoney
The Enid Blyton Dossier   Brian Stewart and Tony Summerfield